The Poetry of Thought

Also by George Steiner
AVAILABLE FROM NEW DIRECTIONS

My Unwritten Books
George Steiner at The New Yorker

The Poetry of Thought

From Hellenism to Celan

George Steiner

A NEW DIRECTIONS BOOK

Copyright © 2011 George Steiner

All rights reserved. Except for brief passages quoted in a newspaper, magazine, radio,
television, or website review, no part of this book may be reproduced in any form
or by any means, electronic or mechanical, including photocopying and recording,
or by any information storage and retrieval system, without permission
in writing from the Publisher.

Published by arrangement with George Steiner and his agent, Georges Borchardt.

PUBLISHER'S NOTE
At New Directions' request, the author has provided translations
of some of the longer passages quoted in the original in *The Poetry of Thought*.

Manufactured in the United States of America
New Directions Books are printed on acid-free paper.
First published as a New Directions book in 2011
and as a New Directions paperbook (ISBN 978-0-8112-2185-6) in 2014
Design by Erik Rieselbach

Library of Congress Cataloging-in-Publication Data
Steiner, George, 1929–
The poetry of thought : from Hellenism to Celan / George Steiner.
p. cm.
Includes bibliographical references and index.
ISBN 978-0-8112-1945-7 (hardback : acid-free paper)
1. Literature and philosophy. 2. Philosophy in literature. I. Title.
PN49.S74 2011
801—dc23
2011037840

3 5 7 9 10 8 6 4 2

New Directions Books are published for James Laughlin
by New Directions Publishing Corporation
80 Eighth Avenue, New York 10011

For Durs Grünbein
Poet & Cartesian

Toute pensée commence par un poème.

(Every thought begins with a poem.)

—Alain: *"Commentaire sur 'La Jeune Parque,'"* 1953

Il y a toujours dans la philosophie une prose littéraire cachée, une ambiguïté des termes.

(There is always in philosophy a hidden literary prose, an ambiguity in the terms used.)

—Sartre: *Situations IX,* 1965

On ne pense en philosophie que sous des métaphores.

(In philosophy one thinks only metaphorically.)

—Louis Althusser: *Éléments d'autocritique,* 1972

Lucretius and Seneca are "models of philosophical-literary investigation, in which literary language and complex dialogical structures engage the interlocutor's (and the reader's) entire soul in a way that an abstract and impersonal prose treatise probably could not.... Form is a crucial element in the work's philosophical content. Sometimes, indeed (as with the *Medea*), the content of the form proves so powerful that it calls into question the allegedly simpler teaching contained within it."

—Martha Nussbaum: *The Therapy of Desire,* 1994

Gegenüber den Dichtern stehen die Philosophen unglaublich gut angezogen da. Dabei sind sie nackt, ganz erbärmlich nackt, wenn man bedenkt, mit welch dürftiger Bildsprache sie die meiste Zeit auskommen müssen.

(In contrast to the poets, the philosophers look incredibly elegant. In fact, they are naked, piteously naked when one considers the meager imagery with which they have to make do most of the time.)

—Durs Grünbein: *Das erste Jahr,* 2001

PREFACE

What are the philosophic concepts of the deaf-mute? What are his or her metaphysical imaginings?

All philosophic acts, every attempt to think thought, with the possible exception of formal (mathematical) and symbolic logic, are irremediably linguistic. They are realized and held hostage by one motion or another of discourse, of encoding in words and in grammar. Be it oral or written, the philosophic proposition, the articulation and communication of argument are subject to the executive dynamics and limitations of human speech.

It may be that there lurks within all philosophy, almost certainly within all theology, an opaque but insistent desire—Spinoza's *conatus*—to escape from this empowering bondage. Either by modulating natural language into the tautological exactitudes, transparencies and verifiabilities of mathematics (this cold but ardent dream haunts Spinoza, Husserl, Wittgenstein) or, more enigmatically, by reverting to intuitions prior to language itself. We do not know that there are any such, that there can be thought before saying. We apprehend manifold strengths of meaning, figurations of sense in the arts, in music. The inexhaustible significance of music, its defiance of translation or paraphrase, presses on philosophic scenarios in Socrates, in Nietzsche. But when we adduce the "sense" of aesthetic representations and musical forms, we are metaphorizing, we are operating by more or less covert analogy. We are enclosing them in the mastering contours of speech. Hence the recurrent trope, so urgent in Plotinus, in the *Tractatus*, that the nub, the philosophic message lies in that which is unsaid, in the unspoken between the lines. What can be enunciated, what presumes that language is more or less consonant with veritable insights and demonstrations, may in fact reveal the decay of primordial, epiphanic recognitions. It may hint at the belief that in an earlier, Pre-Socratic condition, language was closer to the wellsprings of immediacy, to the undimmed "light of Being" (so Heidegger). But there is no evidence whatever for any such Adamic privilege. Inescapably, the "language-animal," as the ancient Greeks defined man, inhabits the bounded immensities of the word, of grammatical instruments. The *Logos* equates word with reason in its very foundations. Thought may indeed be in exile. But if so, we do not know or, more precisely, we cannot *say* from what.

It follows that philosophy and literature occupy the same generative though ultimately circumscribed space. Their performative means are identical: an alignment of words, the modes of syntax, punctuation (a subtle resource). This is as true of a nursery rhyme as it is of a Kant *Critique*. Of a dime novel as of the *Phaedo*. They are deeds of language. The notion, as in Nietzsche or Valéry, that abstract thought can be danced is an allegoric conceit. Utterance, intelligible enunciation is all. Together they solicit or withstand translation, paraphrase, metaphrase and every technique of transmission or betrayal.

Practitioners have always known this. In all philosophy, conceded Sartre, there is "a hidden literary prose." Philosophic thought can be realized "only metaphorically," taught Althusser. Repeatedly (but how seriously?) Wittgenstein professed that he ought to have set down his *Investigations* in verse. Jean-Luc Nancy cites the vital difficulties which philosophy and poetry occasion each other: "Together they are difficulty itself: the difficulty of making sense."

Which idiom points to the essential crux, to the creation of meaning and poetics of reason.

What has been less clarified is the incessant, shaping pressure of speech-forms, of *style* on philosophic and metaphysical programs. In what respects is a philosophic proposal, even in the nakedness of Frege's logic, a rhetoric? Can any cognitive or epistemological system be dissociated from its stylistic conventions, from the genres of expression prevalent or under challenge in its time and milieu? To what degree are the metaphysics of Descartes, of Spinoza or Leibniz conditioned by the complex social and instrumental ideals of late Latin, by the constituents and underlying authority of a partially artificial Latinity within modern Europe? At other points, the philosopher sets out to construe a new language, an idiolect singular to his purpose. Yet this endeavor, manifest in Nietzsche or in Heidegger, is itself saturated by the oratorical, colloquial or aesthetic context (witness the "expressionism" in *Zarathustra*). There could be no Derrida outside the wordplay initiated by Surrealism and Dada, immune to the acrobatics of automatic writing. What lies nearer deconstruction than *Finnegans Wake* or Gertrude Stein's lapidary finding that "there is no there there"?

It is aspects of this "stylization" in certain philosophic texts, of the engendering of such texts via literary tools and fashions which I want to consider (in an inevitably partial and provisional way). I want to note the interactions, the rivalries between poet, novelist, playwright on the one hand and the declared thinker on the other. "To be both Spinoza and Stendhal" (Sartre). Intimacies and reciprocal distrust made iconic by Plato and reborn in Heidegger's dialogue with Hölderlin.

Fundamental to this essay is a conjecture which I find difficult to put into words. A close association of music with poetry is a commonplace. They share seminal categories of rhythm, phrasing, cadence, sonority, intonation and measure. "The music of poetry" is exactly that. Setting words to music or music to words is an exercise in shared raw materials.

Is there in some kindred sense "a poetry, a music of thought" deeper than that which attaches to the external uses of language, to style?

We tend to use the term and concept of "thought" with unconsidered scattering and largesse. We affix the process of "thinking" to a teeming multiplicity which extends from the subconscious, chaotic torrent of internalized flotsam, even in sleep, to the most rigorous of analytic proceedings, which embraces the uninterrupted babble of the everyday and the focused meditation in Aristotle on mind or Hegel on self. In common parlance "thinking" is democratized. It is made universal and unlicensed. But this is to confound radically what are distinct, even antagonistic phenomena. Responsibly defined—we lack a signal term—serious thought is a rare occurrence. The discipline which it requires, the abstentions from facility and disorder, are very rarely or not at all in reach of the vast majority. Most of us are hardly cognizant of what it is "to think," to transmute the bric-à-brac, the shopworn refuse of our mental currents into "thought." Properly perceived—when do we pause to consider?— the instauration of thought of the first caliber is as rare as the crafting of a Shakespeare sonnet or a Bach fugue. Perhaps, in our brief evolutionary history, we have not yet learned how to think. The tag *homo sapiens* may, except for a handful, be an unfounded boast.

Things excellent, admonishes Spinoza, "are rare and difficult." Why should a distinguished philosophic text be more accessible than higher mathematics or a late Beethoven quartet? Inherent in such a text is a process of creation, a "poetry" which it both reveals and resists. Major philosophic-metaphysical thought both begets and seeks to conceal the "supreme fictions" within itself. The bilge-water of our indiscriminate ruminations is indeed the world's prose. No less than "poetry," in the categorical sense philosophy has its music, its pulse of tragedy, its raptures, even, though infrequently, its laughter (as in Montaigne or Hume). "All thought begins with a poem" taught Alain in his commerce with Valéry. This shared incipience, this initiation of worlds is difficult to elicit. Yet it leaves traces, background noises comparable to those which whisper the origins of our galaxy. I suspect that these traces are discernible in the *mysterium tremendum* of metaphor. Even melody, "supreme mystery among the sciences of man" (Lévi-Strauss), may, in a certain sense, be metaphoric. If we are a "language-animal," we are more specifically a primate endowed with the capacity to use metaphor, so as to relate with arc lightning, Heraclitus's simile, the disparate shards of being and passive perception.

Where philosophy and literature mesh, where they are litigious toward one another in form or matter, these echoes of origin can be heard. The poetic genius of abstract thought is lit, is made audible. Argument, even analytic, has its drumbeat. It is made ode. What voices the closing movements of Hegel's *Phenomenology* better than Edith Piaf's *non de non*, a twofold negation which Hegel would have prized?

This essay is an attempt to listen more closely.

1

We do speak about music. The verbal analysis of a musical score can, to a certain extent, elucidate its formal structure, its technical components and instrumentation. But where it is not musicology in a strict sense, where it does not resort to a "meta-language" parasitic on music—"key," "pitch," "syncopation"—talk about music, oral or written, is a suspect compromise. A narration, a critique of musical performance addresses itself less to the actual sound-world than it does to the executant and the reception by the audience. It is reportage by analogy. It can say little that is substantive of the composition. A handful of brave spirits, Boethius, Rousseau, Nietzsche, Proust and Adorno among them, have sought to translate the matter of music and its significations into words. On occasion, they have found metaphoric "counterpoints," modes of suggestion, simulacra of considerable evocative effect (Proust on Vinteuil's sonata). Yet even at their most seductive these semiotic virtuosities are, in the proper sense of the idiom, "beside the point." They are derivative.

To speak of music is to foster an illusion, a "category mistake" as logicians would put it. It is to treat music as if it was or was very close to natural language. It is to transfer semantic realities from a linguistic to a musical code. Musical elements are experienced or classified as syntax; the evolving construct of a sonata, its initial and secondary "subject" are designated as grammatical. Musical statements (itself a borrowed designation) have their rhetoric, their eloquence or economy. We incline to overlook that each of these rubrics is borrowed from its linguistic legitimacies. The analogies are inescapably contingent. A musical "phrase" is not a verbal segment.

This contamination is aggravated by the manifold relations between words and musical setting. A linguistically ordered system is inserted within, is set to and against a "non-language." This hybrid coexistence is of limitless diversity and possible intricacy (often a Hugo Wolf *Lied* negates its verbal text). Our reception of this amalgam is to a large extent cursory. Who but the most concentrated—score and libretto in hand—is capable of taking in simultaneously the musical notes, the attendant syllables and the polymorphic, truly dialectical interplay between them? The human cortex has difficulty in discriminating between and re-combining entirely distinct, autonomous stimuli. No doubt there are musical pieces which aim to mime, to accompany verbal and figurative themes. There is "program music" for storms and calm, for festivities and lamentation. Mussorgsky sets to music "paintings at an exhibition." There is film music, often essential to the visual-dramatic script. But these are justly taken to be secondary, mongrel species. Where it is per se, where it is according to Schopenhauer more enduring than man, music is neither more nor less than itself. The ontological echo lies to hand: "I am what I am."

Its only signifying "translation" or paraphrase is that of bodily motion. Music translates into dance. But the enraptured mirroring is approximate. Stop the sound and there is no confident way of telling what music is being danced to (an irritant touched on in Plato's *Laws*). But unlike natural languages, music is universal. Innumerable ethnic communities possess only oral rudiments of literature. No human aggregate is without music, often elaborate and intricately marshalled. The sensory, emotional data of music are far more immediate than those of speech (they may reach back to the womb). Except at certain cerebral extremes, associated mainly with

16

modernism and technologies in the west, music needs no decipherment. Reception is more or less instantaneous at psychic, nervous and visceral levels whose synaptic interconnections and cumulative yield we scarcely understand.

But what is it that is being received, internalized, responded to? What is it that sets the sum of us in motion? Here we come upon a duality of "sense" and of "meaning" which epistemology, philosophical hermeneutics and psychological investigations have been virtually helpless to elucidate. Which invite the supposition that what is inexhaustibly meaningful may also be senseless. The meaning of music lies in its performance and audition (there are those who "hear" a composition when silently reading its score, but they are rare). To explain what a composition means, ruled Schumann, is to play it again. To women and men since the inception of humaneness music is so meaningful that they can hardly imagine life without it. *Musique avant toute chose* (Verlaine). Music comes to possess our body and our consciousness. It calms and it maddens, it consoles or makes desolate. For countless mortals music, however vaguely, comes closer than any other felt presence to inferring, to forecasting the possible reality of transcendence, of an encounter with the numinous, with the supernatural as these lie beyond empirical reach. To so many religious people emotion is metaphorized music. But what sense has it, what meaning does it make verifiable? Can music lie or is it altogether immune to what philosophers call "truth functions"? Identical music will inspire, and seemingly articulate irreconcilable proposals. It "translates" into antinomies. The same Beethoven tune inspired Nazi solidarity, communist promise and the vapid panaceas of the United Nations hymn. The selfsame chorus in Wagner's *Rienzi* exalts Herzl's Zionism and Hitler's vision of the *Reich*. A fantastic wealth of variant, even contradictory meanings and a total absence of sense. Neither semiology nor psychology nor metaphysics can master this paradox (which alarms absolutist thinkers from Plato to Calvin and Lenin). No epistemology has been able to answer convincingly the simple question: "What is music for?" What sense can it have to make music? This crucial incapacity more than hints at organic limitations in language, limitations pivotal to the philosophic enterprise. Conceivably spoken, let alone written discourse are a secondary phenomenon. They may embody a decay of certain primordial totalities of psychosomatic awareness still operative in music. Too often, to speak is to "get it wrong." Not long before his death Socrates sings.

When God sings to Himself, He sings algebra, opined Leibniz. The affinities, the sinews which relate music to mathematics have been perceived since Pythagoras. Cardinal features of musical composition such as pitch, volume, rhythm can be algebraically plotted. So can historical conventions such as fugues, canons and counterpoint. Mathematics is the other universal language. Common to all men, instantly legible to those equipped to read it. As in music, so in mathematics the notion of "translation" is applicable only in a trivial sense. Certain mathematical operations can be narrated or described verbally. It is possible to paraphrase or metaphrase mathematical devices. But these are ancillary, virtually decorative marginalia. In and of itself mathematics can be translated only into other mathematics (as in algebraic geometry). In mathematical papers, there is often only one generative word: an initial "let" which authorizes and launches the chain of symbols and diagrams. Comparable to that imperative "let" which initiates the axioms of creation in *Genesis*.

Yet the language(s) of mathematics are immensely rich. Their deployment is one of the few positive, clean journeys in the records of the human mind. Though inaccessible to the layman, mathematics manifests criteria of beauty in an exact, demonstrable sense. Here alone the equivalence between truth and beauty obtains. Unlike those enunciated by natural language, mathematical propositions can be either verified or falsified. Where undecidability crops up, that concept also has its precise, scrupulous meaning. Oral and written tongues lie, deceive, obfuscate at every step. More often than not their motor is fiction and the ephemeral. Mathematics can produce errors, later to be corrected. It cannot lie. There is wit in mathematical constructs and proofs, as there is wit in Haydn and Satie. There may be touches of personal style. Mathematicians have told me that they can identify the proponent of a theorem and of its demonstration on stylistic grounds. What matters is that once proved, a mathematical operation enters the collective truth and availability of the anonymous. It is, moreover, permanent. When Aeschylus is forgotten, and already the bulk of his work is missing, Archimedes' theorems will remain (G. M. Hardy).

Since Galileo, the march of mathematics is imperial. A natural science gauges its legitimacy by the degree to which it can be mathematicized. Mathematics play an increasingly determinant role in economics, in prominent branches of social studies, even in the statistical areas of history ("cliometrics"). Calculus and formal logic are the source and anatomy of computation, of information theory, of electromagnetic storage and transmission as these now organize and transform our daily lives. The young manipulate the crystalline unfolding of fractals as they once manipulated rhymes. Applied mathematics, often of an advanced class, pervades our individual and social existence.

From the outset, philosophy, metaphysics have circled mathematics like a frustrated hawk. Plato's exigence was clear: "Let no one enter the Academy who is not a geometer." In Bergson, in Wittgenstein the mathematical libido is exemplary of epistemology as a whole. There are enlightening episodes in the long history of the philosophy of mathematics, notably in the early investigations of Husserl. But advances have been fitful. If applied mathematics with its inception in hydraulics, agriculture, astronomy and navigation can be located within economical and social needs, pure mathematics and its meteoric progress pose a seemingly intractable question. Do the theorems, the interplay of higher mathematics, of number theory in particular, derive from, refer to realities "out there" even if as yet undiscovered? Do they, at however formalized a level, address existential phenomena? Or are they an autonomous game, a set and sequence of operations as arbitrary, as autistic as chess? Is the unbounded, one may say "fantastic" forward motion of mathematics from Pythagoras's triangle to elliptical functions, generated, energized from within itself, independent of either reality or application (though, contingently, the latter may turn up)? To what psychological or aesthetic impulses does mathematics answer? Mathematicians themselves, philosophers have debated the issue across millennia. It remains unresolved. Add to this the luminous puzzle of mathematical capacities and productivity in the very young, in the preadolescent. An enigmatic occurrence analogous with, and only analogous with virtuosities of the musical prodigy and the child chess master. Are there links? Is some transcendent addiction to the useless implanted in a handful of human beings (a Mozart, a Gauss, a Capablanca)?

Being condemned to language, philosophy and philosophic psychology have found themselves more or less helpless. Many a thinker has echoed an ancient sorrow: "Would I have been a philosopher if I could have been a mathematician?"

In regard to the requirements of philosophy, natural language suffers from grave infirmities. It cannot match the universality of either music or mathematics. Even the most widespread—today it is Anglo-American—is only provincial and transient. No language can rival the capacities of music for polysemic simultaneities, for manifold meanings under pressure of untranslatable forms. The enlistment of emotions, at once specific and general, private and communal, far exceeds that in language. At some points, blindness is reparable (books can be read in braille). Deafness, ostracism from music is irremediable exile. Nor can natural language rival the precision, the unambiguous finality, the accountability and transparency of mathematics. It cannot satisfy criteria of either proof or refutation—they are the same—inherent in mathematics. Must we, can we mean what we say or say what we mean? The implicit generation of new questions, of new perceptions, of innovative findings from within the mathematical matrix has no equivalent in oral or written speech. The forward paths of mathematics look to be self-sustained and unbounded. Language teems with shopworn specters and factitious circularities.

And yet. The very definition of men and women as "language-animals" put forward by the ancient Greeks, the nomination of language and linguistic communication as the defining attribute of what is human, are no arbitrary tropes. Sentences, oral and written (the mute can be taught to read and write), are the enabling organ of our being, of that dialogue with the self and with others which assembles and stabilizes our identity. Words, imprecise, time-bound as they are, construct remembrance and articulate futurity. Hope is the future tense. Even when naively figurative and unexamined, the substantives we attach to concepts such as life and death, to the ego and the other are bred of words. Hamlet to Polonius. The force of silence is that of a denying echo of language. It is possible to love silently, but perhaps only up to a point. Authentic speechlessness comes with death. To die is to stop chattering. I have tried to show that the incident at Babel was a blessing. Each and every language maps a possible world, a possible calendar and landscape. To learn a language is to expand incommensurably the parochialism of the self. It is to fling open a new window on existence. Words do fumble and deceive. Certain epistemologies deny them access to reality. Even the finest poetry is circumscribed by its idiom. Nonetheless, it is natural language which affords humanity its center of gravity (note the moral, psychological connotations of that term). Serious laughter is also linguistic. It may be that only smiling defies paraphrase.

Natural language is the ineluctable medium of philosophy. The philosopher may resort to technical terms and neologisms; he may, like Hegel, seek to crowd familiar idiomatic terms with novel significations. But in essence and, as we have seen, barring the symbolism of formal logic, language must do. As R. G. Collingwood puts it in his *Essay on Philosophic Method* (1933): "If language cannot explain itself, nothing else can explain it." Thus the language of philosophy is "as every careful reader of the great philosophers already knows, a literary language and not a technical." The rules of literature prevail. In this compelling respect, philosophy resembles poetry. It is "a poem of the intellect" and represents "the point at which prose comes nearest to being poetry." The proximity is reciprocal, for often it is the poet who turns to the philosophers. Baudelaire adverts to de Maistre, Mallarmé to Hegel, Celan to Heidegger, T. S. Eliot to Bradley.

Within the disabling confines of my linguistic competence and drawing lamely on translation, I want to look at a pride of philosophic texts as these proceed under pressure of literary ideals and the poetics of rhetoric. I want to look at synaptic contacts between philosophic argument and literary expression. These interpenetrations, fusions are never total, but they take us to the heart of language and the creativity of reason. "What we cannot think, that we cannot think: we cannot therefore *say* what we cannot think" (*Tractatus*, 5.61).

2

The incandescence of intellectual and poetic creativity in mainland Greece, Asia Minor and Sicily during the sixth and fifth centuries B.C. remains unique in human history. In some respects, the life of the mind thereafter is a copious footnote. So much has long been obvious. Yet the causes of this sunburst, the motives which brought it about in that time and place remain unclear. The penitential "political correctness" now prevalent, the remorse of postcolonialism make it awkward even to pose what may be the pertinent questions, to ask why the ardent wonder that is pure thought prevailed almost nowhere else (what theorem out of Africa?).

Manifold and complex factors must have been interactive, "implosive" to borrow a crucial concept from the packed collisions in atomic physics. Among these were a more or less benign climate and ease of maritime communication. Argument traveled fast; it was, in the ancient and figural sense, "Mercurial." The availability of protein, cruelly denied to so much of the sub-Saharan world, may have been pivotal. Nutritionists speak of protein as "brain food." Hunger, malnutrition lame the gymnastics of the spirit. There is much we do not yet grasp, though Hegel sensed its central role, concerning the daily ambience of slavery, concerning the incidence of slavery on individual and social sensibility. It is, however, evident that for the privileged, and they were relatively numerous, the ownership of slaves comported leisure and dispensation from manual and domestic tasks. It bestowed time and space for the free play of intellect. This is an immense license. Neither Parmenides nor Plato needed to earn a living. Under temperate skies, a nourished man could proceed to argue or to listen in the *agora*, in the groves of the Academy. The third element is the most difficult to evaluate. With stellar exceptions, women played a housebound, often subservient part in the affairs, certainly in the philosophic-rhetorical affairs of the *polis*. Some may have had access to higher education. But there is little evidence prior to Plotinus. Did this (enforced, traditional?) abstention contribute to the luxury and even arrogance of the speculative? Does it reach, via the arrestingly modest contribution to mathematics and metaphysics made by women, into our own, now metamorphic day? Protein, slavery, male prepotence: what was their cumulative causation in the Greek miracle?

For let us be clear: a miracle it was.

It consisted in the discovery, though that concept remains elusive, and cultivation of abstract thought. Of absolute meditation and questioning uncontaminated by the utilitarian demands of land economy, of navigation, of flood control, of astrological prophecy prevalent, often brilliantly so, in the surrounding Mediterranean, Near Eastern and Indian civilizations. We tend to take this revolution for granted, being its products. It is in fact strange and scandalous. Parmenides' equation between thought and being, Socrates' ruling that the unexamined life is not worth living are provocations of a truly fantastic dimension. They incarnate the primacy of the useless, as we intimate it in music. In Kant's proud idiom, they aspire to the ideal of the *disinterested*. What is stranger, perhaps ethically more suspect, than a willingness to sacrifice life to an abstract, inapplicable obsession as does Archimedes when pondering conic sections or Socrates? The phenomenology of pure thought is almost daemonic in its strangeness. Pascal, Kierkegaard bear witness to this. But the deep currents of radiant "autism" which relate

Greek mathematics and speculative, theoretical debate, which exalt the hunt for truth above personal survival, launch the great western journey. They impel that "voyaging through strange seas of thought alone" which Wordsworth attributes to Newton. Our devising of theories, our sciences, our reasoned disagreements and truth-functions, so often abstruse, proceed by that distant Ionian light. We are, as Shelley proclaims, "all Greeks." I repeat: miracle there is, but also strangeness and, it may be, a touch of the inhuman.

Philosophic and literary prose, indeed prose itself, come late. Their self-awareness hardly predates Thucydides. Prose is wholly permeable to the dishevelment and corruptions of the "real world." It is ontologically mundane (*mundum*). Narrative sequence often carries with it the spurious promise of logical relation and coherence. Millennia of orality precede the use of prose for anything but administrative and mercantile notations (those lists of domestic animals in Linear B). The writing down in prose of philosophic propositions and debates, of fictions and history is a specialized ramification. Conceivably, it is symptomatic of decay. Famously, Plato views it with distaste. Writing, he urges, subverts, enfeebles the primordial strengths and arts of memory, mother of the Muses. It purports a factitious authority by preventing immediate challenge and self-correction. It lays claim to false monumentality. Only oral exchanges, the license of interruption as in the dialectic, can quicken intellectual inquiry toward responsible insight, insight that is answerable to dissent.

Hence the recurrent resort to dialogue in the works of Plato himself, in the lost books of Aristotle, in Galileo, Hume or Valéry. Because it preserves within its scripted forms the dynamics of the speaking voice, because it is in essence vocal and kindred to music, poetry not only precedes prose but is, paradoxically, the more natural performative mode. Poetry exercises, nurtures memory as prose does not. Its universality is indeed that of music; many ethnic legacies have no other genre. In Hebrew scriptures the prosaic elements are instinct with the beat of verse. Read them aloud and they tend toward song. A good poem conveys the postulate of a new beginning, the *vita nuova* of the unprecedented. So much of prose is a creature of habit.

Demarcations we presume, almost casually, as between metaphysics, the sciences, music and literature, had no relevance in archaic Greece. We know next to nothing of the origins, oracular, rhapsodic, didactic, of what was to become cosmological thought. We know nothing of the shamans of metaphor to whom we owe the identity of the western mind, who laid the foundations for what Yeats called "monuments of unageing intellect." Ascriptions to Orphic covens, to mystery cults, to seminal contacts with Persian, Egyptian, perhaps Indian practices of sagacity remain hypothetical at best. There is reason to believe that Pre-Socratic teachings were recited orally, perhaps sung, as Nietzsche intuited. For a very long time the lines between creation narratives, mythological-allegoric fictions on the one hand and philosophic, propositional dicta on the other were entirely fluid (Plato is a virtuoso of myth). At some unrecapturable stage, abstraction, the *cogito* assumes its imperative autonomy, its ideal strangeness. Theories—themselves a formidably challenging concept alien to so many cultures—as to the components and ordinances of the natural world, as to the nature of man and his moral status, as to the political in the encompassing sense, could be formulated most incisively in poetic modes. These in turn could facilitate recall and memorization. The rhapsodic precedent, its subversions of textuality disturb Plato. Witness the disquieted ironies of his *Ion*. We find it again in Wittgenstein's paradoxes on the unwritten. The belief that Homer and Hesiod are the true teachers of wisdom persists. The paradigm of the philosophic poem, of a seamless fit between aesthetic articulation and systematic cognitive content continues into modernity. Lucretius's aspiration "to pour forth on the darkest of themes the clearest of songs" has never lost its spell.

The aesthetics of the fragment has of late drawn attention. Not only in literature. In the arts the sketch, the maquette, the rough draft have been prized above the finished work. Romanticism invested in an aura of incompletion, in the unfinished graced by early death. So much that is emblematic of the modern remains incomplete: Proust and Musil in the novel, Schoenberg and Berg in opera, Gaudi in architecture. Rilke exalts the torso, T. S. Eliot shores up fragments "against our ruin."

The issues are important. The centrifugal, anarchic motions in modern politics, the *accelerando* of science and technology, the undermining of classical stabilities in our understanding of consciousness and meaning, as in psychoanalysis or deconstruction, make systematic unison and comprehensiveness implausible. "The center cannot hold." The encyclopedic ambitions of the Enlightenment, the leviathan constructivities of positivism as in Comte and Marx no longer persuade. We find it difficult to tell or attend to "the great stories." We are drawn to the open-ended, *la forma aperta*. Levinas discriminates between the coercive claims and foreclosure of "totality," of the totalitarian and the liberating promise, messianic in essence, of "infinity." Adorno simply equates completeness with falsehood.

These antinomies are as ancient as philosophy itself. Consonant, perhaps, with radical polarities in human sensibility, there have been the master builders and the mercurial practitioners of shorthand, of perception in provisional motion. The lineage of Aristotle is that of the attempt at total ingathering and harvest. It inspires the plenitude of Augustine and the *summa* of Aquinas. It underwrites the axiomatic coherence of Spinoza's *Ethics* and Kant's Newtonian universalism. Paramount among systematic builders is Hegel whose very resort to the term "encyclopedia" crowns a millennial ambition. When they promise the passing mariner the revelation of all that has been, is and shall be, the Sirens are setting Hegel to music.

The countercurrent dates back to the Pre-Socratics and the abrupt, parataxic aphorisms of *Ecclesiastes*. Even when they are formally copious and discursive, Montaigne's essays—we must not overlook the literal meaning of that word—proceed by leaps and digressive bounds. They proceed by marginalia and annotate existence. Pascal's *Pensées* achieve the seeming contradiction of fragmented magnitude, of fractured immensities. This model will be realized in the "flash photography" of Novalis and Coleridge, precisely where these thinkers were haunted by the mirage of an *omnium gatherum* (Coleridge's macaronic tag). All Nietzsche, all Wittgenstein is fragment, sometimes willed, sometimes enforced by contingent circumstance. In contrast, Heidegger's writings will run to ninety tomes and the incompletion of *Sein und Zeit* is amended incessantly thereafter. Only those too feeble or vanitous not to do so write, publish books, said Wittgenstein. The truths of the fragment may, given luck, border on those of silence.

The format in which Pre-Socratic thought has come down to us is, to be sure, largely fortuitous. What we have are remnants. So many of the splintered sayings are embedded, inaccurately perhaps, in later contexts, often polemical and adversative (in the Church Fathers or Aristotelian detractors). The material requisites for the conservation of extended written works evolved slowly. They hardly precede the redaction of the Homeric epics. Once only does Socrates consult a written scroll. But there are also substantive motives for the aphorismic and apodictic tenor of these auroral pronouncements.

When the Magus in Miletus declares that all matter is founded on water, when a rival sage in Ephesus affirms that everything is ultimately fire, when a Sicilian seer proclaims the oneness of all things while a wandering Sophist insists on their multiplicity, there is, strictly considered, nothing to add. Step by step demonstration, as expounded in mathematics, comes only gradually to cosmology and metaphysics. Initially, thought and dictum are, as it were, inebriate with the absolute, with the power of a sentence to speak the world. Extreme concision, moreover, draws impact from oral exposition and enlists memory. The sheer volume of Plato's dialogues is not the least of their revolutionary genius. Though here also there is frequent recourse to fictions of orality, to reproductive remembrance. The lapidary teachings of the Pre-Socratics can be spread by word of mouth and memorized throughout a preliterate community. "Pigmy in extent" (Jonathan Barnes' phrase), these archaic vestiges tell of what must have been audacious, in some sense entranced, forays into unknown seas. The simile of philosophic thought as an Odyssey will persist till Schelling.

The obscurity of many of these vestiges may not be accidental, albeit our ignorance of the relevant setting and of linguistic specificities contributes to it. If the "Orphic," the "Heraclitean" or the "Pythagorean" carry connotations of the hermetic, this association implies the possible existence of more or less initiate theosophic, philosophical, even political covens. Wittgenstein's acolytes offer a modern counterpart. They also direct us toward connections between the genesis of philosophic rationality and the far older, at times ritual performance of poetry. The matter of Orpheus is inextricably mythical, but points to what we can intimate of the wellsprings of both music and language. The utter force of the fable has not diminished across the millennia. Already to the ancients Orpheus's visionary wisdom instructs his spellbound listeners about the origins of the cosmos and the instauration of an Olympian hierarchy. To medieval and renaissance mythographers, artists and poets this sung syllabus, as reported in Apollonius of Rhodes's *Argonautica*, made of Orpheus the begetter of cosmological understanding. A tragic begetter, in whose wake philosophy will never evade the informing shadow of death.

The unison of poetry, music and metaphysics continues to haunt philosophy like a fraternal ghost. Near the end, Socrates turns to Aesop and to song. Hobbes translates Homer into verse. Astringent Hegel writes a profoundly felt poem to Hölderlin. Nietzsche thinks of himself as a composer. I have cited Wittgenstein on *Dichtung*. Passages from Plato and the *Tractatus* have been set to music. As we have seen, at their highest reach these pursuits share an enormity of uselessness. Already Thales was said to have rejected all material gains. It is pragmatically absurd to sacrifice one's life in defense of a speculative intellectual hypothesis; to renounce economic security and social esteem in order to paint pictures no one wishes to see, let alone purchase; to compose music without realistic expectations of performance or audition (electronic devices have somewhat qualified this paradox); to project topological spaces forever beyond demonstration or decidability.

It is a comely cliché to associate poetry with the lunacies of love. But the inward solitudes and abstentions from normality which energized logic in Gödel are no less strange. Eros can have its recompense. What makes abstruse philosophical argument indispensable to certain men and women? What disinterested passion or arrogance induces Parmenides and Descartes to identify cogitation and being? We do not really know.

I have suggested that the "discovery" of metaphor ignited abstract, disinterested thought. Does any animal metaphorize? It is not only language which is saturated with metaphor. It is our compulsion, our capacity to devise and examine alternative worlds, to construe logical and narrative possibilities beyond any empirical constraints. Metaphor defies, surmounts death—as in the tale of Orpheus out of Thrace—even as it transcends time and space. Frustratingly, we are unable to locate, even to conceive the hour in which a human agent in ancient Greece or Ionia saw that the ocean was wine-dark, that man in battle had become a ravening lion. Or to grasp how the author of *Job* saw the stars raining down their spears. In what plausible ways, moreover, can music and mathematics be taken to be metaphoric? What is metaphoric in their relation to and radical self-distancing from everyday experience? Of what is a Mozart sonata or the Goldbach conjecture a metaphor?

It is out of a metaphoric magma that Pre-Socratic philosophy seems to erupt (the volcanic is not far off). Once a traveler in Argos had perceived the shepherds on the stony hills as "herdsmen of the winds," once a mariner out of the Piraeus had sensed that his keel was "plowing the sea," the road to Plato and to Immanuel Kant lay open. It began in poetry and has never been far from it.

"The power of Heraclitus's thought and style is so overwhelming that it is apt to carry away the imagination of his readers ... beyond the limits of sober interpretation." So remarked Hermann Fränkel, soberest of scholars. The history of attempted elucidations of Heraclitean fragments, often truncated or imperfectly rendered within later, adversative contexts, is itself among the high adventures of the western intellect from before Plato to Heidegger. Heraclitus is to Blanchot the first virtuoso of surrealist play. To numerous artists and poets he is the very icon of meditative solitude, of aristocratic aloneness. "*Ce génie fier, stable et anxieux,*" writes René Char, spellbound, as was T. S. Eliot, by a voice which consumes the husk of baffled translation. Yet Sextus Empiricus and Marcus Aurelius read Heraclitus as civically engaged and scrupulous in communal observance. For Nietzsche his "legacy will never age." Together with Pindar, rules Heidegger, Heraclitus commands an idiom which exhibits the matchless "nobility of the beginning." Meaning at dawn.

Philologists, philosophers, historians of archaic Hellas, have labored to define, to circumscribe this auroral force. Heraclitus's dicta are arcs of compressed voltage setting alight the space between words and things. His metaphoric concision suggests immediacies of existential encounter, primacies of experience largely unrecapturable to rationalities and sequential logic after Aristotle. The *Logos* is at once performative enunciation and a principle inherent in that which it signifies. Thus enunciation, the decoding of thought, takes on a substantive reality somehow external to the speaker (Heidegger's *die Sprache spricht*). In some respects, Heraclitus bears witness to the origins of intelligible consciousness (Bruno Snell). Thus Heraclitus both celebrates and wrestles with—all celebration is agonistic—the terrible power of language to deceive, to demean, to mock, to plunge deserved renown into the dark of oblivion. Dialectically, the capacity of language to ornament and enshrine memory also entails its faculties of forgetting, of ostracism from recall.

Heraclitus "works in original manner with the raw material of human speech, where 'original' signifies both the initial and the singular"(Clémence Ramnoux, one of the most insightful commentators). He quarries language before it weakens into imagery, into eroded abstraction. His abstractions are radically sensory and concrete, but not in the opportunistic mode of allegory. They enact, they perform thought where it is still, as it were, incandescent—the trope of fire is unavoidable. Where it follows on a shock of discovery, of naked confrontation with its own dynamism, at once limitless and bounded. Heraclitus does not narrate. To him things *are* with an evidence and enigma of total presence like that of lightning (his own simile). What would be the past tense of fire? Not all have been seduced. Contradiction, Heraclitus's chosen instrument, "implies falsity; and that is that" (Jonathan Barnes). He was "a paradoxographer" whose "conceptual inadequacy" is patent. It is a verdict which Plato, though fascinated by Heraclitus, hints at in the *Sophist*.

Already to the ancients Heraclitus was proverbially obscure. A proponent of dark riddles, equally contemptuous of his plebeian inferiors as he was of those, the great majority of mankind, incapable of grasping a philosophic paradox or argument. But what does it mean for articulate thought, for executive discourse to be "difficult"? I have elsewhere tried to sketch a theory of difficulty. The most prevalent is contingent and circumstantial. We know next to nothing of the linguistic and social background to Heraclitus's idiom and terrain of allusion. We cannot "look things up." He crassly dismisses Homer and Archilocus because they have not understood the harmony of opposites which governs human existence, because they waste words on puerile fantasies. But epic hexameters crop up in Heraclitean texts and what may be elements of pre-Aesopian fables in Heraclitus's references to animals. The metaphoric names which he often enlists in place of common nouns point to the gnomic formulations of the oracular. We simply do not know enough about oracular, mantic and Orphic conventions to assess their influence on Heraclitus. Famously, Fragment XXXIII professes that Apollo "whose oracle is in Delphi neither declares nor conceals, but gives a sign" (a Wittgensteinian move). Contrary to an Adamic nomination, Heraclitus does not label or define substance but infers its contradictory essence. Semantic ambiguities, a second order of difficulty, both relate the internal to the external and signal their dissociation. In what may again derive from archaic precedents, riddles are crucial (they are the crux). Puns, wordplay, deceptive synonymity convey the polysemic depths, the constant mobility in phenomena and their presumed linguistic counterpart. Poetic affinities, for example with the etiology of Chaos in Hesiod, are plausible but cannot be demonstrated. Scholars have proposed analogies between Heraclitus's cosmogony and Middle Eastern creation myths. What, if anything, did he know of Egypt? Virtually inescapable is the suggestion that Zoroastrian symbolism in regard to fire finds resonance in Heraclitus. Ephesus neighbors on Iran. Overall, however, the sinews of Heraclitean grammar and vocabulary, of his paratactic constructs and elisions are his own. Only certain choral odes in tragedy, only certain tropes in Pindar provide any parallel. It is not verbally but in music that Heraclitus's suspensions of linear logic, that his simultaneities in contrary motion (inverse canons) have their analogue. Nietzsche felt this affinity. Here also, as in *Zarathustra* and Nietzsche's melodies at midnight, obscurity can be made luminous.

This "darkness" is undoubtedly part of the spell which Heraclitus has exercised on literature. This most mesmeric of *"penseurs poètes,"* is exemplary of a tradition and aesthetic of "dark matter." Of a lineage which includes Pindar, Góngora, Hölderlin, Mallarmé and Paul Celan. One is tempted to say that where poetry is most itself, where it comes nearest the fusion of content and form in music, its inclination toward the hermetic will be strongest. There is an enduring conception of poetry as insurgent against natural language, against all *dialektikē technē*, the sequential criteria of reasoned demonstration and ordered persuasion. The resulting difficulties are what I have called "ontological." Thought and saying seek to transcend their available means, to enforce transgressive potentialities.

T. S. Eliot adverts to this "boundary condition" in the Heraclitean echoes in the *Four Quartets* (the musical citation is evident). Heraclitus presses utterance toward *aporia*, toward antinomies and undecidabilities at the very edge of language, as if language, like mathematics, could generate from within itself innovative, forward-thrusting understanding. Precisely, Char invokes Heraclitus's *"contraires—ces mirages ponctuels et tumultueux ... poésie et vérité, comme nous savons, étant synonymes."*

It is the most "stylish" of philosophers, those most alert to the expressive constraints and resources of stated thought, to its implicit cadence, such as Kierkegaard and Nietzsche, who look to Heraclitus. It is Novalis, practitioner of the Orphic fragment, and Heidegger the neologist, the craftsman of tautology. Rhapsodic and oracular intellects recognize in Heraclitus the fundamental, generative collision between the elusive opacity of the word and the equally elusive but compelling clarity and evidence of things. Immediate or hurried apprehension, the colloquial, misses this decisive tension, that, in Heraclitus's celebrated duality, of the bow and the lyre. To listen closely—Nietzsche defined philology as "reading slowly"—is to experience, always imperfectly, the possibility that the order of words, notably in metrics and the metrical nerve-structure within good prose, reflects, perhaps sustains the hidden yet manifest coherence of the cosmos. A conjecture cardinal to metaphysics. The analogy with Pythagorean and Keplerian models of concordance between harmonious relations and intervals in music and planetary motions is relevant. Again, music is the transit between metaphysical-cosmological speculation, i.e. "mirroring," and semantic articulation.

The occult violence of inspiration fascinated Heraclitus no less than it did Rimbaud or Rilke. He invokes "the Sibyl with raving mouth" whose voice, adds Plutarch, "carries through a thousand years." He refers, though guardedly, to acolytes who "raved for Dionysus" in ecstatic possession. But Heraclitus's eminence as a writer lies in his exponential economy. A very few, terse words unfold into the unbounded (an effect realized in Ungaretti's diptych—*M'illumino / d'immenso*—where immensity illuminates and enlightens). I have already referred to Heraclitus's use of "bow," differentiated from "life" by a mere accent: "The name of the bow is life; its work is death." A concision in which Artemis and Apollo are present like incipient shadows. Grammatical construction can make of an apparent riddle or paradox a font of expanding intuition: "Death is all things we see awake; all we see asleep is sleep." Ring-structures spiral into esoteric depths which we might, mistakenly, sense as psychoanalytic: "Living, he touches the dead in his sleep; waking, he touches the sleeper" (Heraclitus is our great thinker on sleep). With audacity, perhaps alone among ancients, Heraclitus challenges the gods in a tautly balanced aphorism: immortals and mortals are close-knit "living the other's death, dead in the other's life." Nietzsche attends to the implications of this (Fragment XCII) and Euripides will give it echo: "Who knows if life be death, but death in turn / be recognized below as life?" "Kingship belongs to the child." "The thunderbolt pilots all things" which Heidegger makes pivotal to his teachings. A cognitive surrealism virtually defiant of paraphrase.

Nineteen words suffice to stage a cosmic drama: "The sun will not transgress his measure. If he does, the Furies, ministers of Justice, will find him out." The collision between universal metrics and measure (*métra*) and infernal Justice will inspire the Prologue to Goethe's *Faust*. The actual quote may have been a Plutarchian paraphrase, but Heraclitus is unmistakably embedded: "Souls smell things in Hades, they use their sense of smell." As do poets, Heraclitus follows language where it leads him, where he is receptive to its inward and autonomous authority, with somnambular yet acutely lucid trust. Hence his recurrent attempts to characterize, to make us party to the twilight zone between sleeping and waking. Day melting into night, night begetting day in subversion of the trenchant Mediterranean light. There is here no distinction between philosophic or scientific finding and poetic form. The springs of thought are identical in both (*poiesis*). Poetry betrays its *daimon* when it is too lazy or self-complacent to think deeply (Valéry's *astreindre*). In turn, intellection falsifies the shaping music within itself when it forgets that it is poetry.

Ancient report has it that Heraclitus deposited the scroll containing his writings in the temple of Artemis at Ephesus. Wittgenstein notes that he would have wished to dedicate the *Philosophical Investigations* to God. Comparable points of method and sensibility are arresting. Both thinkers are constantly aware of what lies beyond rational saying, of the claims of mysticism and of silence which both abrogate and substantiate the legitimacy of the word. The author of the *Tractatus*, no less than Heraclitus, seems to have distrusted systematic completion. The fragmentary told of thought in provisional motion. It empowered compacted breadth. The timbre, the pitch of their style are often kindred. As is the virtue or drawback of that style to generate the aura of myth, of inspiring strangeness which emanates from both *personae*. Withdrawal, a pulse of secrecy underwrites their propositions: "God does not reveal himself *in* the world" (*Tractatus* 6.432); "All inference takes place a priori" (5.133); "I am my world. (The microcosm)" (5.63); "Philosophy is not a theory but an activity" (4.112).

This oracular economy carries over into Wittgenstein's more technical, heuristic *dicta*. Both sages possess the rare gift of making of logical conundra or didactic provocations something like a flash of pure poetry. "Are roses red in the dark?" "Has the verb 'to dream' a present tense?" Heraclitus and Wittgenstein play "language-games" in which the syntax and conventions of the colloquial are corrected by those of mathematics and of music. In Number 459 of the *Zettel*, Wittgenstein cites Heraclitus on not stepping twice into the same river: "In a certain sense one cannot take too much care in handling philosophical mistakes, they contain so much truth." Just like those riddles at Delphi. We recall Heraclitus's *legein* and its conceivable contacts with *Ecclesiastes* when Wittgenstein notes in 1937: "Thinking too has a time for plowing and a time for gathering the harvest."

And during the darkness of 1944: "If in life we are surrounded by death, so too in the health of our intellect we are surrounded by madness" (those "raving mouths" in Heraclitus). What could be more in accord with the spirit of Heraclitus than Wittgenstein's admonition of 1947: "One keeps forgetting to go right down to the foundations. One doesn't put the question marks *deep* enough down"?

The point is straightforward: in both philosophy and literature style is substance. Rhetorical amplitude and laconic contraction offer contrasting images and readings of the world. Punctuation is also epistemology. Within philosophy resides the perennial temptation of the poetic, either to be made welcome or to be rejected. The nuances of tension and interaction are manifold. Seemingly disparate teachings are made contiguous by affinities of voice. "When you are philosophizing you have to descend into primeval chaos and feel at home there." Was Wittgenstein, in his notebook for 1948, transcribing a fragment of Heraclitus not yet available to the rest of us? Another minimalist of immensity is Samuel Beckett. Echoes out of Spinoza and Schopenhauer are frequent. Again the crossings need not be those of specific doctrine. The matter is that of rhythm, of intonation, of grammatical bent. The barest bones of language are made resonant. Words, often monosyllabic, press against the unspoken. Connectives and disjunctives, formally void, take on normative, monumental finality. "You CRIED for night: it comes. It FALLS: now cry in darkness.... Moments for nothing, now as always, time was never and time is over, reckoning closed and story ended" (not a bad summation of Hegel's ending of history). Consider that Heraclitean tide of perpetual motion, of cosmic flux in *Krapp's Last Tape*: "We lay there without moving. But under us all moved, gently, up and down, and from side to side." In both philosopher and dramatist, the ministry of time is unfathomable: "Now and then the rye, swayed by a light wind, casts and withdraws its shadow." How vivid is Pre-Socratic cosmogony in Lucky's mad monody in *Waiting for Godot*: "in the plains in the mountains by the seas by the rivers running water running fire the air is the same and then the earth namely the air and then the earth in the great cold the great dark the air and the earth abode of stones in the great deeps and the great cold . . . on sea on land and in the air"—where the elision of punctuation declares archaic perceptions of elemental unison prior to the impoverishing, distorting fragmentations of logic and the sciences. Earth, air, fire and water, as immediate to Beckett as to the visionaries before Plato. Just as in Heraclitus, Beckett's brevities safeguard their implosive secrecy. They rebuke "This craze for explication! Every i dotted to death!" (*Catastrophe*). And how could Shakespeare not have intuited Heraclitus on the damned smelling their way in hell when tortured Gloucester is tauntingly bidden smell his blind way to Dover? As between metaphysics and poetry, the air is thick with echoes.

Also with failures. With the frustration of not being able to embody, to communicate in and via language the inchoate, tentative birth of meaning. At best, we intimate that birth in Anaximander, in Heraclitus, in the despairing honesties of the *Philosophical Investigations*. What tumults, what celebrations but also setbacks of consciousness must have attended on the utterly uncanny realization that language can say *anything*, but never exhaust the existential integrity of its reference? When Beckett bids us fail, fail again but "fail better," he locates the synapse at which thought and poetry, *doxa* and literature mesh. "It's the start that's difficult."

That inception, that tenor of thought at dawn, is emphasized by Heidegger in his lectures on Parmenides of 1942–43. Editorial, exegetic attempts to discriminate between poem and cosmology in Parmenides are anachronistic. No such dissociation is valid. Instead of *Lehrgedicht* or didactic verse, Heidegger proposes *sagen*, a "Totality of the enunciated," as the only category appropriate to what we can make out of Parmenides' vision and intent. We find it difficult to do justice to this form because we are inapt "to go toward the beginning," to move upstream where meaning may have originated.

Heidegger's autocratic gloss—founded on the scandalous but not altogether easy to disprove dogma that only ancient Greek and

German after Kant are endowed with the executive means of magisterial metaphysics—has a gnomic fascination of its own. The contrasts which he draws as between Parmenides' allegory, between the alternating pulse of self-disclosure and withdrawal in Greek *aletheia* ("truth") on the one hand, and the celebration of "openness" in the VIIIth of Rilke's *Duino Elegies* on the other, crystallizes almost every facet of the theme and history of the poetry of thought. Heidegger's commentary is virtually untranslatable as is the poetry with which it is interwoven: *"Das Haus der Göttin ist der Ort der ersten Ankunft der denkenden Wanderung."* The journey toward the dwelling of the deity who sets Parmenides' text in motion *"ist das Hindenken zum Anfang."* It is the "thinking of inception." Academic philology and textual criticism find this idiom irresponsible.

Parmenides' uses of rhythm, of symmetrical juxtapositions suggest an archaic frieze. What we need to tease out, argues Karl Rein-hardt in his seminal monograph of 1916, are the rules of archaic composition. In what ways, characteristic of the Pre-Socratics, does Parmenides encapsulate the sum of his arguments in each seemingly discrete section? The mythological lineaments of the poem are not vestment or masque in the baroque sense. The mythological embodies, allows, the only direct access to the invocation and articulation of the abstract where language, prior to Aristotle, has not yet evolved key modes of logical predication. But already Gorgias the Sophist understood that Parmenides' verses have the same imperative alignment as do the motions of thought which they strive to verbalize and unify. For Parmenides, the world is nothing but the mirror of my thought—a proposal whose enormity across the millennia should never escape us. Thus poetic form becomes the natural configuration for the most radical, overwhelming yet also strange and perhaps counterintuitive of assertions: that of the identity of thought and being. This existential identity will be a determinant in the genesis and pilgrimage of western consciousness. In a sense, Descartes and Hegel are footnotes. Parmenides' vocabulary and syntax, so far as we can make them out, enact thought as the voice of being. The cautionary ambience of prose will come later.

There are flashes of poetry in our fragmentary texts. Imitating Homer, Parmenides tells of the moon "wandering around the earth, a foreign light." Another passage, eerily prescient of modern astrophysics, recounts "how the hot power of the stars started to come into being." Scholars have suggested that Parmenides possessed a poet's sensitivity to the psychological undertones and acoustic associations of words. His resort to ambiguity and poetic irony in the address of the Goddess is that of a true writer.

Like Heraclitus, Parmenides uses oxymorons—how were these discovered?—to dramatize, to "perform" his central thesis of conflict leading toward harmonic resolution; the sun blinds us, putting out the stars and thus making objects invisible. Parmenides seems to register a poet's awareness, his audition of the nascent surge and prodigality of language before it stiffens into colloquial, utilitarian usage. Handsomely, the salutations which initiate Plato's *Parmenides* echo the welcome of the Goddess in Parmenides' *On Nature*. These moves bear the imprint of dawn. In contrast, says Heidegger, ours is the *Abendland*, the vesperal land of sundown.

Formally, Empedocles is the finer, more memorable of the two poets. His idiom is both archaic and inventive. The expression of the cosmic cycle exercises "a subtle aesthetic fascination; and Empedocles' poetical style—grand, formulaic, repetitive, hierophantic—adds to that seductive power" (Jonathan Barnes). Aristotle records that Empedocles had also written epic poetry. Empedocles' vivid Ionian is studded with neologisms and local turns. Often its prodigal epithets derive from Homer. The debt to Hesiod is evident. Certain touches may derive from Pythagoras and the formulaic parlance of the mystery cults. Empedocles will surface at moments in Aeschylus, notably in the *Oresteia*. The matrix of doctrine is literary. Empedocles' philosophic verse, particularly his *Purifications*, was declaimed at Olympia by the rhapsode Cleomenes. Thought is sung. Sheer poetry emerges: "Zeus, the white splendor"; "the voiceless throng of profusely-spawning fish" (did Yeats know that line?). Surreal terror marks Empedocles' depiction of the torn but errant bodies of the dead and of the turbulence of Chaos (Dante's *bufera*). There are locutions which, observes Barnes, suggest "a Cartesian artist." Empedocles tells of the bruising onrush of images and knowledge into the human mind. Their pressure is polymorphic: "I have already at times been a boy and a girl and a bush / and a bird and mute fish in the salty waves." Radiant Aphrodite will annul the agonistic scissions, the cruel hatreds and bloodletting which darken our world. Via Empedocles' poetics, the logical constraints of the Eleatic school yield to metaphysical conceits and lyric intuitions. The technique of variant reiterations has its didactic musicality.

Hence Empedocles' recurrent presence throughout western literature. The legend of his suicide, of his sandal (golden?) found on the crater's edge have afforded this presence an iconic status. Empedocles remains the philosopher-poet celebrated in poetry. No document in the mythography of thought, no reconstruction of the sacrificial strangeness and apartness of intellectual creativity surpasses the three successive versions of Hölderlin's *Der Tod des Empedokles*. Commentaries on this towering text constitute a meta-poetic and meta-philosophic genre in their own right. Every issue I try to clarify in this essay is set out in Hölderlin. A cyclical cosmology, the doom of a philosopher-king bringing harmony to the works and days of men, teaching made eros are given both intimate and monumental articulation. No other exegesis comes close to Hölderlin's understanding of the transition in Empedocles from ritual and magic to ethics and politics. To his metamorphic rendition of the self-destructive, almost inhuman demands of pure speculative thought as it entrances and consumes the fragile contours of reason. Hölderlin was Hegel's theoretical peer; but pressed further into the vortex of questioning and experiencing the disaster which he anticipates in his *Empedokles*. Whatever his communicative force, the preeminent thinker is condemned to solitude: *"Allein zu sein / Und ohne Götter, ist der Tod."* Godless solitude is death. Not even the human being we love most can *think* with us.

The pedagogic earnestness of Matthew Arnold's *Empedocles on Etna* cannot altogether dull the ache of self-portrayal:

> Before the sophist-brood hath overlaid
> The last spark of man's consciousness with words—
> Ere quite the being of man, ere quite the world
> Be disarrayed of their divinity—
> Before the soul lose all her solemn joys,
> And awe be dead, and hope impossible,
> And the soul's deep eternal night come on—
> Receive me, hide me, quench me, take me home!

What we have of Nietzsche's several attempts to compose an "Empedocles" is not only intriguing in itself but points forward directly to the figure of Zarathustra. McLuhan directs attention to the inherence of Empedocles' speech on double truth in T. S. Eliot's *Four Quartets*. Empedocles' fiery death is evoked by Yeats, Ezra Pound and Joyce. It is present in Primo Levi's *Ad Ora Incerta* of 1984.

Such literary encounters and permutations extend to the Pre-Socratics as a whole. The afterlife of Pythagoras in mathematical lore, in musical theory, in architecture and the occult reaches from the Hellenistic era and Byzantium to Scholasticism and the present. Zeno and the paradox of his arrow's immobility make their meteoric entrance in Valéry's *Cimetière marin*. The materialist atomism of Democritus is a part of the Marxist pantheon and of Marx's hunger for validating precedent.

Subsequent currents in western thought are manifest, be it embryonically, in Eleatic, Ionian, Pythagorean and Heraclitean pronouncements. These are poetic throughout or, more precisely, they antedate differentiations between verse and prose, between narrative moored in mythology and the analytic. From this hybrid source stems the enduring tension between image and axiom in all our philosophy. The Siren song of the poetic, the potential of subversive metaphor which it comports, inhabit systematic thought. Attempts either to enlist this subversion, as in Nietzsche, or to hold it stringently at bay, as in Spinoza or Kant, are the unresolved legacy of the wonder of voiced meditation which originated (but how?) with Thales, Anaxagoras and their inspired successors.

Doubtless, Lucretius looked to Empedocles for guidance. The suicide of the magus quickens the evocations of Etna in *De Rerum Natura* VI: *flamma foras vastis Aetnae fornacibus efflet*—"how an eddy of fire roars suddenly out of Etna." Santayana ranks Lucretius's poem with the *Commedia* and Goethe's *Faust*. It is the *locus classicus* of our theme. But the differences from these other summits are fundamental. Lucretius aims at a "high vulgarization" of the cosmological and moral teachings of Epicurus, at an exposition of his master's instructions on life and death, though he gives to these a personal torsion. Much may escape us in what could well be an incomplete work. It is clear, however, that Lucretius's reflections and perhaps eclectic, Stoically influenced, worldview have an impetus of their own. The sources of vision are twofold. In the Epicurean mode, Lucretius aims to enfranchise men and women from servility to superstitions and from the fear of death. The gods are distant and possibly mortal (Nietzsche knew this text). As is our world, as are the heavens "which must begin and end." At the same time, Lucretius celebrates and seeks to account for manifold natural phenomena, for organic life whose teeming, transformative wonders and terrors he observes unflinchingly.

The opening hymn to Venus, patroness of generation, has rung through the ages. In Dryden's festive version:

> For every kind, by thy prolifique might,
> Springs, and beholds the Regions of the light.

The very stretches of ocean laugh at this generative wonder: *tibi rident aequora ponti*. Animated by love, by a cosmic *élan vital*, "herds go wild and bound in their pastures"; as does the Latin: *ferae pecudes persultant*. In counterpoint to this exultant naturalism, Lucretius has an implacable sense of "the reality principle," of irremediable human exposure to disaster. Who, save Thucydides, has matched his rendition of the plague? Of that "tide of death" out of Egypt which engulfs Athens, scorching men to madness. Lucretius emphasizes the strengths of reason, of rational diagnosis. But he enforces their limitations. The observation is numbing: *mussabat tacito medicina timore.* In C. H. Sisson's translation:

> The doctors muttered and did not know what to say:
> They were frightened of so many open, burning eyes
> Turning towards them because they could not sleep.

Sleep is instrumental in *De Rerum Natura.* It liberates the spirit from turmoil and anguish. Why fret if it should prove everlasting after the stress of transient life? In as lapidary an axiom as Wittgenstein's, Lucretius concludes that "death cannot be lived," it lies unharming outside existence.

Lucretius is the most *Latin* of Roman poets, the one whose ear and linguistic sensibility concur most intimately with the genius of the tongue where it is least informed, as in Virgil, by exemplary Greek. No other Roman poet matches the weight, the tread as of a legion on the march:

> ergo animus sive aegrescit, mortalia signa
> mittit, uti docui, seu flectitur a medicina.
> usque adeo falsae rationi vera videtur
> res occurrere et effugium praecludere eunti
> ancipitique refutatu convincere falsum.

This simile of truth in combat with false reasoning, cutting off its retreat as it flees and vanquishing error with a two-pronged refutation, is military throughout. The noise of battle is consonant with the fricatives, the *r* and *f* sounds which drive the passage forward. Walter Savage Landor characterized the register of *De Rerum Natura* as being "masculine, plain, concentrated, and energetic." It defines Latinity.

Lucretius makes us feel that there are in certain movements of thought, of abstract argument, a *gravitas*, a material weight (Simone Weil's *la pesanteur*). The syllables, in which consonants energize the packed, sometimes rebarbative syntax, seem to bend and then spring forward under the weight of philosophic speculation. When there is speed in the cadence it is that of an armored swiftness, of a pugnacious *accelerando*. Like that of boys dancing "clad in armor, clashing bronze upon bronze to a measure." No translation matches the mercurial weight, if there is such a thing, of the original:

> cum pueri circum puerum pernice chorea
> armatei in numerum pulsarent aeribus aera.

Lucretius's genius for the "interanimation"—I. A. Richards's term—of moral, cognitive, scientific, medical and political teachings with inspired poetic enactment proved exemplary. Numerous poets of a philosophic or scientific bent strove to rival *De Rerum Natura*. Whenever, wherever western speculative sensibility inclines toward atheism, overt or masked, toward materialism and stoic humanism, Lucretius is talismanic. His tranquil daring, the bracing assent to life's brevity and afflictions which inform his argument were indispensable to Leopardi's poems and philosophic dialogues. As did Voltaire before him, the young Leopardi saw in *De Rerum Natura* a text which, incomparably, compels knowledge into the daylight of reason. Tennyson's *Lucretius* is a meditation perhaps uncharacteristically tinged by the erotic. But its paraphrase of passages in Lucretius is sovereign: "I saw the flaring atom-streams / And torrents of her myriad universe." If at all, the gods merely "haunt / The lucid interspace of world and world." The hour may not be far off when momentary man

> Shall seem no more a something to himself,
> But he, his hopes and hates, his homes and fanes,
> And even his bones long laid within the grave,
> The very sides of the grave itself shall pass,

Vanishing, atom and void, atom and void,
Into the unseen for ever....

Dated 1868, Tennyson's scenario of Lucretius's alleged suicide throws light on his own anxious efforts to reconcile with human trust the bitter scientific and technological disputes of his time.

The characterization of Lucretius by the young Marx in the prolegomena to a projected history of Epicurean and skeptical philosophy is hard to better: "Heroic warfare *omnium contra omnes*, the stark stance of autonomy, Nature emptied of the gods and a God alien to the world." Citing *De Rerum Natura* I, 922–34, Marx notes its "thunderous song." A text which proclaims the "eternal rejoicing of the spirit."

That rejoicing of the intellect figures in the rarely quoted but extensive "Notes on Lucretius" which Leo Strauss included in his *Liberalism Ancient and Modern* (1968). In Lucretius's poem "not to say in Epicureanism generally, premodern thought seems to come closer to modern thought than anywhere else. No premodern writer seems to have been as deeply moved as Lucretius was by the thought that nothing lovable is eternal or sempiternal or deathless, or that the eternal is not lovable." Paraphrasing, Strauss sees the subject as dark, "but the poem is bright." Lucretius shows us that "poetry is the link or the mediation between religion and philosophy." Echoing his own exegetic stance, Strauss finds that "the philosophic poet is the perfect mediator between the attachment to the world and the attachment to detachment from the world. The joy or pleasure which Lucretius's poem arouses is therefore austere, reminding of the pleasure aroused by the work of Thucydides." Elsewhere Strauss will revert to this analogy.

If Lucretius marks the apex of "thought poetry," of poetic instauration and exposition of systematic philosophic intentions going back to the Pre-Socratics, *De Rerum Natura* also signals a prolonged epilogue. What successful philosophic epic has come after?

The case of Dante is exceedingly complex, made more so by the virtually incommensurable secondary literature. Dante's contributions to philosophic theology, to ontology after Aristotle, to political theory, to aesthetics, to cosmological speculations are, of course, momentous. We have proof of no subtler, more compendious intellect, of no supreme poetic powers more endowed with analytic penetration, of no sensibility in which disciplined logical and psychological alertness were brought to bear more creatively on language. Dante's range of philosophic reference is omnivorous. It includes Aristotle's legacy, Seneca, the Stoics, Cicero, the Church Fathers, Averroës, Aquinas and, perhaps, further Islamic sources. It is faintly possible that the *Commedia* reveals indices of contact with Hebraic and Kabbalistic material accessible in Verona. Dante's Thomism is of a strength of assimilation and restatement without rival. At moments, Aristotle comes close to being equated with God. Yet Dante's uses of Ptolemaic astronomy do challenge Aristotelian orthodoxy. And although the evidence remains disputed, the *Commedia* may have flirted with the heretical metaphysics of Siger of Brabant. In short, from the Neoplatonism of the early love poetry with its intricate interplay of eros and intellect onward, Dante's work in both verse and prose is immersed in the idiom, often technical, and in the conceptual determinants of the philosophical. Dame Philosophy never left his side.

It has been said, by Étienne Gilson among others, that Dante envisoned a total metaphysics which would include theology thus unlocking the secrets of being and of the universe. Which would, for example, disclose why the heavens revolve from east to west and reveal the origins of our universe. Such sovereign philosophy and metaphysical cosmology would recompense the labors of reason even as theology rewarded those of faith. Yet Dante knew that this *summa summarum* of the intelligible lies beyond the grasp of mortal minds: "*Iddio lo sa, chè a me pare presuntuoso a giudicare.*" One thing is clear: in Dante's *oeuvre* theology presides over, marshals the intellectual, often abstract discourse, the moral dialectic and the sciences. The arduous pilgrimage of the spirit is theologically motivated and crowned. Dante's prodigiously informed philosophy of history, his political doctrines, his polyglot philology, even his uses of mathematical and musical analogues or symbolism are ramifications from a theological meridian. The reach is vast and, more than once, idiosyncratic. But the constraints are those of a Scholastic armature and prescription, whatever final understanding might lie beyond it.

After Dante, the heroic, the allegoric, the romantic epic has its manifold history. It is, together with aspirations echoing the *Commedia*, alive in Pound's *Cantos*. But the full-scale philosophic poem, the use of verse to profess and expound a metaphysical *doxa* becomes rare. Coleridge planned precisely such an enterprise with fervent resolve. Hearing Wordsworth reciting a part of *The Prelude* on the night of January 7, 1807, he saluted

> —An Orphic song indeed,
> A song divine of high and passionate thoughts,
> To their own music chanted!

Here shone the light of "Thoughts all too deep for words!" To Coleridge it seemed convincing that when completed, Wordsworth's *Recluse* and *Excursion* would realize that fusion of song and philosophy, of the rhapsodic and the cognitive which myth had attributed to Orphic revelation. But the notion of philosophy implicit in Coleridge's encomia is diffuse and metaphoric. It dwells on introspective consciousness rather than systematic thought. Victor Hugo's late eschatological epics remain unread.

If there is an exception, often slighted, it is that of Pope's *Essay on Man* of 1732–33. His was not a philosophic temper though, interestingly, Pope did intuit something of Abélard's stature. The *Essay* draws on Newton and Bolingbroke, possibly on Leibniz, as Lucretius had drawn on Epicurus. Formally, the indebtedness to Horace's *Epistles* is undisguised. But the poised incisiveness of Pope's heroic couplets lends authority to the providential ethics and cosmology which he propounds:

Heav'n from all creatures hides the book of Fate,
All but the page prescrib'd, their present state:
From brutes what men, from men what spirits know:
Or who could suffer Being here below?
The lamb thy riot dooms to bleed to day,
Had he thy Reason, would he skip and play?
Pleas'd to the last, he crops the flow'ry food,
And licks the hand just rais'd to shed his blood.
Oh blindness to the future! kindly giv'n,
That each may fill the circle mark'd by Heav'n:
Who sees with equal eye, as God of all,
A hero perish, or a sparrow fall,
Atoms or systems into ruin hurl'd,
And now a bubble burst, and now a world.

Note the transition from the "book of Fate" to the "page prescrib'd,"
the muted allusion to both *Hamlet* and the Gospels in the fall of the
sparrow and the exact dichotomy of "atoms" and "systems." Kant,
no easy judge, admired Pope's *Essay* for its philosophic message and
poetic economy.

3

Again, as in respect of Dante, the secondary literature is mountainous. To the industry of commentaries on Plato, of commentaries, often polemic, on these commentaries, there is no end. Bibliographies are tomes in their own right. Yet in this perennial tide there seems to be a central void. It is the study of Plato's *literary* genius, of his supremacy as a dramatist and of the ways in which that genius and supremacy necessarily generate the substance of his metaphysical, epistemological, political and aesthetic teachings. There have been ample studies of Plato's initiation and uses of myth. There have been fitful attempts to chart the "play of characters" within the dialogues. There have been rare notices of the presence of one or another historical persona in the conversations (e.g. Critias in the *Timaeus*). We find acute but scattered observations in Kenneth Burke's pioneering rhetoric of motives. The vocabulary, the syntax, the heuristic and oratorical turns in Plato's prose have been minutely dissected.

What we lack (though there are approaches in Lidia Palumbo's work on *Mimesis*, on "theater and world" in the dialogues [2008]) is any adequate analysis of Plato's incomparable dramaturgy, of his invention and placement of characters rivaling that of Shakespeare, of Molière or Ibsen. There have been ingenious inquiries into the scenario of the opening lines in major dialogues; but no systematic critical examination of how urban and rural, private or public settings, *mises en scène*, initiate and inform the subsequent dialectic. I know of no comprehensive look at the role of entrances and exits in the dialogues though these are as paced and shaping as in any great play.

The Platonic account of the trial and death of Socrates has long been regarded, together with Golgotha, as archetypal of western tragic art and feeling in *toto*. We know that Plato began by writing tragedies. Certain dialogues, the *Symposium* and the *Phaedrus* among them, have been staged. Erik Satie's musical setting of *La Mort de Socrate* is crystalline. But we do not have any literary and philosophically authoritative investigation of the manifold ways in which Platonic thought and Platonism are the products of a *writer*, of a dramatic sensibility and technique second to none in both the tragic and, more rarely, comic or ironic vein. What is missing is any thorough analysis of such complex literary devices as Plato's indirect narrations, of the deliberately counter-realistic postulate of a lengthy colloquy as reported by the memory of a witness or participant or, at threefold remove, by one to whom such a participant had brought report (a maneuver of triple "alienation" as Brecht might put it). We need to consider the dramaturgy of absences: that of Plato at the hour of his master's death, that of Socrates—if he is not the Athenian Stranger!—from Plato's final and most compendious dialogue, the *Laws*.

In this essay I am trying to clarify the extent to which all philosophy is *style*. No philosophic proposition outside formal logic is separable from its semantic means and context. Nor is it totally translatable, as Cicero found with regard to his Greek sources. Where philosophy aches for abstract universality, as in Spinoza's *more geometricum* or Frege's epistemology, the resulting tensions and frustrations are unmistakable. Thus it is not only that all western philosophy is a footnote to Plato, as A. N. Whitehead said. It is that the Platonic dialogues and letters are performative literary acts of surpassing richness and complication. In these texts abstract and speculative thought of utmost complexity is embodied or as Shakespeare puts it "bodied forth." Intellectual moves and counter-moves are dramatically voiced. There are occasions on which the *Commedia* or *Faust II* or *Ulysses*—in the inspired debate on *Hamlet*—achieve such incarnation. We have the theological-metaphysical parable of Dostoevsky's "Grand Inquisitor" and Kafka's allegories. But none of these paramount instances, with the possible exception of Dante, matches the compass, the variousness and the immediacies of Plato's theater of the mind.

There is much that remains enigmatic in the capacity of literature, of oral and written words and sentences to create, to communicate to us, to render unforgettable characters. Characters more complex, loveable or hateful, consoling or menacing by far than the vast majority of the living. Personae with whom we may come to identify our own lesser lives and who endure—a radiant paradox which Flaubert found outrageous—far beyond the individual life span of both writer and reader. What *imitatio* of divine or organic creation, what vitalizing technique make possible the begetting and durability of an Odysseus, an Emma Bovary, a Sherlock Holmes or a Molly Bloom? Sartre's contention that these are nothing but scratches on a page is both incontrovertible and risibly inadequate.

No less than the quest for "the historical Jesus" that for the "actual" Socrates remains inconclusive, possibly factitious. We do not, we cannot know with any confidence what the living Socrates was like or what he taught. Scholars incline to the view that he may well have resembled the somewhat pedestrian, domesticated moralist and "economist" depicted by Xenophon. How much authentic reportage is concealed in the satiric portrayal of Socrates in Aristophanes' *Clouds*? My "blameless" intuition (Quine's forgiving epithet) is this: Plato's Socrates is a literary-dramaturgical construct like no other. Neither Hamlet nor Faust, neither Don Quixote nor Captain Ahab, surpass the psychological prodigality, the physical and mental characteristics, the "real presence" of the Socrates quickened to virtually unquenchable life in the dialogues. Or quite match the ironized pathos of Socrates' trial and death as Plato enriched, composed, invented these—we simply do not know. What is more: no other figure in our legacy rivals the cognitive depths and ethical urgency manifest in Plato's *montage*—if that is what it was. Hamlet, Faust, Proust's Narrator are intellectual presences of momentous stature. As is Dante's Virgil. Alyosha Karamazov radiates moral provocation. But even these *dramatis personae* do not equal the philosophic-moral dimensions of Plato's Socrates, dimensions which compel so much of western consciousness and questioning to follow in their wake. It seems to me that there has been no greater "wordsmith" than Plato.

This makes fascinating and central to our theme Plato's notorious quarrel with poets and poetry, a quarrel anticipated, as we saw, by Heraclitus but notable also in Xenophanes and in Hesiod's critique of Homer. Plato who had composed tragedies in his youth, and who confesses in Book X of the *Republic* how painful it is for him to disenfranchise his spirit from the enchantments of the poetic. Yet the verdict is emphatic: nothing but didactic and civically ornamental poetry is to be allowed in either the possible or the ideal *polis*. The peregrine bards and rhapsodes who had played so marked a part in nascent Greek discourse and *paideia* were to be banished. Once more, the corpus of commentary is intractably voluminous and does much to obscure an already complex, perhaps ambiguous issue.

Whenever philosophy and literature engage, elements of the Platonic polemic surface. It is echoed in ecclesiastical condemnations of theatrical spectacles and licentious writings across the centuries. The Platonic ideal models Rousseau's indictment of playhouses. It underlies Tolstoy's fundamentalist iconoclasm. It is implicit in Freud's reading of poetry as an infantile daydream to be outgrown by adult, cognitive access to positive knowledge and the "reality principle." Of even graver consequence is Plato's draconian perception that uncensored art and literature, ungoverned musicality are inherently anarchic, that they sap the pedagogic duties, the ideological coherence and governance of the state. This conviction, set out with chilling severity in the *Laws*, has generated numerous programs of "thought control" and censorship, whether inquisitorial, Puritan, Jacobin, fascist or Leninist. The unfettered poet or novelist energizes, exemplifies the rebellious irresponsibilities of the imagination. He is always to the left of official sentiment. In the economy, always under pressure, of civic means and obligations the aesthetic can entail both waste and subversion. From this point of view Plato does worse than repudiate the "open society" (Popper's celebrated indictment): he repudiates the open mind. He seeks to discipline the sensuous, ungoverned demon within ourselves, a potential in sharp contrast with the *daimon* of justice in Socrates.

The problem is that this position, even stripped of its ironies, compounds metaphysical, political, moral, aesthetic and possibly psychological motives which are exceedingly difficult to disentangle and recapture.

The consensus is that the core of Plato's case is epistemological, that his condemnation of poetry and the arts derives directly from his threefold architecture of being. Abstract, eternal, immune to sensory apprehension are the Ideas or archetypal Forms which alone underwrite ontological truth. These "primes" are only *partly* accessible to philosophic language, to the art of inquiry in the dialectic. The secondary level is that of the transient, mutable, imperfect realm of the empirical, of the everyday world. At dual remove from verity are the modes of representation, of *mimesis*. The carpenter produces a table in the internalized, "remembered" light of its transcendent Form. The painter, incapable of making any such object, provides an image of it. All representation is a shadow play parasitic on reality. Images are mere images: *eidola, eikones, mimemata*. There is worse. These phantasms pretend to being truthful. Every fiction *feigns*. It would pass itself off as authentic. It arouses and cultivates emotions, empathies, terrors beyond those elicited by truthful perception and experience. This fraudulent power, this enactment of the inauthentic literally corrupts the human soul and competes fatally with what should be the schooling, the achievement of maturity in our consciousness and in the city. (In his *Poetics*, Aristotle takes exactly the opposite view.) That seductive corruption is deepened by the rhapsode's or dramatist's uses of myth, by his unlicensed inventions, prodigal in Homer, of scandalous gossip about the behavior of the gods. Tragedies teem with horrors, incest and melodramatic implausibilities (cf. Tolstoy's withering critique of Gloucester's leap from the cliffs of Dover in *King Lear*). It is no accident, suggests Plato, that poets laud tyrants and flourish under their régime. Yielding to lust and cruelty, the despot embodies unbridled desires and *eros*. It is *eros*, in the radical sense, which the poet exalts, generating injustice as does Thrasymachus in the *Republic* (Leo Strauss concurs). That the corrupting enchantments of the fictive, of the "phantasm" take hold most intensely on the young, on sensibility when it is embryonic, accentuates the danger. The pedagogic centrality of Homer in *paideia* is nothing less than culpable. Blind Homer who contrives Achilles' feats while knowing nothing of battle, who narrates the travels of Odysseus while himself wholly ignorant of navigation. T. E. Lawrence will meditate on this falsehood in the preface to his version of the *Odyssey*. He, at least, had built rafts and "killed his man." Hence the imperative need for bowdlerization and censorship, for renditions of Homer appropriate to education, of art and music which accompany and celebrate martial skills and the harmonies of law. Hence the injunction, more or less courteous, to the poets, mimes and flute players to leave the *politeia* and peddle elsewhere the narcotics of pretense.

The epistemological indictment is cogent and subtle. The connections in depth between "truth-functions" and law and order are persuasively set out. The associations between the poet and the Sophist, Pindar as referred to in the *Republic* and the *Protagoras* being a stellar instance, remain unsettling. Our present-day perplexities as to the possible legitimacy of censorship in regard to pornographic and sadistic material in the media point to the vitality of

Platonic discriminations. But a more personal conflict may have been instrumental.

When he proposes to banish the singers and the tragedians (though like St. Paul he quotes Euripides), when he picks his quarrels with deceiving Homer, Plato may at the deepest level be wrestling with himself. He is seeking to keep at bay the supreme dramatist, the mythmaker and narrator of genius within his own powers. Even in as stringently abstract a dialogue as the *Theatetes* or the arid stretches of the *Laws*, the gravitational pull of literary art is discernible. Observe the adroit *mise en scène* which sparks off the debate on knowledge in the *Theatetes*. The perennial temptations and threats are those of style, of mimetic art, of the deflection by literary techniques of the metaphysical, political or cosmological issues. The rigorous thinker, the teacher of *doxa*, the logician and celebrant of mathematics grapples with the inventive, lyrically inspired *writer*.

The struggle is the more vehement because both parties, as it were, know of their unison or intimate kinship. Indivisible from natural language, philosophy will enlist or seek to excise the magnetic attraction of the literary. Bergson yields to it. Hence his uneasy relations to Proust, a *malaise* paralleled by that between William and Henry James. Spinoza, Wittgenstein resist to the utmost. It is Heidegger's almost despotic belief that philosophy will overcome this generic dualism and internal scission by hammering out an idiom of its own. Yet even here the presence of Hölderlin is at once a paradigm and an inhibition.

The tension between the poetic and the dialectic, the schism of consciousness pervades Plato's work. The shadowboxing is key. In both the *Phaedrus* and the *Seventh Letter* the praxis of the written word with its functional relations to literature is challenged. Writing lessens the seminal role and resources of memory. It enshrines a factitious authority. It blocks the salutary immediacy of questioning, of dissent and correction. Only *viva voce* exchange with its openness to interjection can achieve either fruitful polemic or consensual accord. The written alphabet and script have been a mixed blessing.

Socrates does not write. It is difficult to know what *gravitas* attaches to these astute animadversions. Irony is a recurrent Platonic move. There may be filaments of humor in even the most magisterial of Plato's contentions. This rebuke to writing stems from a towering writer. It has something of the self-negating thrust of the pronouncement that "language ends" at the close of Shakespeare's *Timon of Athens*. Socrates' abstention from the written word is allowed to press on Plato, on the literary genius of his configurations and dramatizations of his master.

The ironies, the teasing in the *Ion* are sparkling. The rhapsode, the entranced bard is, much in the vein of Molière, unaware of the deconstruction to which he is subject. He who cannot manage a skiff depicts storm-tossed argosies. In innocent vainglory Ion speaks for strategists and heroes. He justifies this incompetent expertise by laying claim to an oracular afflatus. Which is in truth a species of childish madness, shared in *A Midsummer Night's Dream* by the lunatic and the lover. In this early satire, so directly aimed at Homer, the victim occasions more merriment than harm. Matters darken in the *Republic* and the *Laws*.

The *Laws* 817b seems to me as decisive as it is opaque. This passage has often been ignored, even by Leo Strauss and his disciples for whom this final dialogue is canonic. Asked why there is no place for tragedians, though they are eminent, in the *polis* which Plato is designing, the Athenian replies:

we are ourselves authors of a tragedy, and that the finest and best we know how to make. In fact, our whole polity has been constructed as a dramatization of a noble and perfect life; that is what *we* hold to be in truth the most real of tragedies. Thus you are poets, and we are also poets in the same style, rival artists and rival actors, and that in the finest of all dramas, one which indeed can be produced only by a code of true law.

What is Plato telling us in this "shocking dialogue" (Thomas L. Pangle)? And in this passage above all? I have found no satisfactory elucidation.

Certain statements in modern contexts may throw an oblique light. Croce—but this might be a mere echo—qualifies political actions as "grand, terrible" and ultimately tragic. Trumpeting the "Tasks of the German Theater" in May 1933, Goebbels declares that "politics is the highest art there is, since the sculptor shapes only the stone, the dead stone, and the poet only the word, which in itself is dead. But the statesman shapes the masses, gives them statute and structure, breathes in form and life so that a people arises from them." In one of her final notes Hannah Arendt says that more than any literature the *polis* guards and transmits remembrance, thus ensuring the prestige of future generations. But again, this dictum may paraphrase Plato. Closer to the source we find Pericles' assertion that Athens no longer has need of Homer or Democritus. Human beings attain fulfilment through "the highest art" which is indeed that of politics. A finding echoed in turn in Machiavelli's republicanism.

Is this not to slight the crux of rivalry, of agonistic kinship in our text? "We are also poets in the same style, rival artists and rival actors...." The poetic however inspired is not only subversive: it is superfluous because political understanding and the codification of "true law" contain what is best in drama. They provide reasoned sensibility with both ideals and practicalities of social order, of institutional ripening, richer, more adult (Freud's criterion) than those feigned by mimetic enactments. Once more, one senses, Plato is laboring to dominate or rather incorporate—Ben Jonson would say "ingest"—the great stylist and dramatist within himself. He is seeking to abolish the distance between thinker and poet but to the former's advantage.

But as so often in Plato, a wider implication hovers on the horizon like light after sunset. Even at its best and most truthful politics, the instauration of the just city is, at the last, "the most real of tragedies." Politics belongs ineluctably to the sphere of the contingent, of the pragmatic. It is, therefore, transient and, ultimately, destined to fail. This is the aged Plato speaking, the would-be legislator and counselor to princes twice defeated in Sicily. What scenic tragedy, what poetic pathos surpasses the moral and psychological desolation of the sack of Miletus or the humbling of Athens by Spartan victors?

Nonetheless, whatever his ambivalence, Plato could not evade his literary genius. He could not excise from his dialogues the myth-laden language, the dramaturgy in which they are composed. No philosophy is more integrally literature. "Rival artists" but himself both.

Such is the wealth of material that I can touch only on a few examples.

As on stage or in the novel Plato's settings are often thematic. The pastoral prelude to the *Phaedrus*—that summer's day on the banks of the Ilissus near the spot where the wind-god Boreas snatched the nymph Orithya—sets the lyric, magically lit yet at moments poignant tone for the ensuing discourse on love. When the heat abates, Socrates offers a valedictory prayer to Pan and the sylvan deities. Now "let us be going." The intimations of locale in the *Laws* are of the subtlest. Three old men meet on a road in Crete. The distance from Knossos to the cave and sanctuary of Zeus is considerable, preparing us for the length of their colloquy. The day is sultry, almost concordant with all that is oppressive in Plato's political blueprint. But "shady resting places" can be hoped for, among them a "grove of prodigiously fine tall cypresses," trees at once sepulchral and cooling.

The stage setting for the *Protagoras* is a comic miniature. The illustrious visitor is lodging in the house of Callias. Where he spends most of his time indoors—a delicate barb coming from Socrates committed to open and public spaces. It is not yet daylight. At Callias's door, the porter, a eunuch, is in a foul mood. Cursed be the Sophists and their swarm of acolytes. There follows one of the most arresting passages in western prose. Protagoras is walking in the portico with a long line of eager listeners on either side. His voice, as did Orpheus's, has charmed men from numerous cities. The choreography is notable. Socrates is "delighted to notice what special care they took never to get in front or to be in Protagoras's way. When he and those with him turned round, the listeners divided this way and that in perfect order, and executing a circular movement took their places each time in the rear. It was beautiful." This ballet exactly mimes and teases the circularities of Sophistic rhetoric. Identifying the rapt auditors, Socrates quotes the *Odyssey* 11, 601: a celebration of martial discipline. Knowing Plato's suspicions of Homer, we can gauge the irony. Yet also the part of admiration. The dialogue will close on a complimentary note. Protagoras predicts that his young challenger "may become one of our leading philosophers." The *Euthydemus* gets under way with a telling vignette. Socrates is talking and conversing in the Lyceum. Crito wants to listen but the surrounding crowd is so thick that he cannot get close: "However I stretched up and looked over."

The indirections in the *Parmenides* are "counter-realistic" to a degree. Four interlocutors meet in the marketplace in Athens. The visitors from Clazomenae have been told—a further interposition—that Antiphon "has been much in the company of someone called Pythodorus who has related to him the conversation which Socrates once had with Zeno and Parmenides." Antiphon is said to have heard this relation so often "that he can repeat it by heart." This hyperbolic conceit, perhaps self-ironizing, illustrates the Platonic cult of the gymnastics of memory. Antiphon's house is close by, in Melite. He is at home instructing a smith about forging a bit for one of his horses, objects of his main interest. Somewhat reluctantly he agrees to reproduce the entire dialogue. Might it be that these seemingly gratuitous complications and "distancing effects" serve to situate a philosophic text characterized by uncertainties and incompletions?

As the *Charmides* gets under way, Socrates has just returned from the bitter battle at Potidea. Spotting him close to the sanctuary of Basile, Chaerephon "who always behaves like a madman," rushes toward him, seizes his hand and cries out: "How did you escape from the battle, Socrates?" Virtually always Plato signals precise locations, many of whose implicit references or symbolism are bound to elude us. Thus Socrates is walking from the Academy to the Lyceum along the road which skirts the outside of the city walls. He "has reached the little gate where the Panops has its source" when he chances on a cluster of young men eager to engage him. From this unpremeditated encounter springs the *Lysis*, one of the determinant treatments of Socratic pedagogy.

The performative virtuosities which place the *Phaedo* and the *Symposium* among the very summits of all literature need no emphasis. Plato's account of the death of Socrates has informed western consciousness. Comparable only to the Gospel narratives it has been a touchstone of moral and intellectual aspirations. Abstractly, propositionally, the Socratic "proof" of the immortality of the soul may be feeble. As poetry in action it is transcendent. The compositional marvels of the *Symposium* have been endlessly acclaimed. Inexhaustible are Plato's dramaturgical resources—the feast in Agathon's house after his victory in the theater, the nocturnal street outside, the scenario of the porch, the coming of dawn—and the formidably calculated, dialectical play of exits and entrances. Socrates' belated arrival and solitary sober departure are wonders of implied and enacted significance. Alcibiades' arrival, both riot and consecration, is hardly surpassed in any drama or novel. Aristophanes' intervention is astutely suggestive of his comic genius. The wise woman of Mantinea, Diotima, is both absent and formidably present via Socrates' report of her doctrine of love, a report at the roots of Neoplatonism and of Hölderlin's life and work. Inebriation, exhaustion, sleep lap around the protagonists and their oratory. Every move is plotted by a supreme director. Even that of the flute-girl who helps the besotted Alcibiades stagger in "with a mass of ribbons and an enormous wreath of ivy and violets sprouting on his head" (assuredly Caravaggio had come across this image). The graphic vivacities light every gesture. Only a supreme artist could have devised the epilogue. First Aristophanes then Agathon succumb to sodden sleep. Pellucid Socrates "tucks them in comfortably" and leaves for the Lyceum and a bath. I have tried to show elsewhere what fatalities shadow this apparently auroral exit, what deep analogies obtain between the "going into the night" of the *Symposium* and the Last Supper.

Does a Hamlet, a Falstaff have greater "real presence" than Plato's Socrates, is there a more various sum of humanity in Don Quixote? I have expressed my conviction that only an ear deaf to language can doubt that the Socrates presented by Plato is to an eminent degree a product of intellectual, psychological and stylistic creation, that the ripening complexity of his role across successive dialogues is proof of Plato's art. That it enlists the compositional and corrosive agencies of time as does Proust.

A mosaic of snapshots testifies to Plato's craft. Socrates both tranquil and lost in thought during the vexed retreat from battle; Socrates pondering and immobile on his way to Agathon; Socrates returning to Aesop and song at the approach of death. Philosophical and psychological points being made via physical figures. In the shadowboxing of the dialectic—Plato's own simile—Socrates is neither unfailingly upright nor always victorious. He does not prevail against Protagoras. In the *Republic* the incensed Trasymachus, himself a striking *persona*, is not convincingly refuted. The key debate over the ontological status of Ideas in the *Parmenides* ends inconclusively, even confusedly. There are controlled modulations and shifts of key within dialogues. At the close of the *Cratylus* playful ironies and teasing yield to a tidal impulse at once lyric and philosophically charged in praise of goodness and beauty "beyond words." In the *Timaeus*, for so long the most influential of Platonic writings, a tangible incapacity to resolve certain cosmological dilemmas initiates a confident "poetics of eternity." The epistemological labors in the *Theatetes* may, as one authoritive commentary has it, "leave us more in the dark than ever." But there ensues in a major key an exultant recognition of "unknowing," of what Keats will entitle "negative capability" and what Heidegger will commend as *Gelassenheit*. Thought is made cadence and character.

Dramatic animation reaches far beyond Socrates. We saw the silhouette of vainglory in Ion. The gallery of Sophists tells of a complicity between verbal acrobatics and moral or logical insights which Plato may apprehend within himself. "Bristling" Protagoras who "does battle with his answers" is allowed an oratorical sweep consonant with his age and eminence. Gorgias's dazzling eloquence literally tires, unravels under Socrates' needling queries. The Sophist falls totally silent, an unforgettable touch. Polus and Callicles "leap" into the breach. Consider the discriminations, the nuances of intellectual weight as between Glaucon, Ademantus and Trasymachus in the *Republic*. Or as between Critias and Timaeus in the two possibly unfinished dialogues which bear their names. Seeking to best Timaeus and, beyond him, Socrates, Critias turns almost childishly arrogant, a *miles gloriosus* of shallow but blustering argument. The diverse representations of Alcibiades, of his immature grandeur, of his amorous, frustrated wooing of Socrates, whose ugliness is made erotically plausible, exhibit dramatic techniques of the highest caliber. Consider the fragile nascence and unfolding of doubt, of upright bafflement in the voice of Parmenides. The similes at the outset of his great monologue are at once rhetorical and poignant. He is an aged racehorse at Ibycus, trembling at the starting line; an aged poet forced, like Yeats, "into the lists of love"; his own memories "make me afraid of setting out at my age to cross so vast and hazardous a sea." But sitting at his feet "after all these years" are Zeno, Aristotle, Pythodorus and Socrates himself. Was there ever a more stellar seminar? Everywhere, the poets are present. Socrates disputes Protagoras's valuation of Simonides. He contests Antisthenes' conception of Odysseus as an exemplary sage. In a crucial passage of the *Protagoras* (347–48), Plato rejects the uses of poetic interpretation for philosophic ends. Yet there is between poetry and thought an "exultant antagonism" (Maurice Blanchot). The riddling images of the poetic allow philosophic intuitions to reach daylight. Perhaps, suggests Blanchot, this "strange sagacity" is too ancient for Socrates.

Tolstoy bids us take note of the distributive justice whereby a writer brings to memorable life a minor, transient personage, a footman. Who can forget the slave boy in the *Meno* or momentary Theodorus whose arithmetic gaffe launches the *Statesman* on its tortuous way? Voices, motions, embodiments rivaling Shakespeare's but at the service of philosophy.

4

The dialogue genre predates Plato. Aristotle's dialogues are lost. Of all forms, dialogue comes nearest those ideals of query and refutation, of correction and *reprise* enjoined by Plato in his critique of writing. Dialogue performs orality; it suggests, even in writing, possibilities of anti-authoritarian spontaneity and fair play. Thus this genre will play a signal part in western philosophy.

Metaphysical and theological dialogues, the two rubrics being customarily indistinguishable, continue to be produced throughout late antiquity, Hellenism and early Christendom. The library at Cluny, available to Abélard, contained examples by Cicero, Justin, Athanasius and Boethius. First and foremost, he would have known the extensive heuristic and speculative dialogues of St. Augustine. Abélard's *Dialogus inter Philosophum, Judaeum et Christianum* looks to be his final work and remains incomplete. Scholars date it as c. 1140. The visionary dream of three figures approaching the narrator-arbiter from three directions is traditionally allegoric. But the ground bass of melancholy, the delicate intimations of a justice beyond dogma and orthodoxy are wholly Abélard's. They make of this text a spellbinding document of the humane.

The disputants share a fundamental monotheism. Otherwise no substantive exchange would be feasible. The Jew draws exclusively but proudly on the Old Testament. On the Mosaic perception of God as *mysterium fascinans, augustum et tremendum*. He does, however, seek to satisfy the Philosopher's demand for rationality, for ethical demonstration. Grimly he invokes the status of the medieval Jew in "the fiery pit of suffering ... despised and hated." Nonetheless he cites Psalm XVII and its exultant prospect of an eschatological reunion with Jahweh: "I will behold thy face in righteousness: I shall be satisfied when I awake with thy likeness." Abélard may never have heard this Psalm intoned but his own experience of suffering and pariahdom gives to his figuration of the Jew a singular equity and pathos (it is of a theological ballast beyond that of Shylock). Abélard allows Judaism a unique religious and historical condition. He registers but does not share the Philosopher's insistence on Jewish acerbity and exclusivity. Echoing his own previous commentary on *Romans*, Abélard defines the election of the Jew as "preliminary." The *circumcisio Abrahae* will become "a circumcision of the heart." Though in a manner the Jew would not concede, the future is one of promise and homecoming.

The Philosopher disputes the claims to universality of the vengeful and tribal deity of Sinai. He argues his *imperfectio caritatis*. Later history, he contends, has shown the inadequacies of Mosaic law. The Philosopher refers to the logical but also moral defects of God's answer to Job. Scholars suggest that this dialectic is inspired by Islamic exegetes then active in Spain and known to Abélard. The *vera ethica Christi* combines and develops the Judaic call for ethical prescriptions, for submission to the Almighty with the Philosopher's demand for rational evidence. The Christian affirms that Law (*Nomos*) is enclosed in the revealed Word (*Logos*). Abélard's logic and metaphysics are conjoined in this Christological version of the *summum bonum*. In the Christian's confident eloquence Pauline and Augustinian echoes abound. Incarnation alone can validate that *promissio illae vitae aeternae* made by Judaism. It alone can fulfill the tremendous assurance given by Psalm CXXXIX of a divine presence even in Hell. At the same time the Christian debates with the Philosopher without slighting the latter's legitimate objections. This dialectic leads to the pivotal insight that there are verities inaccessible to, inexpressible by either language or deductive reasoning. It may be, and Abélard is here at his inmost, that silence becomes the only consequent mode of prayer. Throughout it is the dialogue format which empowers a fairness, a psychological justice which will not recur in European literature until Lessing's *Nathan the Wise*.

Galileo's informed, critical interests ranged beyond the natural sciences and mathematics. They included literature, music, the fine arts (cf. Erwin Panofsky's classical article of 1954 on "Galileo as a Critic of the Arts"). Already Galileo's contemporaries marveled at his myriad-minded concerns. We have his *Postille* (notes) on Ariosto and Petrarch and two public lectures delivered in Florence in 1588 on the cosmography of Dante's *Inferno*. There are the polemic *Considerazioni al Tasso*. Some scholars assign these to the years between 1589 and 1592; others to the 1620s. Their somewhat haughty asperities, at which later readers such as the romantic poet Foscolo took umbrage, suggest youthful work. Comparisons between Ariosto and Tasso, embedding those between Homer and Virgil, were a routine exercise. Galileo brings to the argument a distinctive vehemence. Fantastication is overt and licit in *Orlando Furioso*, which Galileo cherished. Tasso's indecorous, playful eroticism is unworthy of heroic epic. Galileo is put off by *Gerusalemme's vaneggiamento*, by the "wildness" and hyperbolic anarchy of its conceits. Later on, in the *Saggiatore*, there are hints that Galileo is tempering this judgment.

As Alexandre Koyré puts it: in the *Dialogo dei Massimi Sistemi*, published in February 1632, withdrawn under ecclesiastical pressure in August, the dialogue form "is as important as it is for Plato: for analogous reasons, very deep reasons related to the very conception of scientific knowledge." This magisterial text sets out to persuade the layman, *l'honnête homme,* as well as the courtier of the correctness of the Copernican system, though expressed in Galileo's prudent, almost tentative interpretation. The reader is to be induced into personal reflection; he is to grasp and evaluate for himself complex, partly technical propositions. This is a pedagogical model, a critique of Aristotelian, Thomistically sanctioned principles in the light of a Galilean Platonism. The *Timaeus* lies near to hand. Aristotelian theories of motion presuppose axiomatically what in fact needs to be demonstrated. But they are treated with scrupulous courtesy. Commonsense empiricism, the innocently apparent voiced by Simplicio is allowed fair and ample representation. Hence the repetitiveness and prolixity of the *Dialogo*. Giordano Bruno goes unmentioned; Kepler is referred to only in passing. However, as Giorgio di Santillana said, these four days of *conversazione* "carry with them a whole world of ancient, rich, and also somewhat undetermined meanings ... The *Dialogo* is and remains a masterpiece of Baroque style." It proceeds often with dramatic abruptness from relaxed good humor to "the solemnity of prophetic invective."

Salviati, a Florentine aristocrat who was to die young, welcomes his two guests at his *palazzo* on the Grand Canal. He has tarried "a long hour at this window expecting at every moment the gondola he sent to fetch his friends." Sagredo is also a historical personage, a *bon vivant* and *amatore* in the most attractive sense of the word. Galileo's construct is profoundly philosophical. Though it virtually founds the modern understanding of dynamics, the issues at stake are epistemological and ontological. What is reality in relation to perception? In what legitimate respects is analytic thought counterintuitive and defiant of good sense? In a foreshadowing of Bergson, Galileo's universe is vitalist and subject to change. It contradicts what was taken to be Aristotelian fixity (hence the alarm of the Holy Office). As the copious debate ends, the participants set out to "enjoy the cool of our evening in Salviati's gondola." A parting touch out of Plato. And just as in Plato's saga of Socrates there is for the reader a tragic intimation: the *Dialogo* will trigger the hounding of Galileo and his desolate end.

•

Hume was more politic. Portions of the *Dialogues Concerning Natural Religion* may date back to 1751. The Lisbon catastrophe of 1755 was to make theodicy and divine providence burning issues throughout European theology and metaphysics. Witness Leibniz and Voltaire. Hume was revising his text immediately prior to his death. He cherished the *Dialogues*. They circulated in manuscript among Edinburgh friends and tolerant divines. Time and again, Hume seemed set on publication. One inhibition was censorship; the lack of an appropriate London publisher was another. More than once, Hume seems to have deplored his own abstinence from avowed, public statement. As it was, he left instructions for publication "any time within two Years of my Death." The *Dialogues* did not appear before 1779 and 1804.

Lucian's *Dialogues* had been immensely influential. Scholars list more than one hundred imitations of Lucian between the 1660s and Hume. Among these are works by Dryden, by Shaftesbury and most famously by Berkeley. Though there are allusions to Plato and Platonism in Hume's debate, the principal model is that of Cicero's *De natura deorum* with its exchanges between a Skeptic, a Stoic and an Epicurean. Hume's triad—Cleanthes who is largely modeled on Bishop Butler, Demea and Philo, the voice nearest to Hume's own—recall Cicero's cast. The argument is conducted in the "natural spirit of good company" and with a relaxed urbanity truly Ciceronian. Set in Cleanthes' library, the *Dialogues* draw unforcedly on such tropes as "the book of nature" and "the book of life." The narrator's prelude is in some ways as contradictory as Hume's dialectic. Panfilo remarks on the inferiority of dialogue to systematic exposition. Yet allows that for the consideration of themes at once salient and important but also obscure and uncertain, the provisional fluidity of civil conversation and tolerant mundanity have their benefits.

Hume's stylistic adroitness permits a subtle but significant differentiation of tonalities. Cleanthes inclines to oratory, to the manner episcopal. Though within the bounds of Enlightenment deism, he tends toward a "fundamentalist" directness. Philo's articulation is as lucid, as consequent as Hume's *Enquiry Concerning the Principles of Morals* whose objections to miracles and providential design it frequently echoes. At a pivotal moment in Part II, Philo invokes Galileo, "that great genius, one of the sublimest that ever existed," and the cautious advancement of the Copernican hypothesis in the *Dialogo*. As in Galileo so in Hume the arts of dialogue license, invite the tidal flux of intellectual questioning.

In Parts XI and XII Philo resorts to virtual monologue. In what has too readily been regarded as a *volteface* induced by "preventive self-censorship" (cf. G. Carabelli's study of Hume's rhetoric), Philo comes to acquiesce in Cleanthes' argument from design. In fact, matters are more intricate. Only close reading clarifies the nuanced tactics, almost the duplicity of Hume's intent. As he signaled to Adam Smith in a letter of August 1776, "nothing can be more cautious and artfully written." Philo's "unfeigned sentiment" is shot through with ironic reservations, with that dry smile peculiar to Hume. "Design" turns out to be nothing more than "order." The causes of order in the universe "probably bear some remote analogy to human intelligence"—a hint which Kant will exploit and deepen. Philo's minimalist stance entails agnosticism. There can be no verifiable access to the sphere of the supernatural. Although echoing Cicero, Hume's prose attains a tranquil eloquence:

Some astonishment, indeed, will naturally arise from the greatness of the object; some melancholy from its obscurity; some contempt of human reason that it can give no solution more satisfactory with regard to so extraordinary and magnificent a question.

Pamphilus's valedictory remark that the principles espoused by Cleanthes "approach still nearer to the truth" looks to be little more than courtesy toward an older teacher and benevolent host. The real riposte to Hume, the trenchant dialogue between dialogues will be found in that somber masterpiece, de Maistre's *Soirées de Saint-Pétersbourg*. A comparative reading of these two texts yields substantive evidence for the ways in which literary means, the poetics of the human voice, inflect and energize abstraction.

Paul Valéry made of Leonardo his tutelary spirit, for he too strove to span an arc extending from aesthetics to mathematics, from architecture and the fine arts to the natural sciences. It was not the polymath he valued but the unifier, the artisan of unifying metaphor. The genius of the poet was to find its mirror in that of philosophy. Though he professed to be bored when reading Plato in unavoidable translation—boredom being one of his tactical avocations—Valéry shaped his philosophical dialogues in the explicit light of their Platonic precedent. In a vein altogether different from that of the baroque, Valéry was truly a metaphysical poet.

He was drawn to the philosophy of mathematics as practiced by Poincaré. Zeno's paradoxes fascinated him. Descartes was a constant presence, in style and spirit. He found confirmation as well as grounds for dissent in Bergson. It was in Nietzsche that Valéry located that symbiosis between the lyrical and the argumentative which he himself aimed at. *Monsieur Teste* is an epistemological fable, a parable of ontology which, said Gide, has no parallel in world literature. It is a concise allegory of the absolute whose ascetic idiom seeks to scour from language the disheveled demands of contingency, the waste and vulgarities of the empirical (what Husserl might have called the *Lebenswelt*). Monsieur Teste attempts to "think thought." As in Fichte, though there is no evidence of direct contact, thought alone validates self-consciousness. If there is in the economies of Teste's meditations a proximity to nihilism, it is a nihilism animated by the condition of mathematics and physics at the turn of the century. The axiomatic was in crisis. Liberated from the evident and the pragmatic, the mind is at liberty to generate a boundless play of theories and cognitive hypotheses of which non-Euclidean geometries and the physics of relativity are beautifully, counterintuitively representative. Valéry found this in Descartes.

For the early Valéry the capacity to transmute pure intellect into aesthetic form is demonstrated by what he called da Vinci's "method" (the late Valéry will attach this metamorphic potential to Goethe). It is this very quest for symbiosis in which mathematical purities and executive shapes are all at last fused which occasions the incompletion, the auto-destruct of a number of Leonardo's capital works and projects. Valéry's Leonardo exemplifies Poincaré's assertion that invention is discovery. Lines of force as set out in Maxwell's equations quicken the spatial perceptions of the artist. Witness the live geometries in Piero della Francesca, in Leonardo's *Last Supper*. But also in Cubism of which Valéry is a guarded witness. In turn, architecture deploys analogies in depth with music as both do with mathematics. Of this congruence and "vanishing point" on the horizon of meaning a Platonic beauty is born.

Valéry treasured constraint. "What is most beautiful is necessarily tyrannical." When the publishers of a glossy magazine on architecture commissioned Valéry they insisted that his text, in luxurious typography, number exactly 115,800 characters! Thus *Eupalinos ou l'architecte* (1921) embodies that antithetical duality which Valéry inherited from Mallarmé: that of hazard, a chance assignment, and of strict, contractual necessity, chance and the absurdly coercive imperative of lettering.

Dwelling in the underworld Socrates and his interlocutors are freed from bodily servitude but recall, achingly, their sensuous past. The question under debate are the relations between understanding and creation, between imaginative conception and actual realization. Preeminently it is architecture which conjoins conceptual totality with constructed detail, stable form with internalized motion. It alone "fills our souls with the total experience of human faculties." In the edifice the architect's inner blueprint achieves "clarity and distinction"—the two criteria of Cartesian truth. Almost paradoxically inspiration is *willed*. This anti-romantic principle, founded on disciplined "exercise," another key word, is for Valéry canonic. More than any other aesthetic realization, moreover, architecture can communicate the immediacy of divine presence. Here Valéry anticipates the late Heidegger's reading of a Greek temple as the existentially informing expression of transcendence. Higher than poetic speech, contends Socrates, is the language of the intellect itself, impenetrable but penetrating all. In ideal essence this language is, as Plato decreed when founding his Academy, that of geometry. In the final analysis philosophic meditations and conjectures trapped as they are in even the most austere, purged modes of discourse are *niables*. They are subject to denial or falsification. Only the embodiment of intellectual vision in Eupalinos's buildings achieves validity. To "know the world is to construct it" as did the Demiurge, that master builder in the *Timaeus*. Valéry's Socrates is haunted by the vanity of his dialectical enterprise.

L'Ame et la danse is saturated to the point of preciousness by implicit reference to Mallarmé and Debussy. The raptures of the dance come to possess the speakers in the dialogue as they did Zarathustra. They generate a dynamic perception of time. "The instant engenders form and form makes the instant visible." Socrates asserts that dance articulates the successive, metamorphic appearances of universal flux. But it does so in stringently ordered, quasi-algebraic fashion (i.e., choreography). Mallarmé spoke of "summary equations of all fantasies." In the background lies the ancient *topos* of the dance of celestial bodies. It in turn sets in blessed motion the ballet in Dante's *Paradiso* and in Matisse's murals. Ultimately, concedes Valéry, the human body reclaims its mortal limitations, its infirming gravity. But the pulse of signifying motion continues to beat inside us.

Written in the grim year 1943 the brief *Dialogue de l'arbre* lies at the heart of our theme. It looks to a Latin precedent—Valéry was translating Virgil's *Bucolics*. The topic is that of organic crescence, of the unfolding from within of both natural agencies and human thought. Composed in prose reflecting Valéry's lifelong commerce with Gide, *L'Arbre* is "a dance of ideas" and explores once again the paradox of calculated formal spontaneity, of the organic within the organized which Valéry had come upon in Poe's ballads and Poe's treatise *Eureka*. Dialogue creates as does eros, itself a phenomenon of dialogue. Our binary or dialectical probings oscillate between a thrust toward the absolute and the self-ironizing recognition that this *élan* is vanity and will end in renunciation. But words continue to vibrate magically in the soul of the speaker, in the echo chambers where intellect and imagination meet. Valéry's essay on Bossuet crystallizes this persuasion: "The structure of expression has a kind of reality whereas the meaning or the idea is only a shadow." In forms, be they verbal or material, there is "the vigor and elegance of *acts* ... in thought there is only the instability of *events*." When the sacred precinct lies deserted "the arch regains." Philosophy endures by virtue of stylistic performance.

Valéry was fortunate in his elective reader. In Alain, moralist, student of the arts and of literature, commentator on Plato, on Hegel and Comte, *maître à penser* to successive generations. Alain accompanied Valéry's poems like a luminous shadow. His readings take us directly into the workshop where philosophic hermeneutics and intuition experience the immediacies of poetry, where both are made metaphor as, perhaps, "are the relations of body and soul."

Alain reads line by line. After which, responds Valéry, the poem remains unaltered but enabled to assume new significance. "Paul Valéry is our Lucretius." Instinctively, his art resists the suspect immobility of cognition. In a lyric such as "*La Dormeuse,*" form "devours thought." In "*Palme*" song is always song: "The idea must be in concord with the motion" of the verse, a "miraculous coincidence which presupposes a secret labor." "*Ébauche d'un serpent,*" one of Valéry's greatest, raises the possibility that thought "was an error in the Universe." This philosophical poem which derives from Mallarmé "has kept a theological imprint." Because thought is "death anticipated," the serpent, as Descartes knew, does not think. It is the mark of a great poet that his thoughts contain the conflict between existence and essence, itself a lifeless abstraction. If there is in

"*Cantique des colonnes*" an elemental idea, "that idea is young, as of an Ionian." It is of the morning, before perception parts from song. Valéry, in this and related poems, teaches us that at their outset "our thoughts are arrows," those "winged arrows" of the Pre-Socratics.

Is there any poem more accomplished than *La Jeune Parque*, a quality redoubled by the uncanny wonder of Paul Celan's translation? Alain's commentary of 1953 goes deep. As Valéry said, "the poem has found its Philosopher." What would man be, deprived of mystery? Even a foolish person is adorned by the enigmas of death. If *La Jeune Parque* is obscure, it is only because the reader stands still instead of launching himself forward, for "the key to thought is always to be found in tidal waves." Alain hears in Valéry's text the eternity of the self within transient life: "I have learned this great mystery from the German metaphysicians" (Alain is a passionate expositor of Kant). Again Valéry answers: "Reason bids the poet prefer rhyme to reason.... It is through this happy door that the idea gains entrance." And both men agree that only poetry can realize the *a priori* of philosophy by achieving forms which circumscribe knowledge before there is knowing. In *La Jeune Parque* the font of form, incomparably near, is silence.

The concentrated exchanges between Valéry "who does not forgive himself for not having been a philosopher" (Cioran) and Alain who may not have forgiven himself for not being a great novelist, like his beloved Balzac, are themselves components of a cardinal dialogue. Shorthand and the tape recorder have restored to modern philosophy some of the *viva voce* spontaneities and openness to questioning advocated by Plato. A considerable measure of Wittgenstein's teaching survives in the guise of notes taken by auditors and conversations as recalled by pupils or intimates. On the banks of the Cam as on those of the Ilissus. Even so mountainous a word processor as Heidegger propounds his considered views on language in dialogue with a Japanese visitor. The counter-authoritarian, anti-systematic tenor of twentieth-century philosophic instruction is restoring to orality something of its ancient role. Innovation, stimulus emanate from a Strauss or Kojève seminar. Disciples differ fruit-fully over the master's dicta and intentions. Already there is something dusty and self-defeating about vast, magisterial tomes such as Jaspers on truth or Sartre on imagination, treatises as monologue. "Dreams are knowledge" taught Valéry in his "*Cimetière marin*" and dreams tend to be brief.

5

Philosophers, historians of science and of mathematics, social historians studying the genesis of modern western culture, read Descartes. The assiduous do so in Latin which so often impresses one as having been his first language. Husserl entitled his meditations "Cartesian." But the singularity of the case lies elsewhere.

The immense majority of French women and men hardly read these demanding writings. At most, and from childhood on, they retain that single definition of the self, the *cogito* which may well be the most famous in all philosophy. Nonetheless French consciousness both public and private, the image France cultivates and projects of itself, the claims France makes to preeminent rationality, logic and intellectual prestige are "Cartesian" through and through. The shibboleth *"la France c'est Descartes"* or *"notre père Descartes"* has been trumpeted by both left and right, by radicals and conservatives. Descartes's "method" and reflections are appropriated by Thomist believers and agnostic positivists. Streets, squares, schools are named after this most discreet, private of men who chose to live and produce much of his oeuvre in Holland and who died in Sweden. "I am French *ergo* Cartesian" proclaimed communist leaders in 1945. So had the Vichy acolytes only months before. No other nation has made of a metaphysician-algebraist its totem.

Learned commentaries, elucidations, controversies on every facet of René Descartes's works abound. They began during his lifetime and persist uninterruptedly. He himself solicited objections and embedded them in successive versions of his tractates. What philosophic classic has benefited from more close reading than the *Discours de la méthode* in Étienne Gilson's line-by-line explication? What more attentive recension can one wish for than Ferdinand Alquié's edition of the *Meditationes de prima philosophia*? But Descates's appeal, his *rayonnement* extends far beyond technical, historical or controversial examination. He is the incessant occasion of literary brilliance and creativity in others. Let me cite two examples from amid a multitude.

Incomplete, dating from the last days of his life in the summer of 1914, Charles Péguy's *Note conjointe sur M. Descartes* is, characteristically, nothing of the kind. It does salute the philosopher's "*audace aussi belle; et aussi noblement et modestement cavalière.*" The sinuous argument however bears on Corneille and Bergson and was meant to illustrate Péguy's conviction that major philosophies are harvests deep-rooted in national earth. It is the somewhat earlier *Note sur M. Bergson*—Péguy's "notes" are monumental—which focuses on the *Discours*. Fundamental is the Cartesian "denunciation of disorder," the perception of logic and the human condition as divinely underwritten "order." There are lacunae, discontinuities in Descartes's exposition.

But a great philosophy "is not that which has no breaches. It is that which has citadels." Himself a prodigious marcher and proud conscript, Péguy fixes on the military cast of Descartes's life and prose. His was "a philosophy without fear." Cartesian motion is one "of advance, of return, of renewed advance." Initially the *Discours* proceeds step by step, as in training. Then in Part IV occurs "the most prodigious leap ever, perhaps, to be found in the history of metaphysics" (the alignment of valid thought with divine reinsurance). It is the genius of Cartesian thought to have taken the form of "deliberate action." Thus states Péguy: the opening words of the *Dis-*

cours have proved to be "the starting point of an immense tremor, of a tide, of an immense circular wave in the ocean of thought."

No less than Valéry who wrote to Gide in August 1894 that the *Discours* is "assuredly the modern novel as it might be achieved," Alain treasured Descartes. This "educator of the Third Republic," teacher of teachers, Simone Weil ardently among them, turned to Descartes time and again. As one whose professed aim is "the good conduct of human understanding" where "conduct" conveys every inference of moral and civic behavior. To think straight is to behave responsibly. No man, taught Alain, has ever "thought more closely to himself" ("*nul n'a pensé plus près de soi*"). None ever succeeded better in locating the pulse of the tangible, the irrecusable presence of the world within abstraction (this will be Husserl's starting point). At the same time and in essence the *Discours* is "the poem of faith." No text is more adult, yet there is at its wellspring of discovery and awe "*toujours un mouvement d'enfance*." It is precisely this "motion out of childhood" which generates René Descartes's astonishment at the overwhelming yet mysterious self-evidence of the created world, at the forward-thrusting certitudes of mathematics. Like Aristotle, but with greater humility, a virtue Alain prized, the author of the *Discours* and the *Méditations* is perpetually amazed. Alain knew that wherever modern French prose and sensibility attain their native cadence the Cartesian precedent is not far off.

Yet in respect of philosophy and scientific theories, Descartes's first language can indeed be said to be Latin. The *Discours* is an exception, directed at the layman. But it too is often internalized translation from the Latin of Cicero and Tacitus. The anatomy, the innervation of its supple, seemingly mundane idiom are those of Latin nomination and syntax (Milton and Hobbes provide analogous examples). The dilemmas of transfer are exactly those which Heidegger cites when he posits the untranslatability of Greek philosophic terminology and the enduring distortions caused by erroneous or approximate renditions. *Cogito ergo sum* is at once more concise and absolute than its proverbial French counterpart. As is *ego cogito, ergo sum, sive existo* which can only be imperfectly mirrored by "*Donc moi, qui pense j'existe.*" *Esprit* is as distant from *ingenium* as either is from Hegelian *Geist*. It encompasses memory and imagination which *raison* does not. *Formes* and *natures* are imports out of Latin versions of a medievalized Aristotle. Descartes's decision to compose and publish the *Discours* in French echoes Dante's adoption of the vulgate for his *Commedia* and Galileo's for his dialogues, which Descartes had annotated. "Let those who confide in ordinary good sense rather than scholastic and antiquarian authority read me in their native tongue." For the *Discours* Descartes is, after Cicero and the Roman moralists, the first philosopher to envisage, to educate toward his work a general literate public. Harking back to Epicurus, it will include women.

His own stance regarding literature is ambivalent. Virgil, Horace, Ovid's *Fasti*, Cicero's orations and Seneca's tragedies are integral to Descartes. He confesses that he was in his youth "in love with the poets" ("*non parvo Poëseos amore incendebar*"). During the night of ontological revelation, November 10th to 11th, 1619, the tome offered to him in one of his three epiphanic dreams is a *Corpus poetarum*. It includes a poem by the Gallo-Roman Ausonius. In it the verse *Quod vitae sectabor iter?* will point Descartes to the journey and purpose of his life. The precedent of Lucretius is unmistakable in the atomism and concept of Chaos as set out in the *Discours*. As we saw, at the point of death Socrates turns to Aesop and song. Hegel's poem to Hölderlin is masterly. To the last Heidegger writes verse. Near his end in frozen Stockholm Descartes produces lyrics for a *divertissement* at Queen Christine's court. Overall, however, Descartes stresses the differences between poetics and philosophy, between the inspiration which impels the arts and the calculable methodology of the sciences. Fiction is the Siren-song antithesis to rational truths. Exactly like Freud, Descartes assigns poetic invention to the daydreams and childhood of men. It cannot match, let alone surpass the pure beauty of Euclid or of algebraic geometry as devised by René Descartes himself.

This makes the more noteworthy the extent of Descartes's literary arts, his sheer greatness as a writer. He is a virtuoso of the subjunctive and the pluperfect, anticipating Proust. Montaigne's astute serenities, especially in the *Apologie*, may have instructed Descartes, but the voice is wholly his own. His is the tactical *rallentando* when the argument turns knotty, the summons to objections, to animadversions which make the proposition coil back on itself while the ground bass of demonstration presses steadily forward. Both the *Discours* and the *Méditations* belong to that arc of intellectual and spiritual autobiography which reaches from St. Augustine to Rousseau and Freud. These are not treatises in Spinoza's or Kant's manner. Descartes's self-scrutinizing ego is made immanent under cover of reticent urbanity.

As in Proust the password is *recherche*. Witness the incomplete *conversazione* c. 1647 on *La Recherche de la vérité*. Always there is the resort, revolutionary in systematic philosophy, to the first person singular, to the genesis of all verifiable truths in the disciplined self. The existential is prior to the cognitive. In turn it is out of self-evidence, giving that term its full weight, that springs the indubitability of God's existence and the phenomenological gamble on his benevolent guarantee of an intelligible world. Human liberty and the otherwise inexplicable concept of infinity are the rewards of this certification.

Observe the deft ironies, the cadence, literally "the fall" of the following passage:

je comparais les écrits des anciens païens qui traitent des moeurs à des palais fort superbes et fort magnifiques qui n'étaient bâtis que sur du sable et sur de la boue: ils élèvent fort haut les vertus, et les font paraître estimables par dessus toutes les choses qui sont au monde, mais ils n'enseignent pas assez à les connaître, et souvent ce qu'ils apellent d'un si beau nom n'est qu'une insensibilité ou un orgeuil, ou un désespoir, ou un parricide.

The descent from *insensibilité*, almost a modernism, to the unexpected and unnerving *parricide* which may have been directed at certain Stoic inhumanities, is a stylistic stroke. Or consider the move which inspires Husserl:

examinant avec attention ce que j'étais et voyant que je pouvais feindre que je n'avais aucun corps, et qu'il n'y avait aucun monde ni aucun lieu où je fusse, mais que je ne pouvais pas feindre pour cela que je n'étais point, et qu'au contraire, de cela même que je pensais à douter de la vérité des autres choses, il suivait très évidemment et très certainement que j'étais....

Feindre (*fingere*) is made to beget its own refutation. The scandalous totality of doubt, the abolition of the human body and of the world it no longer inhabits—a thought experiment whose surrealist extremity borders on madness—is deliberately masked by the elegance of Descartes's grammar (*où je fusse*). It is immediately attenuated by the renewed appeal to fiction, to *feindre*. Note also the nuanced verification which proceeds from "evidently" to "certainly."

Sleep and dreams preoccupy Descartes. They complicate crucial discriminations between reasoning and imagining: *"Pour ce que nos raisonnements ne sont jamais si évidents ni si entiers pendant le sommeil que pendant la veille, bien que quelquefois nos imaginations soient alors autant ou plus vives et expresses ..."* Here "vivacity" with its implications of speed leads directly to *expresses*, a complex word which conjoins both clarity and swiftness. These felicities from one who had *"jamais eu l'humeur portée a faire des livres,"* whose procrastinations and resort to anonymity sometimes suggest those of Henry Adams's *Education.*

The Baroque delights in illusions: optical, scenic, psychic, in *trompe-l'oeil* either arcadian or macabre. Hence Corneille's masterpiece *L'Illusion comique*, Calderón's *Life is a Dream*, the misprisions which frame *The Taming of a Shrew* or which activate *A Midsummer Night's Dream*. Hence also the iconographic obsession with Narcissus.

Descartes's conceit is among the most gripping. In his *Meditatio prima* he summons a *"genium aliquem malignum, eundemque summe potentem et callidum,"* a deceptor of supreme power capable of rendering illusory the whole of Descartes's stringently deduced perceptions. Capable of making mendacious phantasms of what we had taken to be reality and its rational order. Descartes's tone remains calm but the epistemological and spiritual tension is palpable. This *mauvais génie* could come out of Gogol or Poe. Error stands for evil. The menace of cosmic irrationality presses on the hard-won privilege of the *cogito*. Exorcism is achieved in the *Seconde Méditation*. To yield to this "most potent of deceivers" would be to succumb, as Gouhier puts it, to "a methodically pessimistic myth of an Almighty who mocks the world and whose irony drives thought to despair," to a Gnosticism bleaker than Kafka's. Refutation lies in the axiom that God's perfection *cannot* harbor deceit, that *"Dieu n'est point trompeur."* Descartes's deity does not want to deceive or madden the human intellect though He could of course do so. He has created and made intelligible eternal verities of which the theorems and proofs in mathematics are exemplary (could God alter these, a vexed point?).

Already contemporary critics noted the circularity in Descartes's argument, a circularity analogous to that in Anselm's celebrated "proof" of God's existence. In the final instance, Descartes's invocation of certitude is a moral imperative rather than a cognitive demonstration. Construing error and illusion as imperfections to which the Almighty is immune, the Cartesian model equates truth with goodness (*bonté*). The precedents are Augustinian and Thomist. The cost is that of a marmoreal stasis in the resulting image of God. Nor has the menace of the malignant illusionist been altogether refuted. Poe's "imp of the perverse" lurks in the shadows. The metaphysical melodrama is there as it is in Hamlet's tortured doubts as to the veracity or hellish deception of the Ghost. There is a touch of supplication in the *Meditatio sexta*: *"Ex eo enim quod Deus non sit fallax, sequitur omnino in talibus me non falli."* The utterance is always that of a first person, of the self in "a history of his own mind"—a title envisaged by Descartes. The inward Odyssey on seas as yet uncharted anticipates that of Hegel and of Schelling. Thus Descartes's literary strengths endow the drama of reason with fragility, with a recurrent strain of psychological *Angst*.

Perhaps only a poet acutely alert to philosophy can recapture that condition. In Durs Grünbein's *Vom Schnee* (2003), subtitled "Descartes in Germany," the voice of a metaphysician and his dreams set alight the imaginings of a major poet. A sequence of forty-two poems meets with, encircles René Descartes in the hut in which he hammered out his demonstrations and logical proofs of the substantive status of the self. The landscape is one of relentless snow seen, as it were, in Cartesian trigonometry. A bone-chilling cold besieges the famous oven by whose fitful glow Descartes pondered, dozed and dreamt. Marauding soldiery, starving wolves, the brutish *misère* of harried villagers constantly threaten the solitude, the peace which the philosopher regards as indispensible to his quest. His Sancho Panza-like valet, Gillot, is sleeping with a local girl. Thus bringing the world too close. The most insidious gremlins however seep from within. Descartes suffers bouts of malaise, of feverish distemper. His body, fortified only by the bastion of long hours in bed, is at once the guarantor of his questioned identity and the natural enemy of pure, ice-sharp intellection. Snow drifts into every cranny of Cartesian algebra and physics, it traces geometric patterns:

> Er modelliert, wohin er fällt.
> Er rundet auf und ab und übersetzt in schöne Kurven,
> Wofür Physik dann, schwalbenflink, die Formel findet.
> Monsieur, bedenkt, was Euch entgeht, verliert Ihr Zeit.
> Für Euch hat es, für Euch, die ganze Nacht geschneit.

"I am nothing except *Geist*." The author of the *Discours* can only substantify his ego in the act of writing. He is a marmot in a paper burrow. With masterly penetration Grünbein renders both the spectral uncertainties and flashes of revelation in Descartes's snowbound dreams. Can a dream dream itself? The philosopher recalls the lightning stroke which disclosed the *cogito*:

Ich war erlöst. Ich war ein neuer Mensch. Erst jetzt
War ich mir sicher: ja, René—du bist, du bist!

In "René" we are meant to hear the epiphany of "rebirth." Yet this luminous realization ends in twilight. "Am I I?" or is that *hoc corpus meum* (the sacramental echo is inescapable) nothing more than a phantasm, the mocking shadow in a dream? Outside the hut, moreover, as in derision of the great navigator of ideas, war, injustice and misery prevail. A thoroughly German winter's tale. But a poetic "inscape" of thought rivalled only by Valéry's Monsieur Teste and the figure of Adrien Sixte in Paul Bourget's *Le Disciple*.

To consider Hegel as a *writer* verges on *lèse-majesté*. Is there any great philosopher seemingly less stylish, more averse to "spirited language" and elegance—*"geistreiche Sprache"*—as he found it in the French *philosophes*? Friends amended Hegel's tortuous syntax, so often derived from laboriously spoken, opaque lectures, abounding in rebarbative neologisms and Swabian locutions. The young Heine, even before a brief personal contact in 1822, was among the first of many who parodied the master's leaden idiom. But the crux is not one of literary, rhetorical finish or welcoming suavity, let alone poetic inspiration.

Hegel's spell is borne out by the volume and distinction of commentary; surpassed only by that on Plato. His impact on philosophy, political theory, social thought has been, if only via Marxism, global. Yet from the time of Hegel's contemporaries to the present the response, adverse as in Goethe, positive as in Lukács or Kojève, has confronted the issue of intelligibility. Is the *Phenomenology*, is Hegel on logic to be understood in any normal sense? Does he mean to communicate the inmost of his doctrines? The case of the prose of Heidegger, so complexly anti-Hegelian, has both legitimized and obscured the question. The topic of willed opacity—Mallarmé and the Surrealists read Hegel—is pertinent. Is intelligibility a deliberately withheld category of Hegelian theory, a potentiality held in suspense as is the verb in German syntax, an open-ended promise which the reader can only intuit? That eventuality exasperated Bertrand Russell but may have inspired Husserl. More importantly, does the "Hegel complex" help initiate those inaccessibilities which characterize modernism? Does difficulty in the *Phenomenology* and the *Enzyklopädie* prepare that in Mallarmé, Joyce or Paul Celan, the displacement of language from the axis of immediate or paraphrasable meaning as we find it in Lacan or Derrida (an annotator of Hegel)? Are we to read Hegel as we try to read, say, *Finnegans Wake* or Celan's *Schneepart*? Nevertheless Hegel was a pedagogue through and through, aiming not merely at academic philosophic influence but at a magisterial role in public and political affairs. Is it possible to reconcile the hermetic with the didactic?

Alexandre Koyré's *"Note sur la langue et la terminologie hégéliennes"* is dated 1931. It marks an intense revival of Hegelian studies in the light of Soviet ideology and of the deepening social crisis in the capitalist west (Hegel's notorious "end of history"). Koyré asks whether we require a *Hegel-Lexicon* on the model of the glossaries available for Plato and Aristotle? What are we to make of Hegel's insistence on concreteness, when no idiom is more abstract? We are called upon, finds Koyré, to learn to think differently, as does the physicist in the counterintuitive sphere of relativity or indeterminacy. Hegel's style, occasionally enforced by provincial parlance, is intended to inhibit the shopworn facilities of the colloquial. Hegel purposes to bring to manifest awareness the inner history of philosopical and psychological terms, a process of genetic anatomy which is that of reason "at hard labor." Thus the self-construction of human consciousness, the realization of *Geist* occurs by means of linguistic processes such as the Adamic act of nomination to which Hegel specifically adverts. Nomination wakes the spirit from the anarchic drift of dreams and fables (cf. Plato's *Cratylus*). The history of language, the life of language are at the same time the history and life of the human spirit. Or as Hegel himself puts it: language is "the visible invisibility of the spirit"—though whether "spirit" or *ésprit* come near to rendering *Geist* worries Derrida.

However, if nomination and intelligible articulation validate the self and open consciousness to rationality, they can also obscure and disperse them. We "hear ourselves being" in Hegel's arresting formula. This incessant process of ontological audition depends wholly on language. In turn, communication to others, imperfect as it is, restores the heard self to itself. This reciprocal motion is in the deepest sense dialectical. The German language possesses a distinctive capacity to move and move reversibly between subject and predicate. It can make circularity fruitful (a key Heideggerian maneuver). Playing on the contiguities and differences between *bekannt* and *erkannt*, the "known" and the "recognized," Hegel reminds us that knowledge is not necessarily recognition or cognition. Hence the need for a new terminology, a need heightened by the social, political, ideological revolutions in the midst of which Hegel composes his works. Thus the Hegelian coinages or idiolectic usage of such seminal terms as the famous, polysemic *Aufheben* ("sublate"?), *Meinung* with its implicit entailment of *mein*. Hence the activation of the dynamics latent in *Er-innerung*, *Ein-bildung*, *Ver-mittelung* or *Ein-fluss*, nouns whose "verb-motion" had been staled or forgotten by inattentive currency. Derrida plunges merrily into this Hegelian whirlpool. What was, lazily, deemed fixed, eternal in the conceptual—that Platonic legacy—is made actual and fluid by the breaking open of words. In Lutheran German— Hegel speaks of being "the Luther of philosophy"—the energies of inception must be restored to the present, but without being archaicized. The instability, the resistant novelty of philosophic style mirror, perform that unsettledness, that unhousedness of being within crisis ("history") which is Hegel's abiding insight.

Alexandre Kojève looked to Koyré's indispensable analysis. His own *leçons* on the *Phenomenology*, a line-by-line, sometimes word-for-word *explication de texte*, extended from 1933 to 1939. The impact of this seminar on intellectual life in France and beyond remains unsurpassed. It reached further than the academic-mandarin community. Kojève's spellbound audience included anthropologists, political scientists, sociologists, historians, metaphysicians. It also included writers: among them Breton, the part-time surrealist Queneau (who was to edit Kojève's notes), and Anouilh, whose *Antigone* is virtually a direct offshoot. Sartre's dream of being both a Spinoza and a Stendhal was quickened by Kojève's uses of Hegel. The seminar inspired Raymond Aron and was the wellspring of French phenomenology as it developed in Merleau-Ponty. Kojève exchanged views on Hegel with Leo Strauss, thus preparing certain aspects of American neoconservatism. This prodigal stimulus, with its role in literature, stems from the fact that the exigent abstractions of Kojève have as their deep structure and subtext the political tensions, the imminent catastrophe of those condemned years.

As in literature so in philosophy intensities of commentary can become "acts of art." They take on autonomous stature. Even on the printed page, Kojève's voice exercises its hypnotic authority, although he insists that all understanding of Hegel is only "possibility," that each express proposition, his own included, is provisional and in incomplete motion (cf. William Empson's readings of Shakespeare in *The Structure of Complex Words*). Hegel's affirmations negate ("sublate") each other as the argument spirals. To say, as Parmenides intuited, is to say what is not. Negation is the axiomatic guarantor of liberty. Hence the positive imperative of death: "*Il faut mourir en homme pour être un homme.*" Malraux and Sartre will elaborate. Self-abolition is concomitant with renovation. Tinguely's "self-destructs" collapse into luminous meaning. Because woman and man are *in-quiétude, Un-ruhe,* dis-quiet in essence, their language and that of Hegel must articulate instability. Consider Virginia Woolf's *To the Lighthouse.* Many of Hegel's key pronouncements are equivocal, "flickering." They resist immediate or normative grasp. The muteness of animals remains vestigial in us. We attain our uncertain humanity via speech acts, born of our rootlessness. The relevance to literature, to expressionist art is obvious.

Abstractions, idealizations are attempts to deny but also to inhabit the real world. Platonic-Christian rhetoric, the Johannine *Logos* alienate (that seminal *Entfremdung*) consciousness both from itself and concrete reality. These strategies of idealizing estrangement make of all modes of romanticism a dishevelled chitchat. *Stricto sensu* consciousness should revert to silence. Beckett is not far off. Yet only language can reveal being. Thus, for Hegel, literature does create (the point is finely made in Peter Szondi's study of Hegel's poetics). The world literature edifice originates in epic, lives in tragedy and dies in comedy. The paradigm is that which unfolds from Homer to Sophocles and from Sophocles to Aristophanes. Philosophy, however, outranks even great literature. "History exists so that the philosopher may attain wisdom in writing a book which contains *absolute* knowledge." From this extravagant maxim derives Mallarmé's notion of *le Livre* "which is the object of the universe." Also, perhaps, the inebriation with totality in Nietzsche's *Zarathustra* and Pound's *Cantos*. Yet where it reaches ultimate self-realization, an articulate concept abolishes the vital singularity of that which it conceives. The concept "memorizes" where and when the object was effaced, exactly as does Proust's Narrator. This allows one of Hegel's most profound suggestions. There is in revolutionary terror and its lust for historicity "*die Furie des Verschwindens*" ("the fury of disappearance"). Kojève cites such a saying as a "text ideogram." Of which the most famous is that of the owl of Minerva setting out on its flight only at sundown. It takes a great writer to find such *figurae*.

At its heart Kojève's reading is almost violently political. He conceives of the *Phenomenology* as Napoleonic-Stalinist. Plato, Hegel, Heidegger and Alexandre Kojève himself exemplify the temptation of the thinker by authoritarian despotism, by the desire to "become the Sage of the State" or in Heidegger's specific case "the Führer's Führer." The culmination of history which Hegel salutes in Napoleon, Kojève reincarnates in Stalin, in that totality of rationalized control and temporalized Utopia which makes of Stalinism at once the apex and the closure of history. This perspective inspires Kojève's elucidation of the "Master/Servant" dialectic in Hegel's *Phenomenology*, the most influential philosophic parable after that of Plato's Cave. In this celebrated narrative, analytic rigor takes on scenic vitality and a difficult to define but somehow lyric tension. It might be enlightening to stage a recitation of Hegel's text in conjunction with Strindberg's *Miss Julie* and Genet's *Maids* and Brecht's *Mr. Puntila and His Man Matti* with Kojève's *Leçons* as program notes.

It was in midst of Stalinist finality that Georg Lukács produced his *Der junge Hegel*, a monumental monograph published in 1948. The sobrieties of Hegel had helped dissociate Lukács from the expressionist exuberance of his own early essays. He now asks himself: what linguistic devices are instrumental in the thought processes of the *Phenomenology*? Threefold repetitions, for instance, act out the underlying triadic construct, the interplay between subjectivity, objectivity and the absolute of *Geist* in which these are subsumed. How, inquires Lukács, can grammar externalize the transit from consciousness to self-consciousness and then to reasoned conceptualization when this transit takes place both within the immediacy of the self and in encounters with others? The question was to preoccupy Husserl and Sartre. It is rendered, unforgettably, in the prison monologue in Shakespeare's *Richard II*:

> yet I'll hammer it out.
> My brain I'll prove the female to my soul,
> My soul the father, and these two beget
> A generation of still-breeding thoughts....
> For no thought is contented: the better sort,
> As thoughts of things divine, are intermixed
> With scruples, and do set the word itself
> Against the word.

Lukács experiences in Hegel's prose "an uninterrupted vibrato" which makes exposition "difficult and obscure." But there are also stellar points of literary accomplishment as in Hegel's depiction of the Greek *polis*. If Diderot's *Neveu de Rameau* is the only modern text referred to in the *Phenomenology* it is just because Hegel was intent on establishing his own modes of dialectic in action.

Hegel is the first western philosopher to equate human excellence with *work*. Not with the accumulation of capital or commercial expansion as preached by Adam Smith and the *Physiocrates*, but with work as the instrument whereby men and women construct their actual world. Where Schelling looks to the *Odyssey*, Hegel seems to internalize *Robinson Crusoe*. Human labor both manual and spiritual defines the realization of the conceptual. This insight translates into the fabric of a Hegelian treatise. The reader must *work* his way through it. Only the laborious in the root-sense can activate understanding. Passive reception is futile. Via the hard labor of concentrated intake "disquiet is made order" in our consciousness. The *Hell-Dunkel*, the *chiaroscuro* of Hegel's prose points toward processes as yet incomplete, toward an unstable engagement with social conditions and ideological contradictions (which Marxism will claim to resolve). It is Hegel's risk to have made of initial bafflement, of polysemic eventualities an instigation to continued attention. Lukács's subsequent and voluminous writings, notably his *Aesthetik*, inherently unfinished, will reflect this strategy, this gamble on patience. *Pace* Descartes, clarity and elegance are in respect of thought treacherous ideals.

Gadamer makes of interpretation his *Leitmotif*. In the wake of Aristotle and of Heidegger he considers experience itself as an interpretive, hermeneutic act. We "read" the world and our place therein as we read a text, seeking to construe meaning. Gadamer meets with Hegel at numerous turns. Hegel's language directs us to the ineluctable gap between that which we have said and that which we wanted to say. Hegel intends to estrange language from its mendacious facilities and *stasis*, precisely as do Hölderlin or Mallarmé. Always, tantalizingly out of reach is that "messianic" moment in which intentionality and truth will coincide, the moment outside history when consciousness will be made *Geist*. It is not only Virgil's *tantae molis erat se ipsam cognoscere mentem* which tells us that introspection falsifies because it must verbalize its findings. There is a perennial danger that abstraction, articulate conceptualization entail a loss of substance. Life drains out of our explicative anatomies. Contemporaries mocked "honestly wooden Hegel" or deplored, as did Goethe, his "thickets of esotericism." But Hegel was grappling with a central paradox: the effacement of substance by that which defines and names it. Only great literature can preserve being within designation. This is why there is no other epistemology in which literature and the arts play a comparable role. What other voice would have dared set Sophocles' Antigone above the Gospel *persona* of Jesus? Gadamer puts forward a stimulating conjecture. The partial collapse of the Hegelian system, the partial failures of its idiom will transfer to the major novelists and poets of the modern era many of the tasks and tactics of sensibility generated by German philosophy. But the impulse toward "failing better" remains with Hegel whose philosophical language "shall, so long as it remains language, endure in human speech." Is there not a sense, perfectly sober, in which the *Phenomenology* is one of the master novels of the nineteenth century?

Like Lukács, Ernst Bloch read and taught Hegel within the despotically vulgar yet also utopian ambience of a quasi-Stalinist society. His *Subjekt-Objekt* of 1951 makes this circumstance manifest. The tone is all but gray. Many of Hegel's sentences "stand like vessels filled with strong and fiery drink, but the vessel has no handles or only few." If Hegel's syntax fractures customary usage, it is simply "because he has unprecedented things to say on which grammar until now has had no grip." As in Hölderlin there is in Hegel a "kind of Athenian Gothic." Almost everywhere Hegel's rebarbative locutions are indispensable. They tell of volcanic striving. The reader must acquiesce if "he wishes to experience the most farflung journey existing hitherto." No less than in Heraclitus or in Pindar "the lightning bolts of meaning" originate in darkness.

Wherever feasible, Adorno yielded to the charms of obscurity.

Even his apprentice work on Kierkegaard and on Husserl flirts with impenetrability. Did he glance ambiguously at the Kabbalistic hermeticism of Walter Benjamin? Adorno's smokescreens render somewhat ironic his parodistic polemic against Heidegger's "jargon." There is however a real empathy in his *Drei Studien zu Hegel* (1963). It is not pejoratively that Adorno concedes that the signification of certain elements in Hegel remains uncertain and "has till now not been securely established by any hermeneutic art." In first order philosophy Hegel may be the foremost example of a writer about whom one cannot always decide unequivocally what he is on about. The parallel is that of Hölderlin's prose in those very same years. The contrarieties between "dialectical-dynamic moments and those of conservative affirmation" are left unresolved or "deferred" in Derrida's sense of the word. The reader's stance is that demanded by great poetry, by a work such as Rilke's *Duino Elegies*. Thus, advances Adorno, there are passages in Hegel in "which there is strictly speaking nothing to understand." As always in Adorno the informing analogy is that with the unparaphrasable meaningfulness of music.

The historicity of thought, consciousness embedded in historical motion cannot be expressed in the algebraic grammatology of a Descartes. Linguistically also the Hegelian principle of negation liberates. As Adorno reads him, Hegel is the adversary *par excellence* of Wittgenstein's *Tractatus*. It is precisely of that of which we cannot speak that philosophy must endeavor to find articulation. Famously Hegel said of the darkness in Heraclitus that it was both necessary and vital "even if it made mathematics seem easy."

Throughout this essay we encounter a polarity. There are thinkers, notably in the Anglo-American vein, who insist on clarity, on direct communication. There are those on the other hand, Plotinus, the German idealists, Heidegger among them, who see in neologisms, in densities of syntax, in stylistic opaqueness the necessary conditions of original insight. Why repeat what has been said plainly before? The dilemma is familiar to the icebreakers in literature, to Rimbaud, to Joyce, to Pound urging language "to make it new." Hegel produces "anti-texts" aiming at collision with the inert matter of the commonplace. They are, says Adorno, "films of thought" calling for experience rather than comprehension. Every good reading of Hegel is "an experiment."

Hegel questioned translation which is "like Rhine wine that has lost its bouquet." In a letter of 1805 he sets himself the task "of teaching philosophy to speak German," to complete a development initiated by Luther (cf. T. Bodammer's *Hegels Deutung der Sprache*, 1969). The potentialities are there as in no other modern tongue. Only ancient Greek possessed comparable resources. Consider the inexhaustible resonance of a word such as *Urteil*—"judgment" but also "origination." What other nation attaches to *Dichtung* the values at once aesthetic, theoretical and virtually corporeal—the density in *dicht*—implicit in German? It alone reaches back to that fusion of the lyric with the analytic which affords Pre-Socratic utterances their enduring spell.

In all this, literature is essential. Even as Homer and Hesiod "create" the Greek pantheon, so the history of poetry and drama prepares the human intellect for its reception of religion and philosophy. We cannot match the *Iliad* or Aristophanes but their finality is indispensable to the clearing of the ground for metaphysics. This complex interdependence persists. We would not have the *Phenomenology* without Shakespeare, Cervantes and Defoe. This symbiotic evolution is the decisive, though always provisional circumstance of human freedom.

The relationship is reciprocal. I have referred already to the dramaturgy of Hegel's "Master/Servant" where *Knecht* connotes more of submission than does "servant." The context in section A of Part IV of the *Phenomenology* is that of the struggle to achieve authentic self-consciousness. This dialectic demands recognition by "the other," by a rival consciousness. "The other"—after Hegel and Rimbaud *l'autre* carries a specific charge—embodies, paradoxically, a mirror image which is also autonomous. Its absence, like that of our shadow, would deprive identity of substance. This reciprocity is empowered by the logic and poetry of death. An acceptance of death and the infliction of death on "the other." Very possibly it was the wrestling match between Jacob and the Angel with its climax of nomination, of the bestowal of identity, which underlay Hegel's agonistic scenario.

The Master objectifies his own being in relation to that of the Servant whom he treats as a "thing" (*Ding*), but whose recognition is indispensable to him. It is in the adverse perception of his *Knecht* that the Master must seek and substantiate his ego. His authority derives from the fact that he is prepared to risk his own life, that his code is that of (archaic?) heroism. His acceptance of self-annihilation determines his magisterial status and ontological-social difference from his Servant. But from within his servitude, and this is Hegel's formidable move, the *Knecht* discovers, is compelled to discover, the dynamic power of *work*. Consciousness which is so to speak static or innocent in Don Quixote is *at work* in Sancho Panza. It is via work that the *Knecht* becomes totally necessary to his Master. Service generates its own form of mastery, a reversal which emancipates the self-consciousness of the *Knecht*. This mastery is never complete. It suffers from an avoidance of death, from that heroic risk which legitimizes the Master's authority. But it entails the potential of social revolution. Ultimately work is more powerful, more progressive than chivalric sacrifice. Whereas the *Herr* depends on "the other" to validate his self, the Servant achieves a realization of consciousness from within the objective status of his labor.

These dramatic equivocations, this "mortal strife," are acted out in Hegel's prose, a prose which is performative of struggle, whose meanings demand to be wrestled with. The duel is incessant; Jacob's encounter lasts through the night of history. But in the final analysis it is the turbine force of labor from within servitude which prepares, which renders ineluctable the social and psychological advance of mankind. This insight, perhaps incipient in ancient Stoicism, sets in motion not only socialism and Marxism but signal aspects of capitalist theory. It will find an inhuman parody in the logo of the Nazi concentration camps: *Arbeit macht frei*.

There are at least four virtuoso responses in the literary echo chamber or orbit of Hegel's parable. These will add the dimensions of class conflict and of the radical antagonism and servitudes in sexuality.

The murderous *pas de deux* of Strindberg's *Miss Julie* (1888) conjoins both. Social tensions and erotic pressure induce an explosive exchange of roles, a reversal of power relations in a characteristically Hegelian perspective. Julie is made her lackey's whore, but her imperious masochism renews his abject servility. The barriers of class are insurmountable. Sexual intercourse in fact sharpens inequality: "I could make a countess of you. You can never make a count of me." Strindberg adopts the Hegelian touchstone. The valet is not ready to die with, let alone for the Mistress. The prerogative of sacrificial death belongs to her. When the Count rings and calls for his boots, Jean succumbs immediately. He chooses self-preservation which is the strategy of the *Knecht*. He bids Julie commit suicide. As in the *Phenomenology* impotence is survival and contains the mechanics of futurity denied to the *Herr*.

The very title of Brecht's *Herr Puntila und sein Knecht Matti* declares a contiguity to Hegel. Brecht's folktale parable of 1948 is modeled on the Hegelian dialectic. But here what is crucial "is the shaping of class antagonism between Puntila and Matti." As in the *Phenomenology*, however, the deep-seated struggle is that for identity: "Are you a man? Before you said that you were a chauffeur. See, I have caught you in a contradiction." "Opinions vary as to what is a man." Is the Master drunk the same as the Master sober? Only the destitute, the exploited can be confident of their humanity. Witness Matti's salute to salt herring, the wretched ration without which the pine forests would not be felled nor the acres sown nor the machines made to run. "If I was a communist," mouthes Puntila, "I would make Puntila's life hell." But the true vengeance and mission of the *Knecht* lie deeper. He will abandon his *Herr*, leaving him helpless. He will become his own Master:

Den guten Herrn, den finden sie geschwind
Wenn sie erst ihre eignen Herren sind.

Matti's assumption of self-mastery which is communism will break
open the millennial cycle of Hegel's scenario.

Which is nowhere more venomous than in Jean Genet's *Les
Bonnes*, also composed during the late 1940s. Genet adds a histrionic twist to Hegel's dualities. He intended the lesbian sisters to be
acted by homosexual adolescents, by rentboys such as he had met
in reformatories and prisons. French *bonnes* signifying both cham-
bermaids and "the benevolent ones" points to the metamorphic
ritual of the Eumenides. The play, suggests Genet, could be staged
at Epidaurus. It is a stylized dance of death (echoes of Strindberg)
in which the Hegelian protagonists exchange identities as they exchange garments. *Les Bonnes* is a primer of hatreds. What, challenges Genet, are the ligaments of loathing not only as between
Master and Servant but within the community of servitude and
subjugation? Has the *Phenomenology* overlooked the dialectics of
humiliation, to which the *Herr* subjects his *Knecht* but to which he
is in turn subjected by the vital need he has of service? "You crush
me under the weight of your humility," says Madame. The masochistic but covertly mutinous fidelity of the maids both flatters and
threatens the Master's despotic dependence. Where Hegel infers
an unfought duel, Genet enlists blackmail. What the *Knecht* knows
of the intimacies of his *Herr*, what the maids know of the erotic
frivolities of their mistress gives them a corrupt and corrupting
power. Cunningly Solange and Claire—the angelic and the luminous—perform a play within the play, a duet of daemonic mirrors:
"I have enough of that terrifying mirror which reflects my image like
a putrid smell." The homicidal hysteria of the *bonnes* gives to Madame a momentary if factitious advantage. The climactic torsion is
in denial of Hegel. Madame exits into privileged, ostentatious life. It
is her domestics who enact the ceremonies of sacrificial death. But
they voice a central insight inaccessible to the Master:

Je hais les domestiques. J'en hais l'espèce odieuse et vile. Les domestiques n'appartiennent pas à l'humanité. Ils coulent. Ils sont une exhalaison qui traîne dans nos chambres, dans nos corridors, qui nous pénètre, nous entre par la bouche, qui nous corrompt. Moi, je vous vomis.

Of this infernal self-consciousness comes not the saving grace of labor, of proletarian futurity, but the wages of suicide. What would Hegel have made of this had he been in the audience?

Samuel Beckett read philosophers closely. He was in frequent exchanges with Schopenhauer. No counterpart to Hegel's diptych of *Herr* and *Knecht* is richer than that of Pozzo and Lucky in *Waiting for Godot* (1952).

Lucky is almost literally a whipped dog, but a dog that can bite. Again the thematic question is that of "what is man?" Grudgingly, the slaver Pozzo concedes the marginal humanity of the two tramps. But to what extent is Lucky human? Held on a leash he performs his master's sadistic commands. Can one treat a human being in this fashion, inquires Vladimir? Pozzo allows that his mastery and the abjection of the slave might have been reversed. Wretched as he is, Lucky provides his tormentor with urgently needed reassurance as to his own status and identity (the essential Hegelian pendulum). If Lucky strives to wake his master's compassion it is so that he can preserve his life-giving dependence: "So that I keep him on." Radicalizing all authority Pozzo bids his *Knecht* "think": "*Pense.*" This imperative transcends the Cartesian *cogito*. In Hegel thought corresponds to the genesis of consciousness, to the potentiality of freedom. Beckett's is an allegory of coercion.

At this ultimatum Lucky bursts into speech. Speech not only defines humanity: it is the sole but immensely consequential weapon available to the slave. Lucky's torrential monologue lays bare the poverty of Pozzo's jargon. His outpouring parodies epistemology, theological speculations, the suspect profundities of modern psychology. Its fractured litany of repetitions, its stumbling onrush are a linguistic *détour de force* unsurpassed in literature and archly deconstructive of Molly's musicalized soliloquy in *Ulysses*. Its self-negating rhetoric hints at what language might have been, might still become if it shook off the banal confines of meaning. After emitting this avalanche of pseudo-grammatical "speech acts," this subversive mimicry of communication, Lucky relapses into comatose muteness. His awesome loquacity ends on the word *inachevé*. Which defines the play itself. Nothing remains but his trampled hat now worn by Vladimir. More than once the Beckettian endgame seems to look to Hegel's trope of the end of history.

The threefold encounter with Sophocles of Hegel, Hölderlin and Heidegger is a summit in that of philosophy and literature. Philosophy reads supreme poetry and is read by it. Both intuit common ground, that originating art and music of thought which inform our sense of the meaning of the world (*der Weltsinn*).

I have elsewhere tried to do justice to Hegel's contentious interpretation of Sophocles' *Antigone* (*Antigones*, 1984). To Hegel this drama was "in every respect the most consummate work of art human effort has ever brought forth." In his late lectures Hegel returns to the *dramatis persona* of Antigone, "that noblest of figures that ever appeared on earth." Hyperbole reaches a climax when Hegel argues that the death of Antigone represents a self-sacrifying lucidity and heroism beyond Golgotha. Jesus could put his trust in resurrection and infinite compensation. Antigone goes freely into the blackness of absolute extinction, an abyss made the more terrifying by the possibility that her stance has been erroneous, that it does not correspond to the will of the gods.

Like no other text *Antigone* makes graphic the polarities, the antagonistic theses fundamental to the evolution of human consciousness. It poses in dialectical terms the conflictual ideals of the state and of private individuality, of civic law and political jurisdiction as against primordial dictates of familial solidarity. The play articulates with almost scandalous vehemence the claims of sororal love as opposed to those of conventional eros and marriage. The ground bass of these confrontations is that of the ontological clash between women and men, between age and youth. There is no axis of determinant antitheses which Sophocles' miraculously compact play does not set out.

Hegel's readings will evolve in a process emblematic of the ripening of consciousness via polemic narrated in the *Phenomenology*. Reexamination persuades Hegel that the Sophoclean paradigm is even more fraught than he initially supposed. It is only within the *polis* and by virtue of the private individual's collision with the *Staat* that opposing ethical values can be defined and brought nearer to the synthesis of the Absolute, that is to say to a *politeia* in which there will be creative collaboration between familial and civic loyalties. Franz Rosenzweig's formulation is apt: "At the outset stood the birth pangs of the human soul, at the end stands Hegel's philosophy of the State." To Hegel "the divine Antigone" and the tragedy in which she endures her passion were the poetic validation of decisive tenets in his own philosophy of the spirit and of history. The "fit" was consummate.

It was the insistence on dialectical equilibrium in Hegel's hermeneutic which had the most immediate and controversial impact. Unquestionably Hegel's successive commentaries and paraphrases contain an apologia for Creon. This advocacy follows on the overarching construct of perfect balance, on the Hegelian definition of tragedy as a conflict in which "both parties are right." A symmetrical reading of Sophocles is necessary if synthesis is to be achieved, if history is to move forward. The Hegelian justification of Creon's embodiment of the state, a state without which the private individual, even as challenger, could not attain self-consciousness, almost certainly runs counter to Sophoclean *pietas*. Witness the chastisement visited on the tyrant. Nonetheless it is the force, the acuity of Hegel's misreading, if it is that, which has compelled attention and revaluation. Even critics of Hegel incline to agree that neither of the two religious-moral positions which *Antigone* dramatizes can by itself be the right one without acknowledging the very thing which limits and contests it.

Written, as it were, at the court of Creon, that is to say under Nazi occupation, Anouilh's *Antigone* adopts the Hegelian interpretation. Creon and Antigone are in fatal balance. Such is the rhetorical and scenic adroitness of Anouilh's staging that Nazi censorship licensed performance and that the playwright came to be indicted for collaboration. Actual staging subtly tilts the equipoise. Creon defeats Antigone in debate. If she chooses insurrection and death it is not out of transcendent piety and moral conviction but out of adolescent disgust. It is Creon's avuncular, patronizing vulgarity, it is the mundane tedium which will come of marriage, which trigger her suicidal gesture. Sophocles consigns Creon to hideous solitude. In Anouilh's play a young pageboy reminds the blighted despot of public duties. There are those who must dirty their hands if life is to go on. There is an important meeting scheduled for five o'clock. Not only does this touch mitigate Creon's aloneness; it proclaims a stoic acceptance of duty and the imperatives of the political vital to Hegel. It is this implicit apologia which Brecht will satirize bitterly in his *Antigone 48*, an anti-Hegelian version reverting both to the Greek source and to Hölderlin's metamorphic rendering of Sophocles.

Whether he knew the *Phenomenology* directly or filtered through Schelling and the Danish Hegelians, Kierkegaard's riposte to Hegel's reading of *Antigone* was highly inventive. He projects an *Antigone* of his own in *Either/Or*. For Kierkegaard tragic guilt is inherited guilt. Oedipus's daughter knows of her incestuous begetting. This knowledge at once unbearable and sanctified makes of her "one of the living dead." It is her bond with her fraternal father and his doom which determines the fate of this "bride of silence" (Cordelia is never far off). Kierkegaardian *Angst* is given a further twist: his Antigone is not certain that Oedipus is fully cognizant of his parricidal and incestuous state. Antigone and her secret make of her an utter stranger in the house of being. She can find lodging only in death. It is she who will force Creon's blundering hand. Only her death can arrest the pollution via inherited guilt which Antigone would perpetuate through the consummation of her love for Haemon.

In a vein alien to Hegel but familiar to St. Augustine and Pascal, Kierkegaard seeks to engage the paradox of innocent guilt. To which became pertinent the biographical circumstances of Kierkegaard's break with Regine Olsen and what he intuited of his own father's moment of despairing blasphemy.

If we add to Kierkegaard's fantastication Hölderlin's philosophic-hermeneutic exegesis of Sophocles, together with Heidegger's analysis of that choral ode in *Antigone* which he deems to be the decisive moment in western civilization (I will return to this exegesis); if we bear in mind Brecht and Anouilh and Derrida on *Antigone* in *Glas* of 1974—the fascination of the "interface" between the philosophic and the poetic initiated by Hegel's interpretation of the play is manifest.

But there are other points in Hegel in which abstract or diagnostic argument is given brilliant "stylishness." We gain access to thought in progress. The lectures on the *Philosophy of History* delivered between 1822 and 1831 contain a disturbingly vivid portrayal of Abraham. Hegel saw in him the suspect source of an enduring rootlessness, of the Jewish repudiation of any at-homeness in the social and political *communitas*. At the same time Hegel felt drawn to the absoluteness of Mosaic monotheism. In oriental faiths even light is sensuous and of this world: henceforth, however, the light is Jehovah, "the pure oneness." "Nature has been diminished to creation"—a striking formulation. Of this fierce monism springs the fatality of exclusion: there can be only *one* chosen people. In language of mounting intensity, Hegel identifies Mosaic Judaism with the totality of the spiritual: "We see in the Jews harsh servitude as related to pure thought." As Spinoza taught—the reference is rare in Hegel—Mosaic law is punitive. But it preserves the Jew from any acceptance of mundanity. This divine appropriation made of Israel a community but not a state. Hence the rapid scission of the two kingdoms. Hegel's prose mimes divisiveness, polarity following on polarity. An organic antinomy lames Judaism: "*So rein geistig der objektive Gott gedacht wird, so gebunden und ungeistig ist noch die subjektive Seite der Verehrung desselben.*" The flowering of subjectivity together with that of the nation state will only come with Hellenism and Christianity. It is the concept of the nation which will banish superstition and ritualized pariahdom.

One could cite numerous such pages, instinct with urgency and concision, having strong winds of self-exploring argument in their sails. Where except in major poetry, drama or fiction are we closer to the immediacies, to the naked energies of "felt thought"? The phrase is awkward and uncomely. That, Hegel would insist, is not the point.

Political theory has bred and enlisted sovereign prose. Consider Machiavelli, Milton on regicide or that great music which Yeats heard in Edmund Burke.

Marx's writings constitute a colossus. In volume, in the spectrum of literary genres, in the diversity of their voices. Marx's sensibility was quintessentially bookish, textual, clerical in the proper sense of the term. Libraries, archives, public reading rooms were his native ground and battlefield. He breathed print. At his death unpublished material ran into more than a thousand manuscript pages. It is in this regard that Karl Marx's vexed Judaism is pertinent. His immersion in the written word in turn generated a strategy of elucidation, of exegetic commentary, of semantic disputation wholly analogous to that of Rabbinic practise and Talmudic debate. The partisan appeal to canonic, secularly sanctified pronouncements, the acrimony of dogmatic conflict and litigation which will pervade the history and fortunes of Marxism-Leninism spring directly from Marx's analytic and prophetic rhetoric. In the internecine quarrels of communism, often homicidal, citation, text criticism and reference are decisive. This will entail a vast secondary and tertiary literature. The communist chieftain and his heretical adversaries, be he Lenin, Stalin, Trotsky or Enver Hoxha, feels called upon to produce theoretical writings, to prove himself a "book man" (Lenin on empirio-criticism, Trotsky on literature, Stalin on linguistics are by no means negligible).

There has been no image of man, no model of history, no political-social program more *written* than Marxism. None since the Torah more fueled by a lineage of textual codification, of "sinaitic" truths which led from Marx and Engels to Lenin and Stalin and in a major ramification to Mao's "red book." With the collapse of Marxism-Leninism, a collapse which mirrors that of theology in the West, an inheritance of scripted *auctoritas* dating back to the Books of Moses and the Pre-Socratics, a reverence for the book—as in the summarizing trope of "the Book of Life"—has probably entered its epilogue, what I have called its "afterword." Marx questions all institutions and power-relations; he brushes aside the self-deceiving illusions and infantilism of religion; his refutation of competing ideologies is pitiless; his contempt for the unexamined clichés of social conventions is unsparing. But at no point does he query the capacity of language, of written discourse first and foremost to represent, to analyze, to alter individual and collective reality, to reshape the human condition. Nietzsche's subversion of the status of propositions, Mallarmé's prophetic uncoupling of signifier and signification, Freud's systematic deconstruction of professed meanings and intentionalities are alien to Marx's classical logocentrism. "Ideas," he taught, "do not exist apart from language." Like Heraclitus, whom he studied, Marx regarded it as axiomatic that "the lightning of thought" as it strikes the scroll or the tome, the compendious volume or the pamphlet, the manual or the poem, could irradiate the dormant spirit of men and women, rousing them to humanity (Marxist régimes are anchored in literacy). It is precisely this faith in the omnipotence of the word which inspired the blind ferocities of communist censorship and the brutal endeavors of communism to create a new language (Orwell's "Newspeak"). In the "free world" license has often been indifference. What potentate in the White House would take note of, let alone dread a Mandelstam epigram? The image of Marx in the British Library rotunda is totemic. It is a celebration, now virtually erased, of the belief that "in the beginning was the Word."

Marx's stylistic repertoire was manifold. His early ambitions were literary and characteristic of the post-Romantic generation. They included a projected translation of Ovid's *Tristium Libri* (an intimation of exile?); a comic novel *Scorpion and Felix*; a scenic fantasy *Oulanem*; lyric verse and disheveled ballads climaxing in the *Wilde Lieder* of 1841. I will return to Marx's doctoral dissertation on Epicurus and Democritus in its more or less conventional academic timbre. Long unpublished, the *Kritik des Hegelschen Staatsrechts* already shows those strengths of close argument and concise irony which were to distinguish Marx's mature works. Composed in collaboration with Engels, *The Holy Family* (1845) was directed against "Bruno Bauer and his Consorts," using those instruments of sustained sarcasm, of contemptuous aggression which make of Marx the most eminent virtuoso of opprobrium after Juvenal and Swift. That virtuosity is again distinctive of the 1847 onslaught on Proudhon, the *Misère de la philosophie*. The exact division of authorship in the *Communist Manifesto* launched with Engels in 1848 is impossible to identify. Rarely has programmatic, hortative speech achieved a more vehement, memorable pitch and impact. The grammatical structure, the *accelerando* of the propositional sequence, the synthesis of diagnosis and prophetic certitude make of this tract one of the most influential pronouncements in all history. Luther's Wittenberg *Theses* were an element in Marx's arsenal. The account of *The Class Struggles in France* (1850) and *The Eighteenth Brumaire of Louis Bonaparte* published two years later are something else again. They fuse analytic precision, satire, theoretical control and immediacies of rage in ways comparable with the best in Tacitus. These epic pamphlets alone would ensure Marx's stature in the poetics of thought.

His journalism was torrential and often inspired. To the Vienna *Presse* Dr. Marx contributed one hundred and seventy-five articles. There have been learned studies of Marx the military analyst commenting on the American Civil War. From 1857 onward drafts, encyclopedic notes toward the *summa* on political economy, in fact a philosophic anthropology, busied Marx. This material, known as *Grundrisse*, was to be published only in 1953. It was to culminate in the first two volumes of *Das Kapital* (1867–79). Few read or have ever read the later sections of this incomplete leviathan. Much therein is uncompromisingly technical and statistical. Yet amid the sandy stretches of economic-sociological inventory there are those flashes of clairvoyant anger, of eschatological promise organic to Marx's genius. In condensed, publicist form these are operative as well in the so-called *Critique of the Gotha Programme* of 1875. Add to all this the wealth of Marx's correspondence with its own gamut of styles, public and familiar, supportive and polemic, forensic and unguarded. A prodigality of "speech acts" which altered our world (for better and for worse).

In Marx the interactions between literature and political philosophy are constant. His literary passions and literary criticism, his contributions to the theory of historical drama and of the novel, his omnivorous readings of classical and modern works—the famous "book-worming"—have been studied magisterially (cf. S. S. Prawer's *Karl Marx and World Literature*, 1976). Marx's distrust of programmatic, *engagé* writings, his formulation of the "Baalam effect" whereby the actual productions of a novelist or poet contradict, negate his express ideology, have been the source of theoretical and critical aesthetics, as in Lukács and Sartre. Marx's literary alertness was encompassing. It extended from the lurid sensationalism of Eugène Sue's *Mysteries of Paris* to the summits of Greek tragedy. Marx reads Aeschylus in the original at the very close of his life. Shakespeare is a perpetual reference. It is not only the melodrama of money in Shylock or in *Timon of Athens*, his preferred play, which fascinated Marx. It is the dynamics of history in Shakespeare and the unrivalled perception of power-relations in the Roman plays and *Macbeth*. No less than his German contemporaries Marx was steeped in Goethe. He found Mephistopheles' sardonic candor exemplary and pondered the allegories of finance in *Faust II*. Marx virtually identifies with the young Goethe's clandestine uses of Prometheus. Prawer shows that even in Marx's journalism such as *Herr Vogt* (1860) there are references to Pope, Sterne, Samuel Butler, Dickens, Dante, Voltaire, Rabelais, Victor Hugo and Calderón. Marxism is a "reading of the world."

Balzac never ceases to engage and astonish Karl Marx. Well before Marx himself, Balzac has grasped the concept of surplus value. In his *Gobseck* Marx finds the acute psychological insight that capitalist avarice is a form of premature senility. Above all there is in the *Comédie humaine* the impartiality of true realism, a clairvoyance which radically subverts Balzac's legitimist and reactionary intent. It is from Balzac, argues Gramsci, that Marx derives the cardinal definition of religion as "the opium of the people."

Dickens's Pecksniff, the depiction of social *misère* and injustice in *Oliver Twist*, Tupman in the *Pickwick Papers*, Martin Chuzzelwit serve Marx and Engels as a shorthand when lampooning their adversaries or substantiating their social protest. Like other eminent artists Dickens achieved "concrete universality," the instancing of historical and social truths via the fictive persona and narrative situation. To Marx he validates the Aristotelian paradox that fiction has a truth exceeding that of history.

Marx's relations to Heine were brief but complex. They were made the more so by the masked Judaism of the two men and by Heine's impassioned albeit journalistic interest in German idealist philosophy. Marx's admiration of Heine's poetic stature alternated with patronizing compassion and bourgeois distaste for Heine's bohemian ways (like that other iconoclast, Freud, Marx was in respect of private mores a conservative). For his part, Heine had abandoned much of his youthful radicalism and found reprehensible Marx's polemic brutalities. Nonetheless via Heine Marx obtained insights into aspects of lyric creation. In the first tome of the *Kapital*, Heine is remembered as a friend and a man of exceptional courage. Marx knew of the poet's fatal infirmities as did Heidegger of Paul Celan's.

Citations from, allusions to Dante are numerous and barbed.

In response to a condescending leader in the London *Times*, Marx invokes Cacciaguida's clarion prophecy: "Happy Dante, another member of that wretched class called 'political refugees' whom his enemies could not threaten with the misery of a *Times* leader! Fortunate *Times* that escaped a 'reserved seat' in his *Inferno*!" A passage from the *Paradiso* illustrates Marx's thesis that "a price therefore implies both that a commodity is exchangeable for money and also that it must be so exchanged." A verse from Dante sends the *Kapital* on its leviathan journey.

It is this enlistment of literature on behalf of often abstractly technical economic, political thought which is striking. Touches out of Schiller's *Don Carlos* and *William Tell* inspire Marx's sensibility. The great bell out of Schiller's "*Glocke*" tolls when Marx addresses the central issue of productive labor. A letter to his daughter Jenny alludes to Goethe's *Faust*, to George Eliot's *Felix Holt* and Charlotte Brontë's *Shirley*.

Marx's syllabus and voice proved to be consequential. His dismissal of *Tendenzliteratur*, of literature which has an ideological, "palpable design upon us" will be a stumbling block to Leninist-Stalinist dogmas of "social realism." The place of Shakespeare, of Goethe, of Balzac in the communist pantheon is reaffirmed in Trotsky's *Literature and Revolution*. The discrimination between classical realism, already Homeric, and modern naturalism in the vein of Zola is fundamental to Lukács and a swarm of lesser critics. The Marxist turn, moreover, is operative far beyond actual communism. Walter Benjamin's studies of fetishism, of the metropolis, of the technical reproducibility of art derive from Marx. As do directive themes in Orwell on literacy and on Dickens. An eclectic reader such as Edmund Wilson draws heavily on Marx as does Lionel Trilling when he places fiction in its social milieu. Jane Austen's incisive focus on class, property and income make of her our proto-Marxist novelist and there is more than a wisp of Marxism in Henry James's *The Spoils of Poynton* or *The Golden Bowl*. Sartre's entire platform of *littérature engagée* is an exercise in "counter-Marxist Marxism."

So are the many key sociological-aesthetic moves in the Frankfurt School, most notably in Adorno. Western efforts to negotiate between Marxist theory and psychoanalysis spawned a veritable industry. Whether in accord or rebuttal we read after Marx as we do after Freud.

Famously, Marx called on philosophy not merely to understand the world but to change it. How often do we pause to take in the proud immensity of that dictate? Marx is convinced that thought *can* alter our world; that there is no greater force. Hence the minimal role of death in Marxism—where the centrality of death in fascism is paramount.

Neverthless Marx engaged closely with the philosophic, speculative tradition. Any study of Marx's uses of Hegel and, to a lesser extent, of Feuerbach must comprise his writings *in toto*. The *philosophes* of the Enlightenment, Voltaire, Diderot, Rousseau, provide a recurrent subtext. Adam Smith, Ricardo, Bentham (whom Marx ironizes) are justly taken to be philosophers. Marx himself redraws the lines between political-economic theory and metaphysical arguments, a revision which can point to Aristotle. At times, as in his demolition of Proudhon and uneasy repudiation of Stirner, Marx attaches to "philosophy" an almost pejorative aura. Elsewhere he is scrupulously attentive. Ancient philosophy pervades his academic training. For young Hegelians the era after the death of the Master seemed parallel to that of Greek thought after Aristotle. Stoicism, Epicurism, Skepticism and the example of the Cynics offered competing readings of the human estate in a climate of religious decay and political despotism comparable to Europe in the 1830s and 40s. Marx asked himself what might be the consciousness of the individual in a context which follows on such philosophic totalities as those of Aristotle and Hegel. He was fascinated by the transition from Greece to Rome. "The death of a hero resembles the setting of the sun, not the bursting of a frog who has puffed himself up." Epicurus and Lucretius, subverters of religion, are crucial to Marx's dissertation on the *Differenz der demokritischen und epikureischen Na-*

turphilosophie (the text has come down to us in incomplete form). The preference for Epicurus is evident. In him the young Marx perceives a robust humanism, a striving to emancipate us from superstition and fear of the gods. Democritus's atomistic determinism abrogates human freedom. In the light of subsequent developments, the anti-materialism of Marx's dissertation is arresting. As are the stylistic flourishes: "Even as Zeus grew up amid the tumultuous armed clashes of the Cretans, so grew the world amid the ringing war games of the atoms." "Lucretius gives us warfare *omnium contra omnes . . .* a nature bereft of God and a God bereft of the world." The notebooks evidence a close study of Parmenides, of Empedocles, of Plutarch's recension of Greek *doxa*. We find that comparison of Socrates with Christ, recurrent in Hegel and pivotal to Kierkegaard. Marx shares the romantic cult of Prometheus who is "the noblest saint and martyr in the philosophic calendar." A calendar which must, as we saw, transmute thought into action.

Marx's prose enlists many voices. He is a master of epigram: "Critique is not a passion of the head; it is the head of passion." He can be emblematic: "If an entire nation could feel shame, it would be the lion crouching before leaping." The lapidary is a key format: "Luther replaced servitude through devotion with servitude through conviction." "German resurrection will be heralded by the song of the Gallic rooster." The entirety of Ernst Bloch and of radical utopia is encapsulated in Marx's "I am nothing, I should be everything." There is a subtle touch, echoing Lucian's *Dialogues*, whereby it ought to be the hope and program of revolution to let "mankind separate itself lightheartedly (*heiter*) from its past." Much of Marx has passed into the general harvest of language: "To be radical is to grasp a thing by its roots. Moreover for man the root is man himself."

When it came to social pathos Marx could match Victor Hugo, Eugène Sue or Dickens at their lachrymose worst. A vignette of the English unemployed appeared in *Die Presse* September 27, 1862. A broken father inhabits a small cottage with his two daughters. The spinning-works close: "Now the family no longer has any means to earn a meal. Step by step *misère* sucked them into its abyss. Every hour brought them nearer to the grave." Soon one child lies dead of hunger; her sister barely has strength enough to recount the horror of her death. The custodian of the poorhouse will "learn to his satisfaction that no blame attaches to him." The jury will crown the solemn comedy with the verdict "died by the visitation of God" ("*Gestorben in folge der Heimsuchung von Gott*"). An implicit reference to Dante's Ugolino prepares the sarcastic use of *Komödie*. And note the wordplay in *Heimsuchung*. Currently the term signifies "pursuit" or "affliction." Here it is made to stand for divine visitation.

Translation is helpless before Marx's volcanic riposte to Karl Heinzen's attack on Engels in October 1847. Marx summons the vituperative grossness and brutalities of the sixteenth century, the flogging cadence of Rabelais:

Platt, großprahlend, bramarbasierend, thrasonisch, prätentiös-derb im Angriff, gegen fremde Derbheit hysterisch empfindsam; das Schwert mit ungeheurer Kraftvergeudung schwingend und weit ausholend, um es flach niederfallen zu lassen; beständig Sitte predigend, beständig die Sitte verletzend; pathetisch und gemein in komischster Verstrickung; nur um die Sache bekümmert, stets an der Sache vorbeistreifend; dem Volksverstand kleinbürgerliche, gelehrte Halbbildung, der Wissenschaft sogenannten "gesunden Menschenverstand" mit gleichem Dünkel entgegenhaltend; in haltlose Breite mit einer gewissen selbstgefälligen Leichtigkeit sich ergießend; plebejische Form für spießbürgerlichen Inhalt; ringend mit der Schriftsprache, um ihr einen sozusagen rein körperlichen Charakter zu geben.... tobend gegen die Reaktion, reagierend gegen den Fortschritt.... Herr Heinzen hat das Verdienst einer der Wiederhersteller der grobianischen Literatur, und nach dieser Seite hin eine der deutschen Schwalben des herannahenden Völkerfrühlings zu sein.

Are we reading Céline? Days later Marx resumes his onslaught with the use of citations from *Love's Labour's Lost* and *Troilus and Cressida* (Marx took pleasure in Thersites). Comparable in the arts of learned derision are Marx's refutations of Proudhon in the *Misère de la philosophie*, composed in French. Proudhon is caricatured as a false Prometheus, "a strange saint as feeble in logic as in political economy." The title of the second chapter compels attention: "The Metaphysics of Political Economy." For Karl Marx political economy as it develops out of Adam Smith and Ricardo is a philosophy. It is a systematic analysis and vision of justice, of ethics, of rationality as comprehensive as Plato's *Republic* and *Laws*. And how indicative it is of Marx's imaginative literacy and refusal of artificial boundaries that this tract, often technical, should close on a fierce quote from George Sand's historical novel *Jean Ziska*.

Der 18te Brumaire des Louis Napoleon remains a classic of irony and anger. Its second sentence became proverbial: when Hegel suggested that decisive events and agents occur twice over, he forgot to add that "they do so one time as tragedy, the other time as farce." In the crises of 1848–51 Marx perceives a macabre parody of 1789. "The social revolution of the nineteenth century cannot draw its creative inspiration out of the past, but solely out of the future." It must "let the dead bury their dead" (scriptural echoes are a frequent ground bass in Marx's idiom). As are mordant allusions to ancient history:

Der 2. Dezember traf sie wie ein Blitzstrahl aus heiterm Himmel, und die Völker, die in Epochen kleinmütiger Verstimmung sich gern ihre innere Angst von den lautesten Schreiern übertäuben lassen, werden sich vielleicht überzeugt haben, daß die Zeiten vorüber sind, wo das Geschnatter von Gänsen das Kapitol retten konnte.

Ironies deepen: "Bourgeois fanatics of law and order on their balconies are shot to pieces by a rout of drunken soldiers; their familial shrine is violated; their homes are shelled as a pastime—all this in the name of private property, of family, of religion and of order." The democrats in the Chamber of Deputies "believe in the trumpets which made the ramparts of Jericho crumble" but brought forth only bleating, impotent rhetoric. Wherein consisted Louis Napoleon's advantage? "As a bohemian, as a *Lumpenproletarier*"— the caustic designation of a proletarian in factitious rags—he could use the grossest and most vulgar means. His sinister mediocrity was the very instrument of his success. There follows a dragon of a sentence, coiling toward venom in ten Latinate abstractions: in a clamorous state of "confusion, fusion, revision, prorogation, constitution, conspiracy, coalition, emigration, usurpation and revolution, the bourgeoisie pants and puffs rather a terrorist end than a terror without end!" The close is exactly prophetic twenty years in advance of 1871: "When the imperial mantle finally descends on the shoulders of Louis Bonaparte, the bronze figure of Napoleon will crash down from the height of the Vendôme column." If there is a poetics of mocking rage, it is here.

Romanticism and the nineteenth century were obsessed by the ideal and prestige of the epic. Chateaubriand, possessed by epic designs, translates *Paradise Lost*. Wordsworth aims for internalized epics in *The Prelude* and *The Excursion*. Balzac's *Comédie humaine* and Zola's *Les Rougon-Macquart* sequences proclaim epic dimensions. *La Légende des siècles* of Victor Hugo was to be an epic panorama of all history. At the close of his career Hugo composes theological-apocalyptic epics in rivalry with Dante and Milton. Consider Browning's *The Ring and the Book* or Hardy's *The Dynasts*. Panoptic immensities characterize post-romantic history paintings, architecture and the titanic scores of both Mahler and Bruckner. How else could sensibility respond to, compete with the Napoleonic saga and the gigantism of the industrial revolution? Three times, moreover, the epic dream was fully realized: in *Moby-Dick*, in *War and Peace* and in Wagner's *Ring*.

Karl Marx's *opera omnia* can be experienced as an epic of thought, as an Odyssey out of darkness toward the far shores of justice and human felicity. Even in the specialized economic-sociological texts there is an underlying drumbeat, a marching cadence toward tomorrow (cf. Hugo's *Les Mages* or the opening thrust in Beethoven symphonies). This tidal motion forward is fueled, as in the prophecies of incensed Amos, by an angry hope. When the 1844 manuscripts adduce a world in which trust will be exchanged for trust and not money for money, the animating dynamism is messianic. No less than Homer's *Odyssey* or the *Aeneid*, Marx's analytic and critical narrative has as its archetype a journey homeward. Ernst Bloch summarizes memorably: a site "which irradiates childhood and where no one has yet been: homeland." That this voyage should have led to despotism and suffering, to monstrous injustice and corruption, that it vainly sought to negate what Hegel had called the tragic essence of history, does not invalidate the grandeur of the dream. It refutes but does not devalue the compliment which utopian socialism pays to mankind's potential for altruism and betterment. When the true revolution comes, proclaimed Trotsky, "the average human type will rise to the heights of an Aristotle, a Goethe or a Marx." The *Manifesto* turns to Shakespeare: with the overthrow of the old order "all that is solid melts into air." The quote from *The Tempest*, the salute to Aristotle and Goethe are no ornamental flourishes. They tell of one of the great, tragic adventures of the human spirit, of philosophy seeking to transmute itself into that other voice of poetry which is action. "In the beginning was the deed."

What is there to add to the voluminous studies of Nietzsche's linguistic genius, of a stylistic virtuosity as innovative as was his philosophy, these two originalities being seamlessly interwoven? A rhapsodic sophist to his detractors, the most mesmerizing of thinkers to his followers worldwide. One aspect, perhaps, needs underlining.

After the Pre-Socratics whom he cherished, Nietzsche is the philosopher in whose writings abstract speculation, poetry and music fuse. Music permeates Nietzsche's existence. He composes. His words are set to music by Gustave Mahler among others. Nietzsche writes poetry. His counter-ethics, his anti-metaphysics inform modernity. What we presume to be threefold interactions between song, *doxa* and the poem in Pythagoras or Parmenides are enacted in Nietzsche. They are essential to his critique of Socratic rationalism and of academic philosophy. In him the poetry, the music of thought are literal.

The *Idylls from Messina* are seven light lyrics assigned to 1882 and not uninfluenced by Heine. They ring characteristic Nietzschean chimes: the insomniac's ache for sleep, the enchantment of birds on the wing, the Mediterranean stars. A major polemic does surface: "Reason?—a bad business" wholly inferior to "song and jest and the performance of *Lieder*." Nietzsche mocks his own poetic avocations: "You a poet? Is your head deranged?" But the woodpecker whose hammering has triggered Nietzsche's metrics will not be denied: "Yes, *mein Herr*, you are a poet!" Three years later the bird was to prove magnificently right.

The "*Nachtwandler-Lied*," the song and nocturne of the Nightwanderer, is both the climax and finale of *Thus Spake Zarathustra*. It is, emphatically, meant to be sung:

> Oh Mensch! Gib Acht!
> Was spricht die tiefe Mitternacht?
> "Ich schlief, ich schlief—
> "Aus tiefem Traum bin ich erwacht:—
> "Die Welt ist tief,
> "Und tiefer als der Tag gedacht,
> "Tief ist ihr Weh—
> "Lust—tiefer noch als Herzeleid:
> "Weh spricht: Vergeh!
> "Doch alle Lust will Ewigkeit—
> "—will tiefe, tiefe Ewigkeit!"

These eleven lines are saturated by depth and midnight darkness, by the penumbras between sleep and waking. Depth, philosophical or poetic, is itself a living mode of darkness. It is not in daylight—and Nietzsche had been the ministrant of the auroral and of high noon—that the world reveals its depth. A depth of suffering (*Weh*), of desire (a lame translation of *Lust* which stands for *conatus* in Spinoza's sense, for that which is libidinal in consciousness and the human soul). No ache in our hearts (*Herzeleid*) is as profound as these contrasting primal impulses or appetites. Sorrow, pain call for transience. But *Lust* wills eternity, "deep, deep eternity." For it is the life force beyond good and evil.

It is difficult to cite a brief lyric under greater emotional and intellectual pressure. The anaphoric structure is already more than halfway to music. The complex punctuation is a means of musical notation. Is it nonsense to hear thought in *contralto*? Here ontology and poetry are in sovereign interanimation. On this text the case being argued in this essay could rest.

6

Noting the concurrent publication in 1890 of his *Principles of Psychology* and of his brother Henry James's novel *The Tragic Muse*, William James declared that this will indeed be a "memorable year in American literature!!" William James's insistence on a robustly democratic, accessible idiom made it difficult for him to appreciate the byzantine convolutions of Henry James's late manner. At best he conceded that *The Wings of the Dove* and *The Golden Bowl* had succeeded "in *getting there* after a fashion, in spite of the perversity of the method and its *longness*, which I am not the only one to deplore." Nonetheless, the advocate of pragmatism could on occasion display stylistic *brio*. He could instance how the passion for intuitive grasp "prefers any amount of incoherence, abruptness, and fragmentariness ... to an abstract way of conceiving things that, while it simplifies them, dissolves away at the same time their concrete fulness." He found that "the rush of our thought forward through its fringes is the everlasting peculiarity of life." Henry James would have concurred in this intimation of the penumbral, though he might have preferred "feeling" to "thought." Not everything has as yet been harvested from the long dialogue, though often internalized, between the philosopher and the novelist. Both were fascinated by the phenomenology of consciousness and by what means, analytic or imaginative, one might gain insight into its dynamics. Where Henry James looked to Flaubert and Turgenev, as indeed did his brother, William James found in Bergson a decisive affinity.

When the Nobel Prize for literature was awarded to Henri Bergson in 1927, this distinction was seen to be appropriate. To Bergson's detractors it confirmed his eminence as being literary rather than philosophical. Equally gifted in mathematics and in letters, Bergson began by teaching classical and modern texts such as Sophocles, Montaigne, Molière and Racine. In 1884, the young instructor edited selections from Lucretius. The choice was representative of Bergson's future. Drawing on classical philosophic sources, Bergson's commentary extends also to Shakespeare and Musset. The lectures on laughter, *Le Rire*, initiated Bergson's celebrity. In this sparkling meditation Thackeray and Mark Twain are present. Bergson cites not only Cervantes and Molière but the virtuosos of boulevard comedy. The discovery of Ruskin was no less instrumental than it would be for Proust. Ruskin's *Modern Painters* of 1843, his tactical symbiosis of theoretical abstraction and lyricism, inspired Bergson's developing model of aesthetic intuition and creativity. Henceforth Bergson's analysis of psychic inwardness and symbolic forms will serve philosophic and epistemological ends.

As in Plato's *Symposium* the concept of *poiesis* both metaphysical and aesthetic, scenic and systematic will generate Bergson's propositions. The central definition is that of *durée*, of the subjective, interior genesis of felt, existential temporality which differs radically from chronometric, linear and neutral uses (rational fictions) of time. Consciousness dances "to the music of time." It teaches Bergson the immediacy of time in motion, a *moto spirituale* internal and incessant. The ego itself is perpetually metamorphic in its intuitive integrations of past, present, future. In a sense Bergson's entire construct elaborates on Montaigne's *"l'homme ondoyant et divers,"* on Montaigne's *"je ne peints pas l'être, je peints le passage"* (and where in the *Essais* can we distinguish the philosophical from the linguistic genius?). For Bergson the introspective intimations which allow us to register these informing vital processes are in substance rational. They are susceptible of cognitive elucidation. Affirmed as early as 1903, this "logical impressionism," this Cartesian Platonism, defines Bergson's originality and the spell which his teachings exercise on his contemporaries. Bergson's intuitionism reveals the "wave motions of reality" (Montaigne's *ondoyant*). By one of those symmetries or chordal harmonies at once puzzling and crucial in the history of thought and of metaphor, Bergson's "wave theory" corresponds to that being developed at that time in atomic physics, in relativity and the understanding of light. "Waves" will characterize electromagnetic and thermodynamic models as they will Debussy's music and the fictions of Virginia Woolf. Bergson stands at the rendezvous of lines of sensibility which, as it were, chime to each other.

This active fluidity and tidal composite of duration is the condition of the aesthetic. Literature gives privileged access to the cadence, to the choreography of internalized experience. Novalis had defined poetry as "absolute reality." But can grammar however supple and inventive translate its linearity into the flux of the immediate? In Bergson's wake Proust, Joyce, Faulkner and Broch will address this epistemological conundrum. The vanguard of modern fiction is integrally philosophical. Only poetics and art (film is imminent) can make sensible that continuum, that pulse of being usually masked or distorted by superficial, conventionalized, statistically ordered realities. This, in his own register, will be Heidegger's exposition of Van Gogh's "Peasant Shoes" or of Rilke's poetry. In lesser art, suggests Bergson, this making sensible produces mere fantasy. In major art and literature it communicates truths more significant of what is human than do the sciences. Only great art or literature authorizes "the study of the soul in its concreteness" where "concreteness" is almost paradoxically an infinite sequence of shadings and nuances. Of this sequence melody is the most faithful agency. At no point does Bergson conceal how much this belief is indebted to the synesthetic musicality of Baudelaire and Verlaine. Tidal energies of human consciousness hitherto unexplored are disclosed, to Bergson, by Virgilian melancholy or Rousseau's "discovery" of alpine sublimity. Such innovations are "surges from the deep," Schiller's exact phrase, originating in the innermost of the psyche. Bergson's intuitionism skirts the mystical. Yet it always aims to step backward or forward into the safeguard of reason. Hence, as Bergson observed, a kinship with Plotinus.

The inherited fixities of vocabulary and syntax can never altogether bridge the gap between articulation and the flow and eddies of consciousness. The struggle to do so is rendered in *La Pensée et le mouvant*: "bottled up when it surges from its source," intuition can only communicate by means of "linguistic symbolism." In analogy with calculus, the linguistic configuration seeks to arrest momentarily the rush, the tides of consciousness so as to make us aware of their inherently unrecapturable vitality. Closely attentive to both the spontaneities and constraints of verbal resources, Bergson concludes that these are less expressive of the manifold spectrum and tints of consciousness than are either colors or musical sounds. Within limitations poetry comes closer than does prose to the font of psychic values. In a perspective reminiscent of Plotinus's emanations, Bergson attempts to trace the generation of images and symbolic structures out of psychic experience. This leads him to a psychological investigation of verbal rhythms and tonalities: "The musical side of style, that's perhaps the essential.... When I write a given paragraph full stops and commas precede the text; punctuation precedes the phrase and the words. An internal motion indicates to me that at a certain moment, if possible (there are benevolent hazards!), there must come words of identical consonance and in sequence." Bergson argues that Descartes's propositions in the *Discours* are energized by rhythms which depend on punctuation. They should like poetry be read aloud. Nowhere are Bergson's "harmonics" more persuasive than in his comparison between laughter and the foam on the crest of the sea:

Les vagues s'entre-choquent, se contrarient, cherchant leur équilibre. Une écume blanche, légère et gaie en suit les contours changeants. Parfois le flot qui fuit abandonne un peu de cette écume sur le sable de la grève. L'enfant qui joue près de là vient en ramasser une poignée, et s'étonne l'instant d'après, de n'avoir plus dans le creux de la main que quelques gouttes d'eau, mais d'une eau bien plus salée, bien plus amère encore que celle de la vague qui l'apporta. Le rire naît ainsi que cette écume.

Bar the child only Nietzsche rivals this incisive lightness. Mercurial *élan*, a word which Bergson made his own, quickens the psychological-epistemological finding.

Bergson's influence on literature, though diffuse and atmospheric, though frequently at second-hand, was pervasive. For a time "Bergsonism" was a climate of feeling and one of the earliest examples of the penetration into the media of academic themes. Much of the spell Bergson cast may have been mundane froth—fashionable Paris crowding his lectures—but the stimulus and impact were real.

As early as 1913, Proust, a distant relative, was labeled an "integral disciple of Bergson." This attribution became a cliché. As Joyce N. Megay has shown in her *Bergson and Proust* (1976), it is a distortion. After an initial meeting in 1890, personal contacts were rare; they virtually ceased after 1913. In the *Recherche* Bergson appears only once in a passage added in 1921. In May 1904 Bergson praises Proust's translation of Ruskin; for his part Proust hardly reads any Bergson later than *l'Évolution créatrice*. In a press interview given in 1913 Proust aims to distance his forthcoming fiction from Bergson's teachings. He underlines the differences between Bergsonian *mémoire* and his own model of both voluntary and involuntary recollection. Proust's views on sleep and dreams are not Bergson's and Proust, unlike William James, is skeptical as to Bergson's interest in spiritualism and faith in the survival of the soul. Bergson in turn was not an assiduous reader of Proust. He never doubted the preeminence of philosophy above narrative fiction. Bergson voiced conventional admiration of Proust's psychological acumen and stylistic resources but found that the *Recherche* did not leave its readers with that sense of "accrued vitality" which distinguishes great works of art. A truly major art must "leave the door open to hope." This Proust fails to accomplish. Late in his august life Bergson stated that in essence Proust had turned his back both on *durée* and *l'élan vital*. A chasm separated their reciprocal readings of the world. What remains to be elucidated is the function of Judaism or half-Judaism, a particularly fascinating rubric, in Montaigne, Bergson and Marcel Proust.

The relationship with the person and works of Péguy was of an altogether more consequential order. It is among the "rich hours" of the encounters between the philosophic and the poetic. Péguy reads Bergson from 1900 onward. He professes him to be his "sole veritable master." He attends Bergson's lectures assiduously. Disillusioned by Bergson's failure to assist his own parlous situation, Péguy abrogates their contacts in 1912. But only outwardly. He writes to Bergson in a vibrant letter of March 2, 1912: "It is you who has reopened in this country the sources of spiritual life." He knows that is "impossible for me to separate myself from Bergson." 1914 brought personal reconciliation. Bergson will become the solicitous guardian of Péguy's orphaned family.

Charles Péguy ingests Bergson in his own cannibalistic manner. He gives to Bergson's elegant optimism a tragic, almost materialist inflection. He echoes Bergson's (Plotinian) valuation of the present moment as potential eternity. Péguy's tidal, repetitive, cresting eloquence seems to realize the forward impetus of *durée*. The tidal wave is about to break into futurity. These concordances and claims to kinship—Bergson kept his *mondaine* distance—inspire the tumultuous tribute, the gloss in *Bergson et la philosophie bergsonienne* and the final *Note conjointe sur M. Descartes et la philosophie cartésienne*, a "note" of leviathan dimensions concerned also and beautifully with the genius of Corneille. These tracts, eminent in the dialogue I am trying to listen in on as between metaphysics and literature, articulate the troubled fidelity of a recusant Catholic to a master whose writings had been placed on the Index. No less than

Péguy himself Bergson, flirting with Catholicism, contravened the "mummification, the bureaucracies, the presence of death" in the official, censorious *ecclesia*. For Péguy "Bergsonism is not a geography, it is a geology" throwing unprecedented light on the buried mysteries of grace, "itself the profoundest of Christian problems" (Simone Weil, steeped in Bergson, would have concurred). Yet the task is not accomplished. Henri Bergson "has once and for all made unsustainable and indefensible materialsm, intellectualism, determinism, mechanistic theories of association." But he has not made them uninhabitable for those who wish to inhabit them nonetheless. These somber previsions are among the very last words Péguy wrote on the eve of his heroic, clearly foreseen death. The dialogue with Bergson breaks off in mid-sentence.

Far more difficult to assess, albeit generally inferred, is Bergson's role in the development of stream of consciousness narrative. Édouard Dujardin's *Les Lauriers sont coupés*, to which Joyce points as technical inspiration, had appeared in 1887. Valéry's interior monologues and attempts to arrest, to crystallize the flux of time date back to the early 1890s. Nevertheless the fashion for fictions of introspective fluidity, of recollection as continuum does seem to echo the widespread authority of Bergson's teachings. "Wave particles" and luminous deployments at the edge or corona of consciousness inspire experiments in narrative from Proust and Joyce to Virginia Woolf, Faulkner and Broch. Narrative is made tidal, in Bergson's sense, in *The Sound and the Fury*, *To the Lighthouse* and *The Death of Virgil*. There is irony here for no prose was more classically pellucid than Bergson's own.

Apostle of mobility, Bergson hardly altered the pitch, the performative invariants of his magisterial style. Its urbane discipline, its seductive poise were operative from the outset. Where our attention bears on a stream of fugitive nuances

qui empiètent les unes sur les autres, elle aperçoit des couleurs tranchées, et pour ainsi dire solides, qui se juxtaposent comme les perles variées d'un collier: force lui est de supposer alors un fil, non moins solide, qui retiendrait les perles ensemble.

Only a small fraction of our past is functional in our thinking:

mais c'est avec notre passé tout entier, y compris notre courbure d'âme originelle, que nous désirons, voulons, agissons. Notre passé se manifeste donc intégralement à nous par sa poussée et sous forme de tendance, quoiqu'une faible part seulement en devienne représentation.

Note the unforced image in *courbure d'âme* and the characteristic horizon of calculus in *intégralement*. A swift stroke refutes Plato's conceit of Ideas: "*Cela revient à dire que le physique est du logique gâté.*" Then the pace quickens:

la vie toute entière, animale et végétale, dans ce qu'elle a d'essentiel, apparaît comme un effort pour accumuler de l'énergie et pour la lâcher ensuite dans des canaux flexibles, déformables, à l'extrémité desquels elle accomplira des travaux infiniment variés. Voilà ce que *l'élan vital*, traversant la matière, voudrait obtenir tout d'un coup.

The intertextual paradigm of electricity remains elegantly unstated. Or consider the treatments of that theme of grace, of mentalities bordering on mysticism in Bergson's late writings, renditions of which the only contemporary parallel is to be found in William James and T. S. Eliot. Throughout, an almost prosaic clarity celebrates the thrust of consciousness toward freedom. Bergson's is a festive aura underlining the contrast with Freud:

au moment où l'acte va s'accomplir, il n'est pas rare qu'une révolte se produise. C'est le moi d'en bas qui remonte à la surface. C'est la croûte extérieure qui éclate, cédant à une irrésistible poussée. Il s'opérait donc, dans les profondeurs de ce moi, et au-dessous de ces arguments très raisonnablement juxtaposés, un bouillonnement et par là même une tension croissante de sentiments et d'idées, non point inconscients sans doute, mais auxquels nous ne voulions pas prendre garde.

"Doubtless not unconscious": an unworried qualification which denies psychoanalysis.

It is a reward to quote Bergson (often Hume's prose conveys the same sensation). The seductions are constant. Unquestionably he continues to be read. His legacy in phenomenology, cf. Merleau-Ponty, in the understanding of aesthetic and religious experience continues to be appreciable. Is he still however a living force? Or does Bergson stand in the half-light of historical and literary significance as do such figures as William James or Santayana or even Croce? What is suggestive is the underlying paradox: that of a stylistic gift so eminent and entrancing that the necessary roughage and density of philosophic content suffer. Bergson remains a writer of the first magnitude. Has his "charm"—he favors that word as did Valéry—subverted his intellectual authority? Returning to his works one experiences a breath at once delightful and dated as of lavender in the linen closets of a *belle époque*. The provocation, the bite are no longer urgent. In contrast with, say, Husserl, difficulty is too often made to seem vulgar. Hegel defines the true metaphysician as one who worries, who feels unhoused. There was darkness also in Bergson's outlook, notably toward its close. But he did not wish to extend such darkness to his readers.

George Santayana is no longer in fashion. His attempts to give a naturalistic interpretation of beauty, his concept of the spiritual as pure intuition, the ways in which he reads Lucretius and Spinoza so as to achieve philosophic calm and a certain epicurean realism have not proved durable. The urbane clarity of Santayana's prose has dated. Yet what philosopher has been the object of two finer poems?

Wallace Stevens is the most metaphysical of American poets. He is alert to Plato's "pure poetry." He is attentive to the greatness of Leibniz. He prefaces the translations of Valéry's philosophic dialogues and composes "A Collect of Philosophy": "A poem in which the poet has chosen for his subject a philosophic theme should result in the poem of poems. That the wing of poetry should also be the rushing wing of meaning seems to be an extreme aesthetic good; and so in time and perhaps, in other politics, it may come to be." Stevens is an epistemologist deeply concerned by the possible relations between imagination and fact. He agrees with Croce that "poetry is the triumph of contemplation." He ponders the validity of analogy and queries A. J. Ayer's logical positivism. For him, as for Schopenhauer, "modern reality is a reality of decreation."

The affinities with Santayana are marked. For both, the mind reflects upon itself so as to register the "flow of substance" and the "hum of change within." Stevens and Santayana see in religion a mode of poetry, a "supreme fiction" whose essences are intuited and actualized in the sensory individuality of privileged moments of time. "To An Old Philosopher in Rome" was published in the fall of 1952 at the time of Santayana's death. It draws amply on Edmund Wilson's interview with Santayana which appeared in April 1946. Stevens himself echoes this dialogue in his "Imagination and Value" of 1948. "There can be lives in which the value of the imagination is the same as its value in arts and letters." Santayana is made Wallace Stevens's alter ego. Rome is perceived as the Augustinian fusion of the City of Man and the City of God. It is at once "threshold," as humble as was Santayana's cloistered lodging, and "Beyond," transcendent in the splendor of its "immense theatre and the pillared porch." Here "the blown banners change to wings." Here "the celestial possible" speaks to the old man's pillow as he dozes in "the depths of wakefulness." Out of silence and humility comes "a total grandeur at the end" and as in both poetry and metaphysics thought is the master builder:

> Total grandeur of a total edifice,
> Chosen by an inquisitor of structures
> For himself. He stops upon this threshold,
> As if the design of all his words takes form
> And frame from thinking and is realized.

Among the "bus-loads of souvenir-deranged G.I.'s and officer-pro-
fessors of philosophy" who came "crashing" through Santayana's
cell after the end of the war in Europe was the young Robert Lowell. A Bostonian visiting a Bostonian "puzzled to find you still alive."
Lowell fixes on what he takes to be Santayana's gentle agnosticism
or even atheism in the midst of his monastic sanctuary. August
shades surround the dying Epicurean: Dante's master Ser Brunetto
undefeated in perdition, the guests at the *Symposium*:

> as if your long pursuit of Socrates'
> demon, man-slaying Alcibiades,
> the demon of philosophy, at last had changed
> those fleeting virgins into friendly laurel trees
> at *Santo Stefano Rotondo*, when you died
> near ninety,
> still unbelieving, unconfessed and unreceived.

At play is not Wallace Stevens's metaphysical serenity, but the halt-
ing intensity of Lowell's own confessional yet agonistic encounter
with Catholicism. Santayana becomes St. Jerome in his consecrated
study, laboring still with his "throbbing magnifying glass"

> where the whirling sand
> and broken-hearted lions lick your hand
> refined by bile as yellow as a lump of gold.

Together with Edna St. Vincent Millay's tribute to "beauty bare" in
Euclid, these two poems are celebrations, not frequent in American
literature, of the aura of intellect.

The quarrel at once bitter and fraternal between philosophers and
poets has echoed throughout the millennial, matchless history of
Greek poetry. From Solon and Plato's repudiation of Homer, from
Byzantine sages to the present. Outsiders such as Anne Carson in
her inspired meditation on Simonides have joined in. But for obvious cultural-linguistic reasons the dialogue remains thoroughly

Greek. Thus in the twentieth century Nikos Gatsos turns to Heraclitus (beautifully translated by Edmund Keeley and Philip Sherrard):

> Cast out the dead said Herakleitos, yet he saw the sky turn pale
> Saw two small cyclamens kissing in the mud
> And as the wolf comes down from the forests to see the dog's
>   carcass and weep,
> He too fell to kiss his own dead body on the hospitable soil.
> What good to me the bead that glistens on your forehead?
> I know that lightning wrote its name upon your lips
> I know an eagle built its nest within your eyes.

Or in a lighter vein Nasos Vayenas's vignette of Spinoza:

> (In his thirst for primary causation
> he very nearly died of starvation)

but like a drummer in the African bush sent signals toward infinity.

Mirror images abound in the *pas de deux* of metaphysicians and poets. Fictive or in *propria persona* philosophers, comical or grave, turn up in poetry, drama and the novel. The oddity of their pursuit, the apartness and pretensions of their obsessed ways within the commonplace community have exercised observers since Xenophanes on Pythagoras. More surprisingly it has engaged composers such as Haydn and Satie. As I have mentioned, bits of Wittgenstein's *Tractatus* have been set to music. One Jean-Baptiste Stuck composes a cantata *Héraclite et Démocrite* in 1722. In his 1962 *Novae de infinito laudes,* Hans Werner Henze uses philosophic texts by Giordano Bruno. The iconography is crowded. Depictions of the death of Socrates are routine in eighteenth- and nineteenth-century paintings. Raphael's "School of Athens" is generated by and in turn generates a lineage of philosophic illustration. It extends from Hellenistic and Roman busts of the master thinkers, almost a genre in itself, to Rembrandt's spellbinding Aristotle. At a level which retains much of its secrecy philosophy itself is made scenic, figural in Giorgione. Blake's, Rodin's transmissions of abstract, speculative thought into corporeal attitudes and gesture have become iconic. Caricature—from medieval representations of Thales falling into a well because his attention is fixed on the heavens to Daumier—has always attended on sublimity. But as so often the summit is at the outset.

Much about Aristophanes' *Clouds* remains perplexing. We know next to nothing about its apparent failure when it was first staged in 423 B.C. Ours is a revised version in which Aristophanes remarks acidly on the imperception of his initial public. Allusions to war, to Spartan inroads are graphic, but their pressure on the comic argument is difficult to assess. Above all Aristophanes' attitude toward Socrates is not merely one of mordant derision. It is more complex. Nevertheless Plato will ascribe to the play significant blame for the subsequent hounding and sentencing of the philosopher. There are in the text ominous flashes of menace and prevision:

> And what a prodigy of madness here—
> your madness, and madder still than you,
> this maddened city which lets you live—
> *you*, corrupter and destroyer of her youth!

Twice the play gives unmistakable warning of Socrates' future doom. There is grim irony in Strepsiades' suggestion that Socrates' forensic virtuosity will ensure his acquittal from any charge. Moreover at least three other comedies seem to have lampooned Socrates. According to Plutarch he did not mind the ragging. At no point is Aristophanes' caricature more distorting than that which he produces of Euripides. We cannot confidently reconstruct the permissible conventions or constraints of satiric mimesis. Plato himself represents Aristophanes, the comic genius, and his beloved teacher as being on distinctly amicable terms in the *Symposium*. Its teasing finale hinges on their shared powers of sobriety. In his labored but thoughtful commentary of 1966, *Socrates and Aristophanes*, Leo Strauss goes further. He discerns in Aristophanes' "wisest" comedy indications of underlying agreement between philosopher and playwright. Aristophanes is not distant from his target when he seeks to reconcile civic virtues and justice with the natural pleasures of the senses. Was the *Clouds*, acted in front of "an unusually quick-witted and exacting crowd"—how does Strauss know this?—meant as a not altogether unfriendly warning?

The structure of dramatic motifs is binary. Its *basso profundo* is nothing less than the destiny of Athens. Can the threatened *polis* revert to its traditional virtues of moderation, of piety toward the gods, of disciplined pedagogy? Can it sustain ideals of veracity and justice such as Socrates enjoined or will it succumb to sophistic mendacity, to the cunning of perjurious venality? Is it already too late, asks Aristophanes, has Athens already yielded to lunacy? This fundamental debate takes manifold forms. The sophistic teachings and *praxis* aimed at by Aristophanes extend beyond Socrates and his stable. They include Anaxagoras, Protagoras, Diagoras, Gorgias, Prodikos. The robust simplicities of rustic pursuits are set against the licentious waste and social snobberies of the urban. Family values, as it were organic, are contrasted with the libertarian associations of philosophic disciples and acolytes, an opportunistic cluster without true fidelity or *eros*. Abstract theorizing and factitious scientific inquiry (Swift follows closely on the *Clouds*) are mocked in the name of plain common sense and civic sagacity. Throughout, the *agon*, the dialectical duel is that between generations, between fathers and sons. The "exquisite tension," as William Arrowsmith put it, "between the obscene and the sublime," climaxes in Pheidippides' threat to beat up his father and, almost unbelievably, his mother. Symmetrically, Strepsiades seeks to impose an archaic, self-defeating authority on his scandalous, raucous son. Aristophanes' rendition of the conflict between Aeschylus and Euripides, between ritual tragedy and ironizing melodrama is another aspect of this encompassing conflict and crisis. But the crux is the clash between natural good sense and sophistic speculation, between just reason, fueled by piety, and verbal skullduggery. Overhead hover the Clouds, ambiguous and changeable.

Language itself is a protagonist. At issue is the bewildering capacity of speech, human or divine, to communicate, to make persuasive either truth or falsehood. This fatal duality is as present to Aristophanes as it is to the third chapter of the Epistle of James. Verbal slapstick of the grossest kind alternates with the poetic luster and musicality of the interventions by the Clouds. Nearly untranslatably, "thunder and farting are the same." The oscillations of linguistic registers are mercurial. Socrates, aloft:

> The earth, you see, pulls
> the delicate essence of thought down to its own gross level.
> Much the same thing happens with watercress.

Would we have the mock-pedantries of Rabelais, of Ben Jonson, of Gulliver's third voyage without Aristophanes' roster of chiropractors, fake clairvoyants, young fops with long hair, dithyrambic bards, astrologers and "New Age" parasites? Where is there a more searching parody of the Socratic techniques of questioning, of his *elenchus*? Ionesco is not far off. Yet the fun, the ribaldry, the circus rides of language turn dark and brutal at the close. The incineration of Socrates' teaching hut, the murderous chase of his disciples point to real loathing. "If *Clouds* made life hard for Socrates, did Aristophanes care?" asks K. J. Dover. The question nags. As does that of the spectators' feelings toward Socrates prominently in view, as tradition has it, during the performance of the play. I know of only one parallel: that of J. Robert Oppenheimer visiting the Paris theater to see himself acted in a fact-fiction dramatization of the inquisitorial hearings which had scarred his life. What torsions of the ego, what self-regard or masochistic humiliations result from such mirroring?

Clouds has its scintillating afterlife in Tom Stoppard's *Jumpers* (1972). The names of the principals are those of the moral philosopher George Moore and his wife Dorothy. Allusions to A. J. Ayer pepper the text. Unless I am mistaken, Stoppard draws mainly on the verbal and gestural idiosyncracies, become legend, of the Cambridge theologian and moralist Donald McKinnon. Academic vainglory and conspiratorial maneuvers, the solipsistic innocence of the abstract thinker in everyday life, the contrast between lofty ethics and lechery are themes which Stoppard shares with Aristophanes. Much of the abstruse tomfoolery, of the juggleries which made *Jumpers* memorable on stage does not transfer easily to the printed page. What persists is the incandescent, eruditely informed brio of George's monologues, indebted as these are to Lucky's fractured but torrential eloquence in *Waiting for Godot*. The logical instruments of Aristotle and Aquinas, the paradoxes of Zeno and of Cantor, the maxims of Descartes and of linguistic philosophy are subtly disoriented and rendered absurd by curvature of context. Bertrand Russell's Theory of Descriptions both authorizes and deconstructs George's considerations on the existence of God: "And then again, I sometimes wonder whether the question ought not to be, 'Are God?'" Stoppard's satiric thrust derives from the interleaving of logical acuity and trivia:

Consider my left sock. My left sock exists but it need not have done so.... Why does my sock exist? Because a sock-maker made it, in one sense; because in another, at some point previously, the conception of a sock arrived in the human brain; to keep my foot warm in a third, to make a profit in a fourth....who made the sock-maker's maker? etcetera, very well, next! see, see I move my foot which moves my sock. (*Walks.*) I and my foot and my sock all move round the room, which moves round the sun, which also moves, as Aristotle said, though not round the earth, he was wrong about that.... and one day!—as we stare into the fire at the mouth of our cave, suddenly! in an instant of grateful terror, we get it!—the one and only, sufficient unto himself, outside the action, uniquely immobile!—the Necessary Being, the First Cause, the Unmoved Mover!!

Even if the audience does not take in the reference to Leibniz on the enigma of existence, Plato's parable of the cave and the paraphrase of Aristotle, it should tingle with "grateful terror." A moment later broad farce intrudes as George looks for his "specially trained tortoise," out of Zeno's disproof of motion, and his similarly schooled rabbit Thumper. The incongruous sparkles: the philosophy faculty is neighbor to the university's gymnastic team, a parodistic nod to the ideals of classical Greece. "The Chair of Divinity lies further below the salt, and *that's* been vacant for six months since the last occupant pulled a hamstring." At the heart of the ironies, slapstick and surrealist stage business lies the conviction that "language is a finite instrument crudely applied to an infinity of ideas." But how will it cope with the merits of "bacon sandwiches underdone, fatty and smothered in ketchup"?

An Aristophanean delicacy; not one to offer to Monsieur Teste. Drafted in a room used by Auguste Comte, Valéry's *La Soirée avec Monsieur Teste* dates back to 1894. Valéry defined language as "the spirit's flesh." No text I know of excels *Teste* in communicating the musculature of thinking. We know next to nothing of the psychic immediacies of concentration. Are they chemical, neuro-physiological, genetic, environmentally fostered or inhibited (Edmund Husserl was reputed to be able to concentrate on a single abstruse point for up to eight hours at a stretch). I have already referred to the opening sentence, become proverbial: "Stupidity is not my *forte*." Teste confesses to a painful ache for precision; to a boundless desire for *netteté*, Descartes's key word. He seeks a coherent, isolated thought system in which the romantic indulgence of infinity plays no part. The "demon" of total intellectual control, the "monster" of absolute reason (do we pause often enough to apprehend what is indeed monstrous in abstraction?) are incarnate in Monsieur Teste. They are his night visitors—Valéry cherished Poe. Teste's ambition is to achieve uniqueness, to be included in the "annals of the anonymous," a status far superior to mundane glory. His Muse is difficulty: "genius is *facile*, fortune is *facile*, divinity is *facile*." No book intrudes in Teste's cell, in this sanctuary of indifference. Yet, as Pascal knew, "to afford something supreme attention" is also to suffer. Such abstention from the vulgarity of mere being frightens Madame Teste. Monsieur's soul is "a singular growth whose roots, not its foliage, grow unnaturally toward clarity!" Her husband is "a mystic without God" (a paradox I met with in that master of the esoteric Gershom Scholem). Teste is aware of the cost. He concedes as much in his logbook:

Ma solitude—qui n'est le manque depuis beaucoup d'années, *d'amis* longuement, profondément vus; de conversations étroites, dialogues sans préambules, sans finesses que les plus rares, elle me coûte cher—Ce n'est pas vivre que vivre sans objections, sans cette résistance vivante, cette proie, cette autre personne, adversaire, reste individué du monde, obstacle et ombre du moi—autre moi—intelligence rivale, irrépressible—ennemi le meilleur ami, hostilité divine, fatale—intime.

In André Gide, Valéry found exactly this destined counterpart and intimate "other." But the aloneness of immaculate thought, the enigma of sadness in mathematics attained enduring expression in Valéry's parable.

Inexhaustible to interpretation, numberless in their variants, three narratives, three primordial tales tell of a fatal kinship between knowledge and retribution. The Tree of Knowledge in Eden provokes humankind to transgression, to lasting exile and *misère*. Prometheus is sentenced to unending torture for his theft of theoretical and practical sagacity from the jealous gods. The striving intellect of Faust overreaches and precipitates his soul into hell. An ineradicable crime attaches to the defining excellence of the human spirit. Measureless vengeance is visited on those who would "teach eternity" (Dante). Hunters after truth are in turn hunted as if some organic contradiction opposed the exercise of the mind and at-home-ness in natural life. Yet the impulse to taste of the forbidden fruit, to steal and master fire, to pose ultimate questions as does Faust, is unquenchable. Be it at the cost of personal survival or of social ostracism.

Moreover this thirst, this *libido sciendi* and "Gnosticism" are immensely more powerful than their objects, than any local intentionalities. These can be metaphysical, aesthetic, scientific challenges of the most exalted kind: the pursuit of "the One," of the "key to the universe" as in Plotinus or current nuclear acceleration. But the object can also be impassioned minuteness, the taxonomy of a million species of insects, the study of cooking utensils out of Sumeria or archaic China. There is an abiding mystery in this imbalance, in this uttermost disinterest. Much may indeed be sought for its actual or potential benefits—that Promethean fire and the technologies which will follow. What matters supremely, however, is the pursuit per se, the new insights, the enrichments of understanding and of sensibility however recondite, however inapplicable. The magnet is the unknown and man is the animal which asks.

The roots of this transcendent fatality remain hidden. The intensity, the exploratory, creative efficiency of this thrust vary profoundly as between individuals and communities, between Athens and Jerusalem on the one hand and large segments of a more pastoral, ruminant world on the other. The "un-quietude" to which Hegel ascribes philosophic, scientific, artistic developments may not be universal. It may be that the seminal allegories of man's fall through knowledge, of his Promethean tragedy and Faustian pact are essentially European. But where this "lust for knowing," where this counter-creativity to innocence obtain, their imperative can be irresistible. Himself an inspired exemplar of this dynamism, Freud overlooked its consuming power. To be possessed by an intellectual problem, pure or applied, by a total hunger for aesthetic form, by a resistant constellation in the sciences is to experience a *libido*—it can enlist madness and criminality—more compelling than that of sex. What orgasmic drive is as potent as the concentrated desire, during eight unblinking years, to find the solution to Fermat's theorem? Even survival can count for less. Women and men have gone to the stake on behalf of theological, ethical, scientific beliefs however abstruse. Today, billions are expended on experiments which may or may not throw hypothetical light on cosmic "dark matter." Like eros, but with greater enforcement and at greater private or public cost, this tireless inquiry into being and substance, this in some sense maniacal lunge after intelligibility is nonnegotiable. Disinterested cerebral and sensory passion can no more be explained than love. It relates to our acceptance and denial of death in ways we can mythologize but not altogether comprehend:

> Cut is the branch that might have grown full straight,
> And burnèd is Apollo's laurel bough,
> That sometime grew within this learnèd man....

But Faust's hunger is inextinguishable, for "only the spirit is ever-lasting" (Husserl).

The initial sketches for Valéry's *Mon Faust* date back to the dark of 1940. A fragment was staged in 1945, shortly before the poet's death. The choice of theme was virtually preordained. It crystallizes the drama of the mind in the western legacy. It incarnates the conflicts between the obsessive solipsism, the soul's autism, in logical and epistemological exploration on the one hand and the seductions of erotic, material, political rewards on the other. Historians of culture have often identified the scientific, technocratic imperiousness of western man, his conviction that "the unexamined life is not worth living" (after all—why?) with the matter of Faust. The bibliography is almost incommensurable. Much about the actual origins and exponential dissemination of the Faust-legend in the late sixteenth century remains uncertain. The literary garland includes master-pieces from Marlowe to Goethe, from Goethe to Thomas Mann, Pessoa and Bulgakov. But other media are crowded: puppet plays (the likely source), operas, ballets, symphonic figurations, films, the comic book. There are "Faustinas." Faust-ballads have been set to great music. There are so many engravings—Rembrandt at his finest—and paintings of differing quality. What western language does not include "Faustian" among its adjectives. The nerve is a central one. Here poetry, art, music, theories of history (cf. Spengler) meet with philosophy, with the acts of philosophic investigation. "All re-incarnations are legitimate" notes Valéry. Faust and the "Other," call him devilish or think of him as *l'Autre* in our divided consciousness, dramatizes as no other scenario does the illicit splendors and vani-ties of philosophic speculation. The fable has lost little of its spell in secular modernity. One of the early sobriquets for research into thermonuclear armament was "Faustus"; the earliest commercially available chess computer was entitled "Mephisto."

Valéry's version is in the key of irony. *Mon Faust* puts in fastidious doubt the entire philosophic enterprise. Even the loftiest of thoughts is a matter of habit, of ephemeral routine. The stately tomes in which philosophers gather their harvest will be consigned to dust. "Everything changes around these crystallized words which themselves do not change; simple duration renders them insensibly insipid, absurd, naive, incomprehensible—or quite simply and sadly classical." Faust finds himself indifferent even to the abyss. Immense labors of thought, of science strive to deny the meager insignificance of earthly existence. Could it be that life is viable only in ignorance of its own triviality? At which point "language grows confused and philosophy starts speaking"—a particular irony and illusion. In the final analysis—the Master's secretary is called Lust—thought of a philosophic order is nothing other than "solitude itself and its echo," a finding which takes us back to Valéry's *Monsieur Teste* and meditations on Narcissus.

This bleak conclusion could serve as motto to Fernando Pessoa's *Faust*, a voluminous torso on which he worked intermittently from 1908 to the very end of his guarded life in 1935. Despite its characteristic polyphony Pessoa's dramatic poem is a soliloquy in metaphysical dread both of solitude and of commitment. Abstention is folly but so is action which severs human gestures and passions from the sanctuary of the private self. In passages profoundly influenced by Schopenhauer, Pessoa equates salvation with sleep, with a sleep so deep that it reaches beyond the unconscious and the vanity of dreams so as to silence the vain tumult of thought. An aching, insoluble contradiction torments Pessoa's magus. Persuaded of the world's irreality he would nonetheless decipher its phenomena (Schopenhauer's "Will" and "representation"). Metaphysical nihilism cannot negate the impulse toward understanding. Repeatedly Pessoa's dramatic monologue reverts to a nightmare horror: possessed by vain but imperative reflection, Faust "suffocates within his own soul." Metaphysical inquiry induces live burial. Pessoa was a close reader of Poe just as Valéry was.

More than philosophy itself, it is the language of literature or, more precisely, of philosophy become literature, as in Kierkegaard or in Nietzsche, which articulates the pathological extremity, the compulsive vainglory of the philosopher's vocation and enterprise. The Faust-theme encapsulates this insight. Going a step beyond Hegel, Pessoa defines metaphysical speculation as nothing but "infinite anxiety."

The presence of Faust implies that of a disciple, a *famulus* whose attitude toward his master can range from loyal adulation to derisive betrayal—a compass set out in Ferruccio Busoni's great opera *Doktor Faust*. Relations between philosophers and their acolytes have exercised the literary imagination since the corpus of Pythagoras legends and since Aristophanes and Plato. Exchanges between teacher and pupil, between the magisterial guru and his more or less self-promoting junior have been satirized by Marlowe, Goethe and Valéry. Hasidic tales of the exigent love or misprisions as between rabbis and their followers, their "court" are legion. As are narratives and parables, often uncannily similar, out of the world of Zen. *Zarathustra* dramatizes the reciprocities, festive and factitious, between the shamanistic master and his students with pitiless lucidity. In chilling isolation Nietzsche cries out for respondent echo. Wittgenstein would have all but an elect nucleus keep their otherwise intrusive distance. Can philosophy be *taught*?

Now neglected, Paul Bourget's *Le Disciple* of 1889 remains arresting. Adrien Sixte (the name is a brilliant stroke) founds his materialist positivism on the doctrines of Darwin, of Herbert Spencer and Hippolyte Taine. Good and evil are a matter of chemistry, God is a childish projection of physiological psychology. Sixte (Monsieur Teste will grow in his shadow) models his daily routine, his monastic devotion to the abstract on the precedent of Spinoza and Kant. His fervent disciple finds himself enmeshed in what appears to be homicide. But has Sixte not instructed him that private, particular horrors merely relate "to the laws of the immense universe," laws wholly deterministic and susceptible of scientific, not ethical, elucidation? Now the master must confront the abyss of his own credo. Bourget raises an unsettling question: how, to what extent is a teacher, a pedagogue responsible for the acts, possibly perverted, possibly founded on misreading, of his disciples? "Go forth," bids the master and "the necessary murder" may ensue. Misread (?) Nietzsche's doctrine of the "superman" and of the decadent tenor of compassion and you get the Nietzsche anthologies distributed by the Nazis. What is the alleged measure of responsibility incurred by the political guru and Spinoza-exegete Antonio Negri in the murderous feats of his Red Brigade faithful? The issue has been fiercely debated.

Herself an academic teacher of Platonic metaphysics and Sartrian existentialism, Iris Murdoch reverts to this dilemma almost obsessively. It is central to such novels as *The Flight from the Enchanter*, *The Bell* and *The Philosopher's Pupil*. To this classical *topos* Murdoch conjoins an alertness to the erotic, to the gamut of sexuality, ancient as the *Symposium*, which quickens and obscures the transmission of philosophic wisdom from the old to the young, from men to women. Consider the blindness of desire between Alcibiades and Socrates, Abélard and Héloïse, Hannah Arendt and Heidegger. The Abélard and Héloïse intrigue has spellbound poets such as Pope, novelists, filmmakers. Logic in the arms of love.

Philosophy has its martyrology. Ancient biographies, always to be questioned, tell of philosophers slain in civic strife, done to death by jealous despots, murdered, as was Ipatia by fanatics. Rumors of violence attend on the death of Pythagoras. An epigram, a metaphysical or cosmological treatise, Spinoza on politics can be the act most dreaded by orthodoxy and absolutism. When it is abroad in the city an ideology can be a menacing specter (Marx's celebrated image). Traditional warning has it that Jerusalem slays its prophets and Athens its thinkers. There is no more dangerous calling than the exercise of reason, itself a constant critique, open or masked, of prevailing norms. In the talismanic wake of the *Apology* and the *Phaedo*, Socrates' final hours have inspired centuries of literature, of the fine arts, even of music as in Satie. In western consciousness, Socrates' is the other defining, iconic death. The epistemological, symbolic interplay with Golgotha is the crux in Hegel, in his riddling statement that "the night is now." In European painting a plethora of academic chill or outright kitsch precedes Jacques-Louis David's *Mort de Socrate* with its poignant falsehood (the presence of Plato). In *imitatio* of this canonic moment, Seneca's enforced suicide and tranquil acceptance of death become emblematic in western morals and the cult of stoic integrity. The libretto in Monteverdi's *Incoronazione di Poppea* is mediocre, but the music which accompanies Seneca's adieu is magical:

> Breve angoscia è la morte;
> Un sospir peregrino esce dal core,
> ov'è stato molt'anni
> quasi in ospizio, come forastiero,
> e se ne vola all'Olimpo,
> della felicità soggiorno vero.

Italian poets of the *Risorgimento* and of anti-Papal emancipation celebrate the death by fire of Giordano Bruno, imaginer of heretical infinities. They honor Campanella tortured for his pioneering naturalism and utopian vision. Nearer our own time there have been eulogies, poems bitter and elegiac in memory of the phenomenologist and historian of ideas Jan Patočka, harried to death by the Czech secret police. How many philosophic scholars, Confucians, intellectual dissenters were humiliated, incarcerated, executed during Mao's bloodlust? We have heard the wonder of Orpheus's inextinguishable song or the testimony to the soul's immortality, we know of Wittgenstein's proposition that death is meaningless in regard to human experience, but the price has been steep. Think at your peril.

A close engagement with philosophy, even of a technical reach, is distinctive of twentieth-century Austrian literature. Hermann

Broch is determined to make substantive contributions to aesthetics and to political-social theory. In Robert Musil's *The Man Without Qualities,* Nietzsche and Alexius Meinong, philosophical psychologist, epistemologist, theoretician of probability, play an oblique but informing role. As Jacques Bouveresse, himself a distinguished rationalist, writes, Musil is an "authentic philosopher," an analyst of the possible distinctions between "soul" and "spirit" of exceptional rigor and cognitive acumen.

Having completed a dissertation on Heidegger, Ingeborg Bachmann turned toward Wittgenstein. Two of her early short stories, which became rapidly famous, represent readings of Wittgenstein's sensibility. Already in the 1950s a halo of legend surrounds the author of the *Tractatus.* The unnamed protagonist of Bachmann's "The Thirtieth Year" cannot bear to live among other human beings. He experiences life as an ontological offense, a falsification from which death is the only rescue. Bachmann intuits what may have linked Wittgenstein to Kierkegaard. It is not language with its shopworn, preordained rules (those "language-games") which is unbearable; it is the routine of thought itself. Bachmann imagines Wittgenstein experiencing a kind of negative epiphany. In the reading room of the National Library in Vienna the *figura* becomes an Icarus. He soars toward the limits of concentrated meditation. Aspiring to become cognizant, an accomplice (*Mitwisser*) of creation, her "Wittgenstein" comes to realize that there can be no communicative exchange with God, that there can be no cleansed, morally acceptable world order without a new language. Thus he perceives that he will live out his days in a gray madness in epistemological and psychological isolation even from himself. Kafka is close to hand.

"Wildermuth" imagines an individual "inebriate with truth," possessed by an imperative of uncompromising veracity while knowing full well that this ideal cannot be achieved in *praxis.* Even trivia in the pragmatic and social spheres defy wholly transparent, verifiable description or explanation. A mesmeric set of similitudes follows: the first-person narrator is involved with truth "like the smith with fire, like the polar explorer with everlasting ice, like a sick man with the night." He loses faith in the significance, in the values of truth itself. Descartes's malignant deceiver has prevailed. Yet the condemned search for a truth "of which no one dreams, which no one wants" will continue.

To Bachmann Thomas Bernhard's bleak oeuvre was exemplary. His loathing of nazified Austria, of the literary-academic circus, of social unction was what she herself aspired to. His monomaniacal addiction to exactitude of thought, feeling and language provided a touchstone. Thomas Bernhard wrote a mordant radio play about Immanuel Kant and spouse on a transatlantic liner. His own imaginative obsession was Wittgenstein, and Wittgenstein's gifted, suicidally inclined family. *Wittgenstein's Nephew* is a novella whose hundred and sixty-four printed pages consist of a single paragraph. The question being whether Ludwig was *perhaps* the more philosophical and his mentally afflicted nephew Paul perhaps the crazier; or the very plausible reverse.

Published in 1975, *Korrektur* is one of the scarcely known masterpieces of modern European literature. Not even expert philosophic commentary yields a more persuasive reading of the "Austrian, late or post-Jewish mathematician-engineer" whom we know as the author of the *Tractatus*. Roithamer's mind—his name is as suggestive as that of Adrien Sixte—is propelled to the edge of madness by the demands of integrity, by disgust in the face of social cant, by disheveled thought processes and emotions spilling into fatuity. It is Wittgenstein the architect, the virtuoso of scrupulous craftsmanship, the aeronautical engineer and algebraist whom Bernhard regards as central. Biographical filaments drawn from Wittgenstein's "anti-career" in Vienna, in Manchester and Cambridge are adverted to. Bernhard recognizes that Wittgenstein's prose and the forms of philosophic investigation which it exercises are wholly at one with the *dramatis persona* which Wittgenstein construed for himself. The action (if Spinoza had written a novel) turns on Roithamer's construction of an isolated dwelling in the shape, never to be fully realized, of a perfect cone. Of a dwelling whose fabric, geometric details and functional features would not only empower undisturbed meditation but represent it. The purposed cone is to spiral upward to an apex of absolute rigor within a more or less hellish forest setting—Bernhard knew of Heidegger's Black Forest hut—itself allegoric of abstention from human commerce. Despite maniacal effort the cone will be left empty. The philosopher's flight to England is simply suicide postponed. That the relevant blueprints require neverending correction, that any attempt at honest existence amounts to inevitably fallible proofreading (*Korrektur*) exemplify Roithamer's conviction that truth has no natural at-homeness in natural life. All culture is at best taxidermy, the stuffing of a corpse. Thought is a mode of slaughter, of "self-slaughter" as Shakespeare had put it:

Aber wir dürfen nicht ununterbrochen solche Gedanken denken, nicht alles, was wir denken und was andere denken und von dem wir hören, immer wieder durchdenken, denn dann tritt der Zeitpunkt ein, in welchem wir von diesem eigenen fortwährenden bohrenden Denken abgetötet werden, ganz einfach am Ende tot sind.

Bernhard's subtle parody of Wittgenstein's style can turn to homage, to celebrating, paradoxically, that tumor of the soul often instrumental in metaphysics and in logic.

Also for Elfriede Jelinek the autistic immaculateness of Bernhard's philosophic parables was a model. Her *Wolken. Heim* of 1988—is *Wolken* a wink at Aristophanes' *Clouds*?—abounds in polyphonic citations from Hegel, Fichte and Heidegger. *Totenauberg* (1992) dramatizes Heidegger's attempts to keep his rustic *Heimat* inviolate from intrusion. Hannah Arendt seeks him out. If, intentionally perhaps, Jelinek's Heidegger is wooden, her Arendt is made poignant. She is an exploited, rejected wanderer, burdened by Judaism and gender. It is as if her rememberance of Heidegger's love was now an additional injustice. She trails a battered suitcase, allegoric of the migrant. Many threads intertwine: Bernhard's solipsism, Ingeborg Bachmann's peregrinations and wretched death,

Jelinek's own agoraphobia. Behind these works, also integral to them, is the voice—the philosophic enactment of the two dominant thinkers of the century.

In this constellation, though of an earlier vintage. *The Man Without Qualities* remains paramount. I have already noted that philosophers turn to Musil as their peer. Schooled in mathematics and engineering, familiar with experimental psychology, Musil published a monograph on Ernst Mach's methodological positivism and cognitive monism. He aimed, says Broch, to make of himself "the most exact poet ever produced by world literature." Musil had worked with Meinong on philosophic psychology. He was steeped in the logical positivism of Carnap and the Vienna Circle. His ironic anti-determinism, his insistence that predicative, inductive reasoning was always probabilistic, were founded on close if polemic study of Hegel, Marx and Spengler. He drew on Max Scheler's humanistic existentialism and explorations of empathy. These in turn pointed to Husserl. Musil ironized Ludwig Klages' overheated dichotomy of "soul and spirit" but made use of it. Musil's awareness of Wittgenstein, a near neighbor, remains conjectural. But *The Man Without Qualities* shares with the *Tractatus* the conviction that logic, rightly understood, relates immediately to ethics. Musil's reflections on the crisis of European values, on a climate of feeling at once profoundly irrational and boastful of its scientific-technological achievements go back to 1912. They thus anticipate Husserl's famous *Krisis* analyses of the 1930s. Early on, Musil senses the totalitarian aspirations incipient in Heidegger, while seeking to adapt Rathenau's doctrines of economic, liberal intuitionism. In short, we are dealing with a philosophically trained and oriented sensibility of the first rank. Together with one of the major novelists in modern fiction. A symbiosis at the very heart of our theme.

The unfinished leviathan of Musil's *magnum* (could it have been finished?), whose protagonist, Ulrich, is himself a mathematician, surfaces out of an ocean of drafts, notes, critical commentaries saturated with philosophy in both the general and the technical vein.

Though conscious that the philosophic enterprise might devour the fiction, Musil conceived of his ideal as unitary. "Men who think are always analytical. Poets are analytical. Because every image is an involuntary analysis." A proper style will "combine the lightness of irony with the depth of philosophy." Poetic creation is intellectual adventure at its most intense. It "pertains essentially to that which one does *not* know; to one's respect for it." What literature, perhaps since Dante, lacks "is intellect in regard to the soul."

The oblique readings of Nietzsche in Musil's novel are revelatory. To a degree unsurpassed by any other philosopher, Nietzsche experienced aphorismic and discursive propositions as *physical,* as inwoven with the life of the body as dance. This difficult, sometimes clouded ideal is given naked expression by the person and utterances of Musil's Clarisse. It is precisely her hysteria which gives graphic embodiment to Nietzsche's choral and choreographic method. What *The Man Without Qualities* achieves is of the rarest: a high comedy of ideas, a *commedia* of thought in the most encompassing yet elusive sense. "From a technical point of view the world is simply comical." Nietzsche's supreme "science" is "gay."

Yet beyond the parodistic lies the undefinable but wonderfully precise truth of Diotima's eros (her name figures prominently in Musil's cast). The transcendent merriment—how else is one to put it?—is celebrated in both the opening and the open-ended finale of the novel as it had been only once before, in Plato's *Symposion.* A fusion which deploys Musil's perception that the poetry of thought is equally the thought of poetry. I noted that laughter within high seriousness is rare in metaphysics. Even rarer, perhaps, is the mystery of the smile (do we imagine Kant smiling?). Musil would have appreciated Scholem's "Abecedarium of the Faculty of Philosophy" concocted with Walter Benjamin for the imaginary State University of Muri in 1918:

> Whoever is ultramodern and ascetic
> Will find Husserl most sympathetic.

Though there is rumor going through the land
He was someone Heidegger could never understand.

Austria generates and experiences the tragedy of psychoanalysis. Freud coveted the Nobel Prize for medicine. He received the Goethe Prize for literature. No physiologist or clinical psychologist spoke at his eightieth birthday: it was Thomas Mann. Sigmund Freud is among the masters of German prose. His style has a clarity, a sinuous suppleness, a control of pace comparable to that of the German classics. Its wellspring is the tension, at times raw, between Freud's positivistic, scientific intent and the inventive genius of the writer. In the later texts that genius tends to prevail.

What now remains of psychoanalytic theory, of its physiological inference? What demonstrable cures has it brought? The typological Freudian neurotic has faded into Central European history, into the vanished era of a bourgeoisie, largely feminine, largely Jewish, from whose contingent historical context her or his troubles arose. The patriarchal, masculine codes of sexuality on which Freudian models and teachings are founded have all but receded into the archaeology of European values. Freudian reductionism, his neglect of the historicity, of the sociology of dreams, his magisterial innocence in regard to the generative structures of language have succumbed to a more complex, biochemically, neurologically, socially informed mapping of consciousness and its pathologies. We now recognize that unexamined trust at the heart of the psychoanalytic method: no less than Aristotle, Descartes or Hegel, Freud took it for granted that syntax relates organically to the realities it segments and articulates, that words speak the world. Only because of their intentional stability, their "truth-functions," can words be psychoanalytically excavated, can their vertical concealments and suppressions be unmasked. The deconstructive proposal that language is in arbitrary motion, that meaning itself is a nonverifiable convention, that there are no insured bonds between discourse and that which is naively, ideologically postulated to exist "out there"—an axiom even of uttermost classical skepticism—the claim that "anything goes" would have struck Sigmund Freud as infantile clowning or madness.

Yet is is precisely such proposals which inspire deconstruction and post-structuralism. Freud's "language-classicism" is the more astonishing as the incipient tremors of the great crisis are at hand around him. They are inherent in Mallarmé's finding that words entail the absence of that which they designate, that language is ontologically void; they inspire the nonsense poetics of Dada, direct begetter of our current rhetoric of nihilism; we sense them in the Vienna Circle's attempt to formalize meaning meta-mathematically, in Karl Kraus's corrosive reflections on the "death of language," in Wittgenstein's exclusion from it of ethical and aesthetic substance. For Freud nothing cataclysmic has happened to the *Logos* since the *Nichomachean Ethics*. How else could pre-Lacanian psychoanalysis operate?

In compensation we have the resources of the writer, of the builder of myths comparable to Plato, of the teller of tales. The accounts of the "Dora" case, of the Wolf Man belong among the masterpieces of the nineteenth-century novel (the Wolf Man himself later raged at what he took to be an exploitative fiction). Freud can narrate, can summon *personae* to dramatic presence as did Maupassant and Chekhov. He shares with the *Republic* or the *Phaedo* the capacity to shape to his purpose representative myths, distorting them blatantly—as he does that of Oedipus—but charging them with intelligible suggestion. Hence the indispensable recourse to legends, sagas, fairy tales, ghost stories, drama and prose fiction throughout his psychoanalytic arguments. Hence the role of Oedipus, of Hamlet, of Cinderella, of the Sandman at nodal points. Hence the ubiquitous reference to the Brothers Grimm, to Shakespeare (whom Freud identified as the appropriately cultured Earl of Oxford), to Goethe, to George Eliot and the ancients. Freud's mythopoetic powers are such that they often disguise their local, circumstantial origin. What is the triplicity of Superego, Ego and Id, for which there is no neurophysiological evidence, other than a mirroring of the bourgeois townhouse with its attic, living rooms and basement, each richly furnished with symbolic requisites and incitements to illicit or treasured remembrance? There was far more than tactical courtesy in Freud's concession that the epochal discoveries of psychoanalysis had been anticipated and voiced by poets, dramatists and novelists. But his own virtuosity as conjuror of myth, as recruiter of the clinching anecdote, was as considerable as that of any major literary artist. Who else would have seen that the daughters of Lear are a variant on Cinderella? It is Freud the writer who endures.

What, however, justifies his inclusion in this essay on the commerce between poetics and philosophy?

If philosophy comports secular morality and "practical reason," if it seeks to circumscribe the phenomenology of death, if its pivotal inquiry is "what is man?" Freud's undertaking is eminently philosophical. His vision of psychoanalysis is indeed heir to Aristotle and Kant.

Freud's concerns extend far beyond the therapeutic. Hardly less than Platonism they address aesthetics and pedagogy, war and peace. They engage politics and the theories of history, the nature of religion and the development of social institutions. Their range is in Hegel's idiom "encyclopedic." Thus there is a "culture," this term being one which Freud questions untiringly, before and after his works. Moreover, like other fundamental philosophical architectures, canonic doctrines elicit a host of derivative and even adverse satellite movements. Almost from the beginning variants, heresies, critiques mushroom. There are virtually as many psychoanalytic schools and techniques as there are disciples. Some of these, most notably in Adler, Jung and Lacan, ripen to full-scale teachings in their own right. In turn, a number of philosophers attend closely, if polemically, on Freud. Wittgenstein's valuation is both fascinated and unsteady. There is admiration for the suggestive acuities of Freud's psychological and social observations. There is a challenge to the necessitarian claims of psychoanalytic explanations of pathological and anthropological data. It could always, insists Wittgenstein, be read otherwise. The scientific pretensions in Freudian theory are inherently suspect. A critique of Freud, inspired by that which it seeks to reject or amend, is crucial to post-structuralism, to deconstruction, to feminist hermeneutics. No *Anti-Oedipe*, no Derridean wordplay without or *contra* the master. Hence the oddity of Sartre's aborted screenplay on Freud. Reciprocally, whatever his wish to keep metaphysics out of psychoanalysis, Freud knew that he had begotten a *Weltanschauung* of a thoroughly philosophic provenance, notably in Schopenhauer and Nietzsche.

Dated 1919, *Das Unheimliche* illustrates that Victorian confidence in language which I have referred to. Freud sets out possible translations of his keyword into classical and romance tongues. None of these embody the determinant play on *Heim* ("home") and *heimlich* ("secret"). This play will be the basis of Freud's hypothesis. "Canny" as in "uncanny," the preferred English echo, points to shrewdness, a semantic field disconnected from Freud's purpose. Yet this localization of his evidence, this reduction of his material to an etymological singularity (cf. Plato's *Cratylus*) does not inhibit the argument. Grimm's dictionary is made to stand for universality. Reference is made to Schelling, but the pivotal testimony is that of E. T. A. Hoffmann's intricate novella "The Devil's Elixir." Here reside the cardinal psychoanalytic motifs of blinding and castration, of the double, of compulsive repetition. Freud ascribes to our intimations of the return of the dead, decisive in Shakespeare's *Julius Caesar*, *Hamlet* and *Macbeth*, a primary function in the experience of the *Unheimliches*. But though such fictions are terrifying they do not occasion the psychic pressures brought to bear on us by actual deaths. These, rules Freud, have their font in infantile traumas of loss. At some points Freud's diagnosis is uncharacteristically blurred. The "aloneness," the "stillness," the "dark" have, as it were, seeped into his argument. Comparison with Heidegger is revealing. The discriminations between "fear" and *Angst* in *Sein und Zeit*, indebted to

Kierkegaard, probe deeper. It is just the difference between identifiable motives of fear and the "nothingness," the *Nichtigkeit* or black hole at the center of the existential which marks the uncanny. Metaphysical terror and unhousedness stem from the paradoxical weight of absence, of negativity (Sartre's *le néant*). They derive from the proximate but insubstantial "I know not what." But behind both the Freudian and the Heideggerian concerns with death, with apparently unmotivated dread, lie the apocalypse of world war and the mutations it triggered in the very status of death. At this point ontology is inseparable from anthropology.

Gravely ill, pondering 1914–18, Freud turned more and more to the theme of death in his meta-philosophical speculations. His stoicism was death-haunted: *Beyond the Pleasure Principle* (1920) belongs with Pascal. Libido, the pleasure principle, the equilibrium of impulse we strive for in our psyche and our daily lives are evident. Yet there is a mechanism of compulsive repetition in the traumatic neuroses suffered by victims of disaster, a drive to reduplicate pain. Freud offers an inspired connection. Why does the very young child repeat and repeat again a game of self-induced loss and deprivation? With the incisive precision, the patience, a key element, which we find also in Rousseau's vignettes of childhood, Freud infers that a compulsion to reenact pain may lie beyond the sovereignty of the *Lustprinzip*.

A morphological excursus leads to the hypothesis, quintessentially Platonic, that all life strives to regain its primal state. A momentous proposition ensues: "The aim of all life is death.... The lifeless precedes the living." The tranquility of Freud's voice empowers statements which are nothing less than "enormous." Properly understood, life is nothing but "a detour" (*ein Umweg*) on the way to death. Freud's readiness to share with us the steps, self-questioning, patient but finally assured, of his meditation give to his conclusion a rare authority. He has "entered the harbor of Schopenhauer's philosophy." He has rejoined the Greek concept, probably archaic, of ineluctable necessity: *anangkē*, the daemonic absolute beyond appeal.

Freud now invokes Aristophanes' fable of the reunion of genders. Sophocles is cited as witness. The poet Rückert underwrites the audacious incompletion of Freud's hypothesis: "It is no sin to advance limping" (a subtle pointer to talismanic Oedipus?). Then comes the stunning rhetorical move: "The pleasure principle seems to be in the service of the death impulse." Freud's theory has not found lasting acceptance, let alone any clinical confirmation. But nowhere in philosophic anthropology is there a clearer example of the unbounded temerities of thought, of what can, without apology, be termed its *salto mortale*. If, as the Stoics and Montaigne have it, true philosophy is an apprenticeship for death, Freud remains a great master of that art.

Both Hobbes and Rousseau are germane to the reflections on war and on death in Freud's *Zeitgemäßes über Krieg und Tod* (1915) whose title neatly reverses Nietzsche's use of "untimely." This time the tonality is one of somber eloquence. The war in raging progress has shown that Enlightenment hopes of civility, of restraint on violence, of distinctions between belligerents and noncombatants were illusory. The presumption of a shared European inheritance of normative ideals, Kant's vision, has proved superficial. A primitive barbarism now engulfs the heartlands of high culture. Why are we amazed? Humanism, declares Freud, was only a veneer, a fragile crust across a primordial chasm. World war merely strips bare the fundamental inhumanity of the species, its inborn impulses toward rapacity and homicide. *Homo homini lupus.* Freud's register mounts toward that of the baroque predicants of mortality. Man's *Urgeschichte,* his genesis, is "replete with murder." World history is "a sequence of genocide." The dead come back to unsettle us. Thus the passing even of intimates wakes in us a defensive *Mordlust* ("lust to kill"). The massacres of war are a distorted attempt to allow death its natural, focal place in biological existence. The analysis could be John Donne's: "*Si vis vitam, para mortem.*" The prose shows extreme tension: as between Freud's therapeutic rationality, his faith in scientific progress and his deepening pessimism. There is an almost mystical resonance in his appeal to the Hanseatic motto: "It is necessary to navigate, it is not necessary to live." The voyage toward the abyss is that of the fearless intellect. Freud knew the outcome. He had read *Inferno* XXVI.

Freud and his movement owe literature an immense, acknowledged debt. In turn, it is difficult to imagine western literature without the psychoanalytic impact. We read, we write differently after *The Interpretation of Dreams*—after the lectures on the psychopathologies of everyday life. Modern drama, poetry, fiction and the media are saturated, often unawares, with Freudian indices. Fascinatingly, it is a resistance to this tectonic shift which energizes the counter-Freudian maneuvers of a Joyce or a Canetti.

Thomas Mann delivered his eulogy in May 1936. His remarks "will be more about myself than about Freud." Who is doubtless an "artist of thought" and a writer of classical stature. Freud's signal achievements, however, are prefigured not only in Schopenhauer and in Nietzsche but in Mann's own early novels and tales. In *The Magic Mountain* or *Tonio Kröger*. But the commanding source is Schopenhauer's affirmation of the primacy of "will" in the economy and preservation of life. It is in Schopenhauer, also in Ibsen's notion of "the life-lie" that we can trace the essentials of the psychoanalytic narrative of unconscious drives originating in a matrix of irrational, primitive magma. What Sigmund Freud has done is to "colonize," Mann's revealing expression, a terrain discovered and to a considerable degree mapped by philosophic pioneers and by Thomas Mann himself. Of whom the nervous ambivalence, the sense of rivalry in this encomium are characteristic.

An altogether different spirit, a clairvoyant largesse animates "In Memory of Sigmund Freud" by Mann's sometime son-in-law W. H. Auden. "Such was this doctor: still at eighty he wished / to think of our life." He had studied "the nervous and the night," neither of which had succumbed to his labors. At the close he was only "an important Jew who died in exile." (Mann had avoided any allusion to Freud's Judaism.) Auden defines definitively:

all he did was to remember
like the old and be honest like children.

Like Dante, Freud had descended among "the lost people" to "the stinking fosse where the injured / lead the ugly life of the rejected." Quite simply, yet overwhelmingly

to us he is no more a person
now but a whole climate of opinion
under whom we conduct our different lives.

Freud wishes us to be free, to love the creatures of the dark and all that is exiled but possessed by a longing for the future. Auden's envoi is matchless:

One rational voice is dumb. Over his grave
the household of Impulse mourns one dearly loved:
sad is Eros, builder of cities,
and weeping anarchic Aphrodite.

What insight, since Socrates' death, has elicited a more perfect valediction?

7

I have already referred to the importance, both formal and substantive, of the fragmentary, of the aphoristic in the compositions of western philosophy. Aphorism's history extends from Heraclitus to Wittgenstein (although there may of course be in the case of the Pre-Socratics a factor of textual loss and contingent survival). Individual impediments, consider Pascal or Nietzsche, play their part as do political circumstances. But an axis of differentiation is at work. There are the builders of systems, the architects of enclosure and addicts of totality such as Aristotle, Hegel or Comte. And there are the raiders, often solitary, on meaning and the world, the technicians of lightning striking as it were from the periphery, "lightning" being in both Heraclitus and Nietzsche a methodological password. I have cited Adorno's counter-Hegelian maxim, itself echoing Flaubert, whereby totality is a lie. His own *Minima Moralia* are a classic of the fragmented, of the parataxic signifying brusque, quantum-like leaps between apparently unrelated topics and propositions. The contrast is truly metaphysical, as between, on the one hand, a presumption of articulate order in reality (a possibility of inclusive "mapping" which underlies a Scholastic or Kantian reading of intelligible existence), and on the other hand the sense of the fractured, possibly random tenor of the phenomenal. Of especial interest are those thinkers whose means or sensibility, whose performative resources were short of breath while their convictions and hopes strained toward a *summa*, toward a *magnum opus* of encyclopedic harvest. I am thinking of Novalis or Coleridge. To this historical and psychological dichotomy the aesthetics, the pulverized context of modernity have given a particular relief.

As early as 1869 the young Mallarmé, in the grip of an epiphanic revelation, sought to break the determinant barriers of language and to liberate syntax from the shopworn linear despotism of logic. Not by force of image or metaphor as Rimbaud had tried to do in his *Illuminations* but by virtue of abstraction, of "absences" made transparent. Hence the mosaic fragments or particles of *Igitur*:

Alors (de l'Absolu, son esprit se formant par le hasard absolu de ce fait) il dit à tout ce vacarme: certainement, il y a là un acte c'est mon devoir de le proclamer: cette folie existe. Vous avez eu raison (bruit de folie) de la manifester: ne croyez pas que je vais vous replonger dans le néant.

Two conceptual and theoretical moves—also rhetoric has its ontology—are in play. Modernist tactics make of blank spaces between the lines, whether typographically declared or inferred acoustically, as in music, something altogether different from nothingness (*le néant*). They can contain the suppressed, the apparently forgotten which exercises a felt pressure. They can be loaded with futurity, with potential eruption into significance on the very edge of deployment. Emptiness is made fertile (*"le vide frais"*), a paradox made fascinatingly actual by the speculations of string theory and dark matter cosmology on "vacuum energized." The second trope is that of silence. The unspoken is made eloquent, even Delphic. Mendacious, imprecise and politically prostituted language, that vast noise (*vacarme* or Heidegger's *Gerede*) of the media, the monstrous amplification of the trivial are set against the decencies, the cognitive and moral cleanliness of silence. Of that which reveals its truth just because it cannot or should not be spoken. Between suspect speech acts, blank spaces—Mallarmé's famous *les blancs*—are custodians or heralds of silence. Which is in turn the poetry of the unspoken. Though couched in an earlier idiom, Keats's "unravished bride of quietness" is a philosophic ideal.

Paramount in the writings of René Char are the formalities of the fragmentary and the interleaving of poetry and philosophy. The Pre-Socratics fascinated Char already in the 1930s. Via Nietzsche, "whose *Birth of Tragedy* is for me fundamental," Heraclitus becomes a tutelary presence. Char pays him exultant tribute in 1948:

L'âme s'éprend périodiquement de ce montagnard ailé.... Héraclite est, de tous, celui qui, se refusant à morceler la prodigieuse question, l'a conduite aux gestes, à l'intelligence et aux habitudes de l'homme sans en atténuer le feu, en interrompre la complexité, en compromettre le mystère, en opprimer la juvénilité.... Sa vue d'aigle solaire, sa sensibilité particulière l'avaient persuadé, une fois pour toutes, que la seule certitude que nous possédions de la réalité du lendemain, c'est le pessimisme, forme accomplie du secret où nous venons nous rafraîchir, prendre garde et dormir.... Héraclite est ce génie fier, stable et anxieux qui traverse les temps mobiles qu'il a formulés, affermis et aussitôt oubliés pour courir en avant d'eux, tandis qu'au passage il respire dans l'un ou l'autre de nous.... Sa marche aboutit à l'étape sombre et fulgurante de nos journées.

An aphorismic sequence such as *A une sérénité crispée* of 1952 exemplifies Char's capacity to energize language with metaphysical intimations more ancient than the servitude of logic, oracular in the Delphic sense of "signaling" possibilities before they are frozen in the banalities of worn usage. "No bird has the heart to sing in a thornbush of questions." "I treasure man uncertain of his ends as is, in April, the fruit-bearing tree." The rendezvous with Heidegger—the last encounter took place in the summer of 1969—was at once predestined and almost vacant. Neither man spoke the other's language. Char could not accept the historicity of Being. If both the ontologist and the poet despised utilitarian technocracies, Char's epicurean hedonism had nothing in common with Heidegger's vision of *Dasein*. Yet a shared apprehension of the mystery of language empowered their mute dialogue. It generated what Blanchot termed "a transparency of thought breaking into daylight via the obscure imagery which would detain it." Both knew of a "strange wisdom already too ancient for Socrates."

At the close, Char placed poetry above philosophy. Philosophy plows the furrow in which poetry will deposit its seed. Creativity is at its most intense in a poet-thinker such as Parmenides or a thinker-poet such as Heraclitus. Heidegger concurred with particular reference to Sophocles and Hölderlin. Char's gnomic utterance spoke for both: "The vessel of rigor" (i.e. of systematic logic, of the schoolmen) "flies nothing but the flag of exile." What homecoming there is lies with the submission of philosophic speculation to the secrecy of the poem. "*Clarté énigmatique.*"

It would be foolish to suppose that there is much that is new or revealing to say about the executive means of the *Tractatus* or the *Philosophical Investigations*. The secondary literature is voluminous. It is also contentious, often self-advertising and prone to preciousness. Time and again Wittgenstein's self-proclaimed disciples and exegetes seem susceptible of that "bewitchment" which he regarded as a prime danger and ambush in philosophic texts. Too often they skate over the problems of translation, always problematic from a very particular German into English, problems which preoccupied and sometimes incensed Wittgenstein himself. To what extent did Ludwig Wittgenstein continue to think in "Austro-German," to enlist German syntax when dictating, lecturing or writing in English? Add to this the question, never so far as I know thoroughly elucidated, of the *oral* foundations of much of the material. As with Socrates what we often have is a reported voice. The articulate epistemology, the devices of monologue simulating didactic exchanges (but with whom?) are at the opposite, say, of the systematic encoding and normative script of a Kant or a Hegel.

Wittgenstein makes confident access even more perplexing. On numerous, salient occasions he stresses the provisional, incomplete, "defeated" tenor of his works. "There is a quite definite limit to the prose I can write and I can no more overstep that than write a poem." Of the *Investigations*: "This book is really only an album" reiterating its fragmented questions and proposals in calculated frustration. He said famously in regard to the *Tractatus*: "My work consists of two parts: the one presented here plus all that I have *not* written. And it is precisely this second part that is the important one." Or "but see, I write one sentence, and then I write another—just the opposite. And which shall stand?" The verdict on his later work is lapidary: "I should have liked to write a good book. It has not turned out so." At best, the *Investigations* are "a photographic album." In stark contrast, there are *dicta* as close to megalomania as any in the final Nietzsche or at the climax to Hegel's *Phenomenology*: the *Tractatus* has resolved all valid philosophical questions. There is no more to be said. Had it been feasible, noted Wittgenstein, he would have dedicated the *Investigations* to God. No other philosopher, save Schopenhauer, is truly worth reading.

Implicit is the exceedingly delicate, "off-limits" element of the Wittgenstein aura, of the mythology which from the outset surrounded his *persona*, his style of being. This mythology contains typological strains known to the history of philosophic meditation and presentment: the spells of extreme solitude, of ascetic retreat to the virtually inaccessible fastness of Skjolden in Norway (shades of Ibsen's Brand) or rural Ireland. There is the halo of sexual abstention, if that is what it was, of the Kierkegaardian anchorite. Wittgenstein elects periods of monastic humility as a market gardener, primary school teacher or hospital orderly. Diogenes and Pascal would have approved. There are, however, also components singular to Wittgenstein: his manifest discomforts, even evasions of his Jewish origins; his renunciation of immense inherited wealth; his caustic indifference to social graces and officious mundanities; his informality of dress and disdain for creature comforts. What is indisputable is the charisma. The mesmerisic impact on his listeners, the capacity of Wittgenstein to alter their lives. The essayist and novelist William Gass puts it memorably:

the total naked absorption of the mind in its problem, the tried-out words suspended for inspection, the unceasingly pitiless evaluation they were given, the temporarily triumphant going forward, the doubt, despair, the cruel recognition of failure, the glorious giving of solutions by something from somewhere, the insistent rebeginning, as though no one, not even the speaker, had ever been there. Without cant, without jargon, and in terms of examples, this abstract mind went concretely forward; and is it any wonder that he felt impatient with twaddle and any emphasis on showy finish, with glibness, with quickness, with polish and shine, with all propositions whose hems were carefully the right length, with all those philosophies which lean on one another, like one in a stupor leans against a bar? ... How no one word was final, how the work was never over, never done, but only, in grief, abandoned as it sometimes had to be, and so, in the manner of the poet, each line of thought was a fresh line, each old problem no older than the sonnet, invented today, to be conquered again for the first time.... How pale seems Sartre's *engagement* against the deep and fiery colors of that purely saintly involvement.

Cadences reminiscent of Beckett or of Nietzsche's neologism *Abstraktions-Künstler*. A record of minimalist authority rivaling that of eastern sages and of Socrates. Though Wittgenstein himself regarded his stance as that of a man helpless, lost in a familiar city, Keynes preferred to entitle him "our newest Spinoza."

Yet one of the few younger philosophers at all close to Wittgenstein defined him as "an awesome and even terrible person." His rebukes, his dismissals could be sulphurous. Gusts of almost hysterical self-abasement in which he confessed to being "mad" or "evil," in which he hinted at scurrilous episodes, left his listeners numb. Verdicts were beyond appeal: Rilke's work was "poisonous" and would cause indigestion. "Each conversation with Wittgenstein was like living through the day of judgment. It was terrible" (G. H. von Wright). When they fell out of intellectual favor, those once nearest to him and most supportive were publicly cut dead. This was the case with Bertrand Russell. Wittgenstein fought with valor on some of the hellish fronts during the First World War—again, that Socratic analogy. He seems to have experienced combat as exhilarating. This may be more significant than his hagiographers and imitators realize. A deep-seated capacity for charring rage inhabited his tensed consciousness, a vital *terribilitá*.

All of which raises the taboo question: to what extent was Ludwig Wittgenstein the deliberate architect (architecture was his expert passion) of his own legend, of the dramatic corona surrounding his presence? What was intentional, at moments histrionic, in his eccentricities, in his uses of anathema, in the props of his abstentions—the famous beach chair in which he was rumored to sleep? What was strategic or allegoric in his confession that only the andante of Brahms's third string quartet had kept him from suicide? This is only to suggest that he was in some sense a virtuoso of a "counter-rhetoric" itself formidably rhetorical. Such a strategy, ensuring indispensable spaces, would be the very antithesis to Spinoza's translucent privacy. Might there have been in his legendary performance just a grain of Viennese *Schmockerei*? In a sensibility of exacerbated genius, vulnerable—but exactly to *what*?—sincerity and theater, authenticity and mask may become indissolubly meshed. As Char says of Heraclitus, so Stanley Cavell says of Wittgenstein: an "obscurity from which clarity comes." The reverse may be valid: concise simplicity, abstention from expressive eloquence can generate darkness. The late portrait photographs are both frighteningly revealing and veiled. Was Wittgenstein posing when he was posing?

How do these opacities relate, if they relate at all, to Wittgenstein's prose, to his cardinal notion of "language-games," itself a suggestive rubric?

Wittgenstein's literary tastes are well documented. He claimed that he had read every sentence of *The Brothers Karamazov* "fifty times." Tolstoy's catechism primer, the *Gospel in Brief*, never left him. Neither did Tolstoy's *Hadji Murad* and "Two Old Men." He treasured Gottfried Keller's fiction and the lyric poems of Mörike.

The bizarre torsion, in the wake of Tolstoy, is Wittgenstein's dismissal of Shakespeare (I have discussed it in detail elsewhere). He echoed Tolstoy's objection to the lack of any declared moral axis in Shakespeare's plays, of stated ethics such as he found in the poetry of C. F. Meyer and Ludwig Uhland! He bridled at the absurdities of plot even in such alleged masterpieces as *King Lear*. Wittgenstein went further. Shakespeare's towering status was a cultural cliché, a matter of banal, unexamined consensus. He lacked "the great heart," the truthful humanity of a Beethoven. His craft was one of verbal virtuosity, of brilliant verbal display often barren of adult content.

This almost ludicrous indictment is the more arresting as Wittgenstein's Viennese background was steeped in Shakespearean translations and performances. Only a sensibility fundamentally extraterritorial to the English language could have entertained and voiced such persuasions. This crux has so far as I am aware escaped notice. When we read Wittgenstein in English, when we attend to his dictations and reported conversations, we are in fact consigned to translations however authorized. At some central level English remains foreign to Wittgenstein. Thus, persistently, he reverts to the universal idiom of music. He knew with Wallace Stevens that "we are men made out of words." Fundamentally these words were in German. Their ideal was that of *Dichtung*. Wittgenstein may indeed have been "a poet of nearly pure cognition," but that poetry was at home in the late romantic and early modernist texture, legacy and stylistic moves of German literature. A condition the more significant for one who proclaimed after Kant that ethics and aesthetics were identical.

The genesis and prehistory of the *Tractatus*, initially entitled *Logisch-Philosophische Abhandlung*, has been minutely examined. The tortuous history of successive rejections by different publishers in what an exasperated Wittgenstein called "this shitty world," its eventual but mutilated publication in Wilhelm Ostwald's wretchedly printed *Annalen der Naturphilosophie*, has been recorded. Details of the process of translation into English undertaken jointly by

F. P. Ramsey and C. K. Ogden remain somewhat indistinct. Nor is it quite certain that the definitive title which like the numeration of propositions echoes Spinoza was suggested by G. E. Moore. It was in any event an inspired *trouvaille,* adding to the aura of authoritative, untimely and timeless strangeness. The precedent of Lichtenberg's aphorisms is undeniable. J. P. Stern finds a "similarity of tone, in the breath of the spoken voice. Wittgenstein appears to share with Lichtenberg a resort to colloquialism, to illustrations drawn from the natural sciences, to short paratactic clauses yet held together, firmly and energetically by a guiding thought." Others have related the *Tractatus*'s "syncopated prose" (C. D. Broad) to the aphorismic techniques in Nietzsche's *Thus Spake Zarathustra*. But the affinities with both these precedents can be exaggerated. One reaches out for possible analogies. Some have made out a kind of poetry and music in the clipped sentences of the *Tractatus* comparable to those minimalist works of modern architecture which Wittgenstein admired and adapted. Parallels have been drawn with the graphic logic and astringent constructivism of Paul Klee. I keep hearing in the *Tractatus* something of the urgent sparsity of Webern. But these are primitive referrals. This "great work of art," this impression of "a veiled face" as G. E. M. Anscombe has it, remains in essence *sui generis.* Neither in philosophy nor in literature is there anything else quite like it. The informing "inscape," as Hopkins might have called it, is decisive from the outset, from the pencilled manuscript known as the *Prototractatus*. As in a rough Cézanne sketch the spell is one of virtually physical intensity.

It is difficult to stabilize those rhetorical tropes instrumental in the *Tractatus*. These can be oracular, anaphoric but also deconstructive of their own affirmations. What attribute other than Delphic is apposite to a whole set of propositions such as that of the celebrated beginning: "*I. Die Welt ist alles, was der Fall ist*"—where English "everything that is the case" excludes the internalized theological connotations of the German *der Fall*. What is more gnomic than the dictate in 5.552 that "Logic *precedes* every experience—

that something *is so*"? Or "there is no privileged number" (ask Riemann or Ramanujan!). Often utterance both makes manifest and disguises (*verkleidet*) an entire program as in 4.112: "Philosophy is not a theory but an activity." Or in the negation of the oracular: "The events of the future *cannot* be inferred from those of the present" (5.1361). Imperative rulings have an awesome resonance: "*The limits of my language* mean the limits of my world" (5.6) (what life does the deaf-mute live?). "There can *never* be surprises in logic" (6.1251) (had Wittgenstein read *Alice in Wonderland*?). Consider the mantic finality of "Ethics is transcendental. (Ethics and aesthetics are one)" (6.421)—where "transcendental" serves as an undefined thunderclap. Nothing in Leibniz, the precedent, is quite as imperious as "God does not reveal himself *in* the world" (6.432). "Not *how* the world is, is the mystical, but *that* it is" (6.44). A vector of assertion which will culminate in the all too illustrious and terminal injunction to silence in proposition 7, a hallowed number if ever there was (the *Tractatus* has its numerology). Propositions, ordinances, definitions, prohibitions graven in stone as in some poetry of commandment. Beyond judicial appeal. Wittgenstein informed Moore and Russell that there was much in the *Tractatus* which they would *never* understand. What did he intend by that?

To demonstrate the anaphoric construct, the undertow of the *Tractatus*, one would want to cite virtually the whole. The decimal numeration acts also as a dramatic device marking a "large number of worked and polished building blocks put together to make a whole" (Anscombe). At certain points—4.011 to 4.024 on propositions or 5.01 to 5.1 on truth-functions—the current is reiterative and cumulative. The reader (listener) experiences a pulse-beat of axioms and arguments progressing toward a pedal point. The effect is so compelling that it enlists—this is Wittgenstein's skill—the gaps, the silences within the serial fabric. An echo of *Anna Karenina* in 6.43 triggers, as it were, the great arc of propositions on death and the world, on the unsayable and the category of the "mystical" leading to the coda. Very short sentences alternate with longer, subtly informal affirmations and asides. The combinatorial cadence is of a literary, poetic quality which set the *Tractatus* closer to Blake's *Proverbs* and to Rimbaud's *Illuminations* than to any other formally philosophic text.

A third major conceit hardly needs emphasis. It is that of a self-ironizing stoicism, of withdrawal for which *Zarathustra* may have been a model. The prefatory note declares that this work will be comprehensible to those who have entertained the same or similar thoughts already. At the last, a true reader will have surmounted Wittgenstein's sentences recognizing that they "are nonsense." Whence the famous simile of thrusting away the ladder on which the reader has ascended. There are admonitions to Ficker and other contemporaries that what has value in the *Tractatus* belongs to its unwritten part. Replying to a member of the Vienna Circle who had requested a copy of the *Tractatus*, Wittgenstein, in July 1925, reported that he owned none. The Indian rope trick at its finest.

Dictation plays a scarcely examined role in the history of western philosophy. As does transmission in the form of lecture notes or recollections at second hand. We have seen how artfully these are staged in a number of Plato's dialogues. Scholars suggest that a key text such as Aristotle's *Poetics* is intelligible solely if we regard it as the notes set down by a pupil or auditor in the lecture hall of the Academy. Failing eyesight compelled Nietzsche to dictate much of his work. Much of Hegel's teaching in Berlin has come down to us indirectly. Dictation may preserve the immediacy, the personal register of the speaker's voice. But it may also stylize and conceal vital processes of hesitation, suspensions of certitude and the economies which qualify a written version. This is of importance in the case of Coleridge. Would that we knew more of dictation in the school of Pythagoras or the seminars of Plotinus.

Wittgenstein dictates the so-called "Blue Book" to his Cambridge class in 1933–34; he dictates the "Brown Book" to two disciples in the course of 1934–35. He regarded the "Blue Book" as nothing more than a set of notes, whereas the "Brown Book" might be a preliminary draft of work in progress, of what would become the *Philosophical Investigations*. Add a further complication: Wittgenstein considered making a German version. He was inwardly translating German when dictating an often labored English. Once again the ironic, self-deprecating touch is there. He tells Russell that he dictated these notes "to my pupils so that they might have something to carry home with them, in their hands if not in their brains." Intriguingly, Wittgenstein reflects on the process of bi- or inter-lingual argument in dictation:

Supposing I had a habit of accompanying every English sentence which I said aloud by a German sentence spoken to myself inwardly. If then, for some reason or other, you call the silent sentence the meaning of the one spoken aloud, the process of meaning accompanying the process of saying would be one which could itself be translated into outward signs. Or, *before* any sentence which we say aloud we say its meaning (whatever it may be) to ourselves in a kind of aside ... A typical example of this is the "aside" on the stage.

Yet it is just these indirections of many-layered semantic means in Wittgenstein's dictations which permit insight into his most influential *doxa*:

If we are angry with someone for going out on a cold day with a cold in his head, we sometimes say: "I won't feel your cold." And this can mean: "I don't suffer when you catch a cold." This is a proposition taught by experience. For we could imagine a, so to speak, wireless connection between the two bodies which made one person feel pain in his head when the other had exposed his to the cold air. One might in this case argue that the pains are mine because they are felt in my head; but suppose I and someone else had a part of our bodies in common, say a hand. Imagine the nerves and tendons of my arm and A's connected to this hand by an operation. Now imagine the hand stung by a wasp. Both of us cry, contort our faces, give the same description of the pain, etc. Now are we to say we have the same pain or different ones? ... Of course, if we exclude the phrase "I have his toothache" from our language, we thereby also exclude "I have (or feel) *my* toothache." Another form of our metaphysical statement is this: "A man's sense data are private to himself." And this way of expressing it is even more misleading because it looks still more like an experimental proposition; the philosopher who says this may well think that he is expressing a kind of scientific truth.

The notion of saying to one's afflicted interlocutor "I won't feel your cold" contains more than a grain of surrealism or Buster Keaton-style slapstick. Note how the "metaphysical" springs abruptly out of a seemingly pedestrian context. Wittgenstein's thought experiments are deliberately down-to-earth, whereas the philosophical entailments are often transcendent. The dismissal of prevailing epistemologies is casually consequential. As the "Brown Book" puts it: "There is a kind of general disease of thinking which always looks for (and finds) what would be called a mental state from which all our acts spring as from a reservoir." The elementary and the most demanding alternate in often concealed patterns. At the turn of a phrase great doors are flung open: "What we call 'understanding a sentence' has, in many cases, a much greater similarity to understanding a musical theme than we might be inclined to think."

The *Philosophical Investigations* cast a spell. They have occasioned a secondary literature adulatory and disputatious, technical and rococo (e.g. readings by Stanley Cavell). These constitute a kind of photographic album traversing and re-traversing a landscape, a comparison advanced by Wittgenstein himself. Diverse angles of incidence are possible. In the background hovers the Spenglerian hint that the grandly systematic or epic is no longer available. At best we must hope for observant description or snapshots. But surface is antithetical to superficiality. All we have is "prose up to a certain point." Yet as Thomas Bernhard insisted, the intellect operative in the *Investigations* is "poetical through and through." The solicitations and pressures of poetry just out of reach are palpable, comparable to the pressures of music on Schopenhauer.

Repudiating the concept of any "private language," the *Investigations* can nonetheless be read as the diary of a diary, an impression strengthened by the notebooks and intimate jottings on which they are based. Once again in echo to the *Tractatus*, Wittgenstein postulates boundary conditions: "What cannot be written cannot be written." A prescription qualified by the wry concession: "My head often knows nothing of what my hand is writing." Here it may be that the historical context and climate of feeling are relevant. The *Investigations* evolve during the time of such experiments in "automatic" writing as André Breton's. At moments they resemble the narrative tautologies of Gertrude Stein. They belong to modes of consciousness without any guarantee of externalized sequence. Wittgenstein was Freud's contemporary, and Bergson's. He affirmed that a homecoming is to be sought even if the voyage has been misdirected or errant. His last academic engagement took him to Ithaca (Cornell University in the State of New York).

Almost illicitly—why is it that reading the *Investigations* often comports a sense of eavesdropping?—one looks to what may have been unexpected sources and subconscious allusions. Proposition 44, for no evident reason, cites the most brutal of Siegfried's arias in the *Ring*. The analysis of distinctions between "knowing" and "saying" in the extended 79th section does seem to reflect Freud's speculations on Moses. In a rare use of that epithet in number 89 Wittgenstein asks "To what extent is logic something sublime?" and adverts once again to St. Augustine. The findings in 97 are lyrical: "Thought is haloed" (*mit einem Nimbus umgeben*). Logic represents the "a priori order of the world" which precedes all experience. It must be of crystalline purity. But here *Kristall* is no abstraction. It is "something concrete and at the same time *hardest*." Striving to apprehend "the incomparable being of language" (is Heidegger on a parallel path?), we forget that such words as "experience," "world," "language" itself, if they can be used at all, must have as humble a utility as do "table," "lamp," or "door." Yet the more closely we consider actual language the more obvious is its conflict with the ideal of crystalline logic (107). This conflict threatens to become unbearable. We are slipping on sheet ice. If we wish to proceed we must have *friction*. "Back to the rough ground!" Husserl is nearby.

Part II, unnumbered, begins with the question of whether animals can hope. Is hope possible only for those beings who can speak? What are the relations between utterance and mien? Terror can be voiced in "a smiling tone." Observe the aptness, but also the beauty of 514–15:

And when I say "The rose is also red in the dark," you see that red formed (*förmlich*) before you.
Two images of the rose in darkness. The one totally black; for the rose is invisible. In the other the rose is pictured in all its particularities and surrounded by blackness. Is one picture true, the other false? Are we not speaking about a white rose in the dark and of a red rose in the dark? And are we not saying that they could not be differentiated in the dark?

Blake would have listened closely.

In many ways, the *Investigations* invite the conjecture that there is "behind" or between their lines *another* text. In which formal logic would irradiate everyday speech. That other text remains just out of reach but its mute presence is ethical. It prefigures a condition in which falsehood would be immediately visible and absurd. This privileged tautology is set out in Swift's fable of ever truthful horses. So far as the human animal goes, such perfect verity may or may not be reserved for death. There is a sense in which the *Investigations*, like so much of enduring poetry, are death-haunted. Referring to Dostoevsky, Wittgenstein notes in his diary for July 1916: "Can one live so that life ceases to be problematic? So that one *lives* in the eternal and not in time?" It may well be that via manifold tangents the *Philosophical Investigations* seem to clarify if not to resolve this question. Which, for all their fragmented "strangeness," does place them in a determinant lineage of morals and metaphysics. But as we have seen, Wittgenstein felt that his teachings should have been articulated in verse.

•

Which brings us to two poems.

Hegel's pronouncements on literature, on literary history, on the theory of poetic and dramatic genres are voluminous. His interest in tragedy was constant. The formative and polemic consequences were profound. Much in the aesthetics of Croce, Lukács and Sartre derives from the Hegelian precedent. But little in Hegel's analytic and argumentative fiber suggests any personal lyric impulse. His voice was prosaic in the best sense of the term. There is one exception: the ode addressed to Hölderlin in August 1796.

Every aspect of the Hegel-Hölderlin relationship, initiated during their schooldays in Tübingen, has been minutely documented and interpreted. Elements in Heidegger's relation to Paul Celan echo that earlier encounter of philosopher and poet. The twentieth century came to identify in Hölderlin's writings, in his poems, letters and theoretical meditations, most notably on Empedocles and Sophocles, philosophic instigations and originalities of an exceptional order. Hölderlin's youthful vision of Hellas, his programmatic adoption of "oneness" in Heraclitus, his instinctive turn toward a Parmenidean equation of thought and being were arrived at and underwritten by close exchanges with the young Hegel. There is indeed a programmatic theoretical text which scholars ascribe to either the one or the other enthusiast. It may well be that the uncompromising rationality of the mature Hegel, the (partial) deflection from pagan Greece in his historicism and political theory reflect, perhaps in unacknowledged depth, Hegel's incapacity to come to terms with Hölderlin's descent into mental derangement. The emotional and intellectual investment in affinity, in celebration had been too great. Here also, the Heidegger-Celan rendezvous invites comparison.

The Eleusinian mysteries are a recurrent topic in western art and poetry. What little is known of them points to rites of initiation into a simulacrum of the underworld symbolized by Demeter.

The figuration of death would lead to some *mimesis* of resurrection, to rebirth in the image of the earth's cyclical return to fertility after the barrenness of winter. In the immediate context of Hegel's ode the sense of a shared immersion in the mysteries of poetic-metaphysical revelation also invokes the libertarian hopes, the ideals of fraternal affinity proclaimed by Rousseau. Add to this the exaltation and the tragedy of the condition of the French revolution throughout 1796.

The summons to the night, custodian of freedom and of contemplation, is conventionally romantic. As is the landscape of veiled moonlight, lake and hills so imitative of that in *La Nouvelle Héloïse*. The image of the cherished friend brings with it an ardent hope of reunion, of a bond which will have ripened. But the vision flees. No private intimacy yields assurance. Together with Hölderlin and Schelling, Hegel now succumbs to, indeed embraces that axiom of universal unison, the *en kai pan* the of the Pre-Socratics which has been the motto of ecstatic hopes in Tübingen. A strangely atticized Spinoza lies close to hand. Would that the portals to the shrine at Eleusis would spring open. Inebriate with enthusiasm—*Begeisterung trunken* derives directly from Schiller—the acolyte could then partake in the sacred rites of rebirth.

There ensues the paradigmatic lament, the elegy of ontological loss which will inspire German poetry and philosophy from the time of Hölderlin to that of Nietzsche, Spengler and Heidegger. The gods have withdrawn to Olympus, abandoning the graves of profaned (*entweihte*) humanity. The genius of innocence is hence. The wisdom of the priests has fallen silent. The quest for ultimate understanding is vain. So is the attempt "to dig for words," an arresting image. Hegel's phraseology grows murky; private, "coded" allusions may underlie our text. But the dominant motif is compelling. Conceptual thought no longer suffices the soul, no longer harbors intimations of infinity. Even if he were to speak with the tongues of angels man would experience the ineluctable poverty of language. He now dreads the impoverishment, the banal corruption which inadequate utterance brings to what had been intuited as encompassing holiness. Almost as in the finale of the *Tractatus* the saving imperative is that of silence. Nothing must be revealed of what had once been glimpsed, of what had been experienced in the night of the mysteries. Lest revelation be made the tawdry plaything of sophists in the marketplace. It is only in the deeds, not in the speech of the elect that divinity persists. In the dark of loss Hegel can still apprehend the goddess. She is the spirit of unspecified acts (*Taten*). Though all else recedes her unspoken presence will endure. Is there in this ode some premonitory intimation of the perils Hölderlin will incur owing to the very vehemence and eloquence of his lyric raptures?

Gershom Scholem, scholar's scholar, mathematician by training and inclination, wrote verse. Some intensely serious but more often of an occasional, humorous and domestic tenor. Frequently it figures in his abundant correspondence. The letters to and from Walter Benjamin constitute one of the most concentrated and illuminating dialogues in twentieth-century moral and intellectual history. There is no more penetrating commentary on Kafka than that developed in their letters during the early 1930s. Their intimate friendship, Scholem's valuation of Benjamin's critical genius, Benjamin's recognition of Scholem's stature in Judaism date back to the period immediately preceding the First World War. Later the exchanges take on a tense, even polemic key. What he regarded as a "treason of the cleric" in Benjamin's Marxism and communism exasperated Scholem. He bridled at Benjamin's fidelity to Brecht. Benjamin's unwillingness to emigrate to Palestine when there was still time and despite reiterated professions of intent angered Scholem who had seen all too clearly what lay ahead for European Jews. For his part, Benjamin felt that Scholem did not rightly evaluate the psychological torment, the material *misère*, the entrapment of the refugee condition in an increasingly apocalyptic Europe. The letters break off in February 1940. Benjamin's suicide did not surprise Scholem but left him irremediably bereft.

Benjamin had acquired Paul Klee's "Angelus Novus," an oil painting with touches of aquarelle. Its hallucinatory power, its allegoric violence and challenge to interpretation became emblematic of Walter Benjamin's own manifold search. The Angelus, storm-driven by the black winds of history, directly inspired Benjamin's last, crowning text, the "historical-metaphysical theses" of 1939–40. After his death the mesmerizing, talismanic image passed into Scholem's hands. From it derives his memoir *Walter Benjamin und sein Engel*.

The seven quatrains of Scholem's "*Gruß vom Angelus*" were sent to Benjamin for his birthday in 1921. In many respects the poem is no less enigmatic than Klee's painting. "I am an Angel-man" (*ein Engelsmann*), perhaps one of those hybrid agents at once sanctified and daemonic whom Scholem had come across in his studies of mystical and occult writings. As early as December 1913 the young Scholem had noted in his journal: "Lurking over me is the sneering face of the angel of insecurity, and it whips me through the silent valleys carved into the depths of my life. It's anyone's guess what my life would look like without this angel, who is for me both fate and doom, but also a severe master and stimulus." Though he be virtuous, man does not concern or interest the Angelus. "I stand under supernatural safeguard / And need no face"—when, in fact, Klee depicts a wildly iconic visage. The world from which the Angelus comes is harmonious, deep and clear. It is solely in our realm that his coherence seems wondrous. The city to which the *Engelsmann* has been dispatched— as in Ezekiel or *Revelation*?—pays no heed. Angelus would gladly return to his true domain, for even if he dwelt in the cities of men to the end of days he would have little chance. He knows what he should proclaim, what message he should deliver "and much else." "I am a non-symbolic thing? Signifying what I am." You rotate the "magical ring" in vain: "I have no sense" (*Ich habe keinen Sinn*). Here interpretation becomes at once arduous and urgent. As is the utterance from the Burning Bush, God's presence, delegated to his messenger, is a perfect tautology. "Do not seek to symbolize or allegorize me": "I am that which I am." Do not diminish me by metaphrase or an ascription of sense. As in music, perhaps, plenitude of significance does not comport "meaning" in any explicit or translatable sense. Scholem's immersion in the paradoxes of mysticism is crucial. As is, by synchronic incidence, Heidegger's meditation on the incommensurable autonomy and resistance to articulations of *Seyn*. Years later Benjamin reread this poem "with undiminished admiration. I place it among the best that I know."

"Mysteries" are at the heart of both "Eleusis" and "Greetings from the Angelus." Both poems modulate complex metaphysical notions into the immediacy of poetic form. In both Hegel to Hölderlin, and Scholem to Benjamin, the poetry of thought and the thought of poetry are fused. A fusion rendered the more persuasive by the tragic fate of the recipients.

Benedetto Croce's dialogue with Hegel was ongoing. Hegel's conviction that a philosophy of human consciousness and a theory of history must include an aesthetic was central to Croce's magisterial prolixity. It generated commentaries on world classics, on Italian writers, on regional (mainly Neapolitan) texts, on literary movements and periods. An embracing system of poetics circumscribes historical, regional and linguistic material.

Croce's *Ariosto, Shakespeare e Corneille* (1920) distinguishes between the intuitive or the aesthetic grasp of a work of art and the intellectual foundations of a critical and historical judgment. An "art for art" approach always falls short. How are we to situate Ariosto's perspective on the "dissolution of the chivalric world," what Goethe called his "wisdom"? Croce's reading of the *Furioso* fixes on Ariosto's tenacious love of poetry itself, a passion in turn erotic. This focus is anti-theoretical in essence. Its ideal is *l'Armonia*. It is ironical, concedes Croce, to identify such a mode of dynamic sensibility with any philosophical-normative discourse. Enchantment is other than understanding. Ariosto's humanism differs from that of his learned, classicizing contemporaries. He aimed for the "incarnation of art as idea" (the Hegelian note). *Armonia* is itself dialectical in relation to concept. Contra Schelling and Schopenhauer's claims for the unique capacity of music to embody "the very rhythm of the universe," Croce attributes this power to Ariosto's language.

Philological inquiry, the study of sources (*Quellenforschung*), licit as they are, is unable to marshal the total cultural matrix, the surrounding arts, the intellectual and political climate. These organize the poet's feelings (*sentimenti*). Ariosto's politics were those of "a private morality." His celebrated ironies both subvert and elevate the teeming particularities of the narrative. His use of the octave allows equilibrium and "*l'eterna dialettica, il ritmo e l'armonia.*" They put in relief the typical, not the individual, even in Orlando's frenzy.

How are we to read Ariosto (a minority avocation already in Croce's day)? We must attend to an intrigue which is in essence always identical but takes on new forms. The magic lies in the "selfsame yet inexhaustible variety of appearance." Ludovico Ariosto is not an orator. He engages us in "conversation" (*conversevole poeta*). Where *conversazione* is a means intensely expressive of Italian sensibility (cf. Giorgione).

What drew Croce to Corneille's ceremonious rhetoric and political sinew? It is wrong to compare him with Shakespeare or Racine, the standard move. Corneille's ideal was an almost Nietzschean "will to power," *an energia di volere*, produced by a sobriety of introspection which endures and overcomes disaster. Following on Schlegel, Croce is fascinated by Corneille's insights into the Machiavellian. He belongs with the Taciteans and political legalists of the late Renaissance. His stringent models of political tragedy are based on a *complessa umanità* and exemplify a "northern energy." Yet his comedies, notably the *Psyché* which he composed with Molière, show that Corneille could have chosen otherwise. Hence the "hybrid" touches, the perennial intimations of tragicomedy. What prevails is poetry, its elevated degree of *sforzo vitale* (Croce must have read Bergson). Croce differentiates "design" from "image," logic of structure from depiction. Most resonant in Corneille are the articulations of death, the terms which allow the protagonist to monumentalize himself, "*scolpire la propria persona in istatua*." Like almost no other critic at the time Croce exalts the late Corneille. He locates in *Pulchérie* that "declamatory song which is the authentic lyricism at once intimate and substantial" of Corneille's greatness. Where there is monotony, this is owing to an "austere inspiration susceptible of few forms."

Poesia e Non Poesia seeks to direct a general poetics toward specific works. Croce defines the criticism of poetry as a "criticism of criticism," as a Kantian determination of the possibilities of judgment. Alfieri's "frenetic hatred of despotism," the powers of his invective lead him to a paradoxical identification with the iron will of the tyrants, of the "supermen" in his dramas. Hence the spell of his masterpiece, *Saul*. Like Seneca's, Alfieri's tragedies are intended to be read. Nonetheless—Croce is echoing Schopenhauer—Schiller is no more than a "frozen Alfieri." Schiller's true merit is to have humanized, to render pedagogic Kant's aesthetic. His best poetry is didactic.

In regard to Kleist, Croce proclaims his own *credo*: the *goia* of great literature derives from its capacity to surpass "passionate agitation" so as to attain the "serenity of the contemplative," what Wordsworth defined as "emotion recalled in tranquility." Hysteria and somnambular violence mar Kleist's eminent gifts. The novellas are "strange, curious, terrifying" rather than truly tragic. *Amphitryon* succumbs to erotic vulgarity. Kleist's strengths were of a secondary order. Croce espouses Goethe and Hegel's strictures. Kleist's suicide is confirmation.

If he comes nowhere near to Lukács's readings of Walter Scott, themselves instigated by Hegel's theories on prose and history, Croce is suggestive on Stendhal. Unusually he dissents from Sainte-Beuve, a constant paradigm. Croce rejoices in the "fantastic tenor" of Stendhal's Italy. He sees analogies with Casanova's chronicles. Stendhal's ideals are at once "ironical and Quixotic." Objectifying himself, Stendhal achieves a "double soul." Astutely Croce discerns the subtle *ennui*, *la sottile noia*, which qualifies the dynamism of

Stendhal's heroes, Julien and Fabrice. During the 1940s Croce took frequent refuge in literature. His range is encyclopedic. He seeks to delineate the operatic quality of Calderón's plays, their analogies with the libretti of Metastasio. Croce notes how "the elemental and populist" character of Tirso de Molina's invention of Don Juan differs from the finesse of Mozart. It is precisely the one-dimensionality of Tirso's Burlador which allows the immense wealth of subsequent variants and enrichments.

Unmistakable is the development of Croce's "Olympian" conservatism, of his distaste for the sources of modernity. He condemns the self-indulgence of Verlaine. He finds Rilke's stature to be exaggerated (we are in 1943). Rilke's poetry lacks "manhood," that vigor of spirit which is nothing else but "force of intuition." Rilke is "intellectually powerless" before the logical problems posed by his hyperbolic invocations of life and death. His substitutions of art for religion lead to the spurious *"soluzione lirica"* in the *Duino Elegies*. Rilke's own life was that of a melancholy *estetizzante,* resorting to vagueness and fragile pathos. (It is fascinating to think of Croce and Heidegger at work on some of the same texts in those tortured years.)

1949–50 finds Croce pondering Mallarmé, a poet in whom modern philosophers often see a litmus paper whereby to test their own stylistic utensils, Mallarmé's hermeticism cuts him off from participation in the great currents of human existence. His art falls prey to "a morbid stasis." Croce contrasts the *Faune* with Pietro Bembo's Renaissance *Fauno*. In Bembo's frank sensuality moral awareness is preserved. Whereas Mallarmé's famous version is one of "morbid desperation" ("morbidity" becomes Croce's shorthand for the enervated aestheticism of modernist precursors). In his very sexuality Mallarmé's Faun remains crudely limited. Nowhere does he attain "the terrifying Lucretian representation" of vain desire, of frustrated eros. Like Rilke, Mallarmé is the object of a cult representative of a decadent epoch. Implicit is Croce's uneasy rejection of D'Annunzio.

His "Reflections on Theory" seek to unify these diverse findings. They voice what Croce's contemporaries and younger readers saw as a profoundly reactionary stance. The "holiness of poetry" is that of Homer, Dante, Shakespeare and Goethe. Linguistics is neither a natural science nor a method adequate to the inner truths and phenomenology of poetry. Pseudo-poetry "afflicts and dishonors present-day humanity." Romanticism contains the germs of decay, despite the salutary resistance of Goethe and Hegel. Rimbaud's failure is "definitive." *Pace* the craft of Ungaretti there can be no genuine poetry in "Husserlian indetermination." After the "blood-soaked orgy" of the Second World War it is the critic's task, Arnoldian in essence, to render justice to what is "sincere" in literature and the arts. Croce's construction of a philosophic hermeneutic ends in self-isolation and myopia. There has been no Hegelian closure of history, only an anarchic and dehumanizing afterword.

As early as 1927, Borges cites Croce: "The sentence is indivisible ... and the grammatical categories that disarm it are abstractions added to reality." Meaning must be taken in "with a single magical glance." In 1936, in *El Hogar*, Borges publishes a capsule biography of Croce which is, of course, pure Borges. After the destruction of his family in the 1883 earthquake, Croce "decided to think of the universe, a proceeding habitual to the desperate." He sets out to explore "the methodical labyrinths of philosophy" (we know what "labyrinths" signify for Borges). At the age of thirty-three, that of the first man fashioned of clay according to the Kabbalists, Croce walks throughout the city sensing an imminent solution to all metaphysical problems. During the First World War Croce remains impartial, foregoing "the lucrative pleasures of hatred." He is with Pirandello "one of the rare important writers of contemporary Italy." Borges invokes Croce in regard to the Ugolino episode in the *Inferno* in his Dante lectures of 1948. Later on, he points to Croce's "crystalline words" on symbol and allegory in the *Estetica*. Considering "The Detective Story" (1978), Borges qualifies Croce's aesthetics and negations of fixed literary genres as "formidable."

The texture of Jorge Luis Borges' genius is a singularity, though there are points of contact with Poe and Lewis Carroll. Borges' imaginings are tangential to the world, oblique to time and space in their customary dimensions. Causal conventions, the seeming facts of reality are vibrant with alternative possibilities, with the strangeness and spectral substance of both dreams and metaphysical conjectures, themselves dreams of the woken intellect. Like Leibniz, Borges cultivates the arts of astonishment. Why there is not nothing—but could there have been, queries Parmenides?—fills Borges with arch wonder and provocation. His *ficciones* enact plots, intrigues, coherent fantastications out of some trove of potentialities more "original," which is to say nearer the days of creation, than are the sclerotic routines, the utilitarian economies of rationality, pragmatism and their Philistine idiom. As does great translation—an exercise which fascinated the polyglot in Borges—his incidence on history, the arts, on textuality as a whole adds "that which was already there"—a paradox yet one which Borges endows with the unsettling authority of the self-evident.

Borges' sensibility, like that of Coleridge whom he valued, was eminently philosophical. It experienced and transmuted abstract thought, metaphysical queries and constructs into immediacy, without conventional interposition, at nerve ends as it were identical with those receptive to poetry and dreams. Borges perceived the choreography, the play of masque and shadow which inhabit the scenic imperatives not only of a Plato or a Nietzsche but also the severities and insistence on the prosaic of a Kant or a Schopenhauer (his true master). More especially, and this is of the rarest, Borges sensed and exploited the play, the elements of charade, of the acrobatic in pure logic. Like *Alice in Wonderland*, like the tales of criminal detection in which his own writings were immersed, Borges' *ficciones* encode—often under the guise of Byzantine, esoteric erudition, often deliberately suspect—the wit, the dialectics of laughter encapsulated in the propositions and rules of pure, even mathematical logic. Out of "the quadruple system of Erigena" and the arcana of medieval scholasticism, out of Gnostic heresiarchs,

Islamic Aristotelians, Talmudic sages, alchemists and theosophists, out of the taxonomies devised by the cosmologists of imperial China and the cartographers of the Baroque, spring Borges' fables of reason. In logic is there a more bizarre contrivance?—which as Bergson puts it "makes use of the void to think the full." And there is no greater inventory, no more teeming catalogue of the conceivable than in Borges' "Library of Babel."

The French scholar J. F. Mattei has counted some one hundred and seventy philosophic presences, some of them only dreamt of in Borges' oeuvre. They range from Anaxagoras and Heraclitus to Bertrand Russell and Heidegger. Plato and Schopenhauer—"the one I would hold on to"—are cited most often. Followed by Aristotle, Hume and Spinoza, that other addict of mirrors. Nietzsche and Heraclitus come high on the list. Plotinus is blessed for his unwavering belief in final oneness. The Islamic masters, Averroës and Avicenna, figure prominently as does their august counterpart Maimonides. The thought experiments of Berkeley, with their elegant abolition of the empirical, catch Borges' eye. As do Davidson and William James on free will or the *Arcania caelestia* of Swedenborg (an interest which Borges shares with Balzac). The "computer languages" of Raymond Llull, the thirteenth-century Catalan polymath, and of George Boole are enlisted, as is blind Ibn Sida, composer in c. 1055 of that ultra-Borgesian resource the *Al Mukham*, a dictionary of dictionaries. Borges seems to have come upon Vico's theory of history via his own concerns with Homer. Campanella and Unamuno take a bow. Had we but Borges' writings, we could reconstruct a "Borgesian" but by no means diminished history of the processional of philosophic exercises in the west and in Islam, in Asia and in Erewhon.

"Keats's Nightingale" of December 1951 illustrates to perfection the crossbreeding of poetics, philosophic logic and bibliographic erudition. Keats's songster is that of Ovid and of Shakespeare. The poet's mortality contrasts pathetically with the frail but imperishable song of the bird. The crux of interpretation resides in the penultimate stanza. The voice of the nightingale in the Hampstead garden is pronounced identical with that heard by Ruth in the biblical story. Borges adduces five critics who in varying degrees of reproach detect a logical flaw. It is sophistry to oppose the life of an individual to that of a species. Though he had never read Keats's ode, Schopenhauer provides the key. He affirms identity across time. The cat bounding before me does not differ fundamentally from that perceived centuries ago. Thus the individual embodies the species and Keats's rhapsode is the same as the one in the night of Moab.

Formally unschooled, Keats had intuited "the Platonic nightingale." He had anticipated Schopenhauer. This observation leads Borges to reiterate the archetypal division between Platonists and Aristotelians, between those for whom there is order and harmony in the universe and those for whom the cosmos is a fiction, possibly a misprision born of our ignorance. Coleridge had argued this radical duality. Borges finds the English to be inherently Aristotelian. They register the particular "concrete" nightingale, not its generic universality. Hence their misreadings of Keats. Yet it is to that very bias that we owe Locke, Berkeley, Hume and the political insistence on the autonomy of the individual. From the time of Anglo-Saxon riddles to Swinburne's *Atalanta*, the nightingale has sung distinctively in English literature. It now belongs to Keats as the tiger does to Blake (as the "dream tigers" do to Borges).

The famous "Tlön, Uqbar, Orbis Tertius" (1940/47) turns on the conceit of mirror-worlds, on imaginary languages, on manifold algebras, on Hume's verdict that Berkeley's deconstruction of the empirical is irrefutable but unconvincing, on Alexius Meinong's theory of impossible objects (which had fascinated Musil). It appeals to the Islamic notion of the Night of Nights in which doors open on hidden worlds. As had Kabbalists, Leibniz, and Russian futurists before him, Borges plays with the concept of imaginary languages. Their generative cell is not the verb but the monosyllabic adjective. They allow no truth-functions in our sense, no necessary concordance between word and object. Language creates at momentary will. Thus there are eminent Tlön poems made up "of a single enormous word" (do we hear its distant rumble in *Finnegans Wake*?). Rejecting the time-space axiomatics of Spinoza or Kant, Tlön metaphysicians seek neither truth nor similitude. They strive for astonishment—both Aristotle and Wittgenstein would have approved. All metaphysics is a branch of the literature of fantasy. "They know that a system is nothing but the subordination of all aspects of the universe to one of those aspects—*any* one of them." One Tlön school of philosophy posits that all time has already passed, that our lives consist of ghostly, crepuscular memories. Another sect compares our universe to a cryptogram in which not all symbols count, in which only that which happens every three hundred nights is real. Yet another academy contends that while we slumber here we are awake elsewhere, that all cognition is a kind of binary pendulum. As in relativity theory, Tlön geometry asserts that as one's body traverses space it modifies the shapes that surround it. Echoing Heisenberg's indeterminacy, Tlön arithmeticians assume that the act of counting modifies the amounts counted.

Works of Tlönian philosophy contain both thesis and antithesis, for only contradiction comports completion (Hegel is not far off). In his postscript Borges hints at the menace of antimatter: contact with the "*habit* of Tlön" could disintegrate our own world. "Already a fictitious past has supplanted in men's memories that other past, of which we know nothing certain—not even that it is false." Borges seems to have known Bertrand Russell's paradoxical supposition that our universe was created an instant ago complete with fictive remembrance. Reversing Mallarmé's dictum that the universe is to result in *un Livre*, Borges' ontological fable suggests that our universe is in essence the product of an eleventh edition of the *Encyclopaedia Britannica* from which the key entries on Orbis Tertius keep vanishing. But then, Borges was a librarian. He knew about lost books.

Drawing on the learning of Ernest Renan, whom he read assiduously, Borges published his "Averroës' Search" in June 1947. It features a coven of medieval Islamic sages, exegetes and lexicographers, foremost among them the illustrious Averroës. In his cool house in Cordoba, the philosopher is composing a polemic treatise on the nature of divine providence. His syllogisms flower as do the delights of his garden. What perplexes Averroës is a conundrum which has arisen in his monumental commentary on Aristotle. The undying wisdom, the deathless poetry "in the ancients and in the Koran" which Averroës has been defending against all attempts at innovation know nothing of theater, of any dramatic genres. How then is he to understand and translate the two mysterious terms recurrent in Aristotle's *Poetics*? Knowing neither Syriac nor Greek, working from the translation of a translation (a characteristic twist in Borges), Averroës has found enlightenment neither in the gloss of Alexander of Aphrodisias nor in the versions of the Nestorian Hunain ibn-Ishaq nor in Abu-Basha Mata. What conceivable meaning can he attach to "tragedy" and "comedy"? At first light, in his library, he experiences revelation: "Aristu (Aristotle) gives the name of tragedy to panegyrics and that of comedy to satires and anathemas. Admirable tragedies and comedies abound in the pages of the Koran and the *mohalacas* of the sanctuary."

The components of the tale are those of playful erudition, of sanctified bibliomania. The epistemological issue, however, is pivotal. What relates words to their intended signification? What proof have we that we construe their purposed function reliably, let alone with any verifiable equivalence, notably in an ancient or foreign tongue? Observe the arch subtlety of Borges' proposal: Averroës' rendition of the two Aristotelian meanings is erroneous, but not altogether so. There is praise sung in ancient Greek tragedy, there are indeed malediction and satire in Aristophanes' or Menander's comedies. Misunderstanding can shed light.

Or consider a miniature such as "Delia Elena San Marco" (1960). A street corner parting. A river of traffic and passersby. How was Borges to know that it was "sad Acheron which no one may cross twice"? Infinite separation underlies a casual farewell. Can Socrates' valedictory lessons as reported by Plato be of help? If these are the truth and the soul is truly immortal, no particular gravitas attaches to our good-byes. "Men invented farewells because they somehow knew themselves to be immortal, even while seeing themselves as contingent and ephemeral." Dialogue will resume when "the city will have vanished into the plains." The slightest of mundane incidents unfolds into the uncertain metaphysics of transcendence.

Borges infers that all philosophic propositions (however stringent), that every formal logic are daydreams, that they manifest the systematic reveries of the woken intellect. In Goya's etching the sleep of reason breeds monsters. In Borges both the night-dreams and the daydreams of rationality engender Zeno's tortoise, Plato's cavern, Descartes's malignant demon or Kant's starlit imperatives. As Hamlet instructs Horatio, the matter of philosophy is "dreamt of." Concomitantly there is no literary text, be it a lyric poem, a detective story, science fiction or romance which does not contain, either declared or veiled, metaphysical coordinates, logical axioms or spoors of epistemology. Man narrates worlds possibly alternative, contrapuntal to his bounded, parochial reality. The philosophical and the poetic are indivisibly conjoined as are "Borges and I" in that parable of mirrors and inevitable duplicity. Both arise from the inexhaustible ubiquity of speech acts.

The young Sartre confessed his ambition: to be both Spinoza and Stendhal. Perhaps no one else has come nearer to being in reach of this symbiosis. "The century of Sartre" was to become a frequent attribution. No other body of work makes as invalid any dissociation between the philosophic and the literary. These are indivisible in a spectrum of genres which extends from world-famous fiction and drama to autobiography, political and social theory, travel writing, ideological manifests, torrential high journalism, and art criticism to voluminous epistemological and ontological treatises. Sartre himself professed that "writing is life," subsuming all energies of consciousness, all experience both private and public, be it technically philosophic or politically polemical under the heading of an incessant prose. No impulse of thought, no phenomenology of perception was wasted. Their access to language was immediate.

It is this imperative fusion which makes of *Les Mots* a masterpiece. Proof that the existential realization of post-Heideggerian ontology and narrative fiction, as in *La Nausée*, that partisan political argument, as in the successive volumes of the *Situations* and theater, as in *No Exit*, arise from, are enacted by the identical, defining instrumentality of words. That text is totality precisely in so far as it articulates the self, our being in the world and the adventures of meaning. In this perspective Sartre's genius is classical. It is a direct beneficiary of the axiomatic conviction—Pauline, Voltairean, Marxist—that the act of writing embodies and alters the human status (*Existentialism is a Humanism*). Nothing infirms Sartre's trust in the executive means of syntax.

In this tidal immensity of print—"words, words, words" as Hamlet instructs Polonius—there are marked differences of quality, of formal mastery and persuasion. If *La Nausée* is indeed of enduring economy, the later novels are feeble. *No Exit* is an astute melodrama of the intellect, wonderfully parodistic of nineteenth-century drawing-room farce. *The Flies* is an arresting but opportunistic device. The later plays have worn badly. The principal philosophic tomes on *Being and Nothingness*, on "dialectical reason," on existential ethics exercised formidable influence and contain pages as dynamic, as abstractly "scenic" as any in Hegel. But they are receding into dusty reverence. Among the essays on art, that on Tintoretto in Venice, that on Giacometti retain their psychological and sociological acumen, their intensities so characteristic of Sartre's analytic and nervous involvement. The celebrated tract on "the Jewish question" is almost certainly erroneous, yet has maintained something of its provocative urgency. There is, moreover, a wealth of autobiographical material whose introspective tension and calculated vulnerabilities rival the self-portrayals of Montaigne and Rousseau.

This vast ensemble comprises numerous reflections on literature and literary works. *What is Literature?* asked Sartre and advocated a program of militant ideological "engagement," now dated. The leviathan apologia for Jean Genet, "saint and martyr," is not only hyperbolic in tone and scale but quite simply illegible. The three compendious volumes on Flaubert, *L'Idiot de la famille*, contain moments of post-Marxist, post-Freudian illumination and notations in depth on what Sartre took to be his own condition, but are again close to unreadable. Rumors persist that they were composed (dictated?) under the influence of stimulants, that they are in some outwardly rational sense "automatic writing." If ever there was a sensibility immune to poetry, as it would seem to music, it was Sartre's. As a result his *Baudelaire* is disastrous.

Though he never rivaled Sartre's global celebrity, Maurice Merleau-Ponty was the more rigorous philosopher. He was, moreover, innocent of Sartre's frequently cynical ideological and political mendacities (in respect to Soviet realities, to Maoism, to the despotism of Fidel Castro). It was over Sartre's equivocations at the time of the Korean war that the two men broke after years of friendship and partisan alliance. Published in October 1961, Sartre's *in memoriam* brings to bear on exceedingly involuted issues—of philosophical-political debate, of personal relationships—the panoply of his psychological, theoretical and narrative resources. Once again this extensive but concentrated text demonstrates Sartre's capacity to incarnate mentality, to make the motions of intelligence visceral (that unlikely confluence of Spinoza and Stendhal).

"We were equals, friends, not alike." The cold war was to break us apart. We drew identically on Husserl and Heidegger. We discovered phenomenology at the same time. The war and occupation drew us close. There was during those black times "an unforgettable transparency of hearts, the reverse of hatred. This was the purest moment of our friendship." But from the outset there was a persistent silence, a privacy in Merleau-Ponty's meditations on perception, on the place of individual singularity within the determinants, the hazards, the irrationalities of history. This inwardness went with an exigence of totality in personal relations. Hence Merleau-Ponty's emotional difficulties and apartness. Hence the anti-dogmatic, necessarily detached tenor of his postwar Marxism. Sartre's image is inspired:

Il eût accepté la doctrine s'il eût pu n'y voir qu'une phosphorescence, qu'un châle jeté sur la mer, éployé, reployé par la houle et dont la vérité dépendît justement de sa participation perpétuelle au branle-bas marin.

Merleau-Ponty found Marxist determinism imperceptive of the essential contingency of human experience. Superpower rivalries were coming to replace class conflicts. "We were blind," concedes Sartre. He at least was one-eyed. Merleau-Ponty welcomed communism but not the Party. His foresights were as somber as Cassandra's.

The analyses which follow are alien to the Anglo-Saxon climate, but fully accessible to Stendhal. They tell of an intelligentsia in which private and public lives were saturated by ideological values, by nuances of dialectical conflict and philosophic-political enlistments eminently French. Sartre and Merleau-Ponty launched *Les Temps Modernes* in the fall of 1945. Merleau-Ponty, for whom the "immortalities of childhood" represented the lost ideal, was *de facto* editor but withheld his name from the cover. This tactical anonymity allowed him to work in tandem with one whose growing fame may have unnerved him. Collaboration remained intimate till 1952. Sartre who had been "a belated anarchist" learned from Merleau-Ponty the limits of autarchy. He would now become a partisan activist. Merleau-Ponty's definition of philosophy as "didactic spontaneity" inspired Sartre's determination to retrieve humanism from the hated bourgeoisie. Both men were still united in condemning what was now known of the Gulag but refused to reject Marxism and its Soviet realizations.

By 1950 Merleau-Ponty's voice had darkened. Sartre infers "a weariness of soul." Can one refuse Stalinism without condemning Marxism itself? Are the concentration camps no worse than western colonialism and capitalist exploitation? In deepening isolation Merleau-Ponty "*se réfugier dans sa vie profonde.*" With the Korean War their reciprocal trust and convictions became "incommunicable." Persuaded that a third world war was imminent, Merleau-Ponty renounced politics. He saw Stalinism as imperialism in a nearing universality of massacre. Sartre's diagnosis is lapidary: "There remains hope in the craziest of rages; in that calm sepulchral (*mortuaire*) refusal there remained none." Sartre propounded his notorious dictate: "An anti-communist is a dog; I do not withdraw from that; I never shall." All that endured between him and Merleau-Ponty was a "mournful rumination." The break became inevitable.

The death of his mother sharpened Merleau-Ponty's solitude. 1953–56 saw the end of any personal contact with Sartre. Merleau-Ponty concentrated on the phenomenology of the human body, of its insertion in the world and of the world's inseparability from our corporeal substance. Painting, Cézanne in particular, became his talisman. His return to Heidegger was qualified by the axiom of man's centrality: "*plus Pascalien que jamais.*" The two men met again at a colloquium in Venice in 1956. The Algerian war found them in accord. Sartre's summation is memorable:

un autre sentiment naquit, la douceur: cette affection désolée, tendrement funèbre rapproche des amis épuisés, qui se sont déchirés jusqu'à n'avoir plus en commun que leur querelle et dont la querelle, un beau jour, a cessé faute d'objet.

Note the wonderfully concise classical turn of phrase, itself Pascalian.

They were now "pensioners of friendship." At a further meeting Sartre was out of sorts and gloom prevailed. Merleau-Ponty died a few days later, turning his deliberate muteness into "an eternity of absence." It is we two who did not know how to love each other well ("*qui nous sommes mal aimés*"). Now, concludes Sartre, that long friendship "remains in me like an indefinitely exasperated wound."

It was not only to painting that Merleau-Ponty turned when

striving to "transport philosophy into the circle of fire of the visible, of that which can be named, which can be thought." When seeking to hear what Hermes Trismegistus had called "the cry of light." Philosophy speaks. Its discourse (*parole*) backs on silence. It speaks from within being, not at some elevation or distance. Philosophy, phenomenology "speaks as trees grow, as time passes, as men speak." It never ceases being uncertain as to its own existential status. It is inseparable from literary, performative expression. It is this expression which enables thought to "give us a sign" (is there here an echo of the *Tractatus*?). Such "signs" transform our lives as does our reading of a Platonic dialogue or of Valéry's "*La Pythie*." It is in the initiators and masters of modern literature that Merleau-Ponty seeks to anchor his teachings on the simultaneities of perception, on consciousness as act.

Literature is decisive in the lectures Merleau-Ponty delivered at the Collège de France in 1958–59. Mallarmé restored a certain muteness to language, retrenching it from the "positivity of the world." Rimbaud does not evade that positivity. On the contrary: he plunges without reticence into the pre-logical unison of experience. He wakes the savage resources in articulation: "clusters of words as there are grape clusters of colors, of qualities in objects themselves." Both these innovative poetics are taken up by Surrealism, which at once destroys and makes sacred literature. For Breton "words make love" though they derive from "the mouth of shadows." After Proust, Joyce and the American novelists, it is prose fiction which signifies indirectly, which deliberately intermingles the self, the other and their worlds. Consider Faulkner's *The Sound and the Fury*. In Proust not everything is falsehood: it is truth within falsehood. The fog of the stream of consciousness, of the interior monologue in *Ulysses* is pierced by interruptions stemming from other voices, as "the folds of the sea melt into a single wave." Hemingway generates propositions without commentary. These produce the highest pitch of anguish and neighbor on the anarchic license, on the absence of contradiction in dreams. In modern writers, "objects are given utterance" as Heidegger posited. "The sensible world is hieroglyphic and it is the discourse of the writer which captures these speech-objects (*choses-paroles*), which deciphers them."

Merleau-Ponty read Claudel via the notations of his fellow philosopher, the Kierkegaardian Jean Wahl. He found in Claudel the cohesion of time and space and man's insertion in that temporal space. The Claudelian landscape is a way of spatializing and temporalizing which enables human awareness to apprehend being. Only distance allows us to adhere to others. He paraphrases Claudel's "mysteries": "The land of shadows, the sun at night ... are that which is most real." Here is a fundamental anti-Platonism in which only the shadow has substance. Merleau-Ponty is perfectly alert to the abyss which separates him from Claudel's ecstatic, ritual Catholicism. "But a writer does not always know how and in what ways he changes the world—and his contemporaries."

Claude Simon was another practitioner of aloneness. He thought in words as Cézanne had thought in paintings. His novels achieve "a kind of eternity of the visible." For Simon space is the relation between our flesh and that of the world. "We must never tire of that sumptuous magnificence of the world on condition that we are made conscious of it." Like Merleau-Ponty himself, Simon celebrated epiphanies which convey in their perceptual splendors an ultimate homecoming to the repose of death. Encountering these narratives Merleau-Ponty found confirmation of his final certitudes. Both the visible and literature are infinite. Style is vision. In both philosophy and literature "ideas" grow laterally, out of hidden roots. When successful the literary work will signify that nothing can be as it was before. Like metaphysics (and Rilke) it bids us change our lives. Art teaches us the most enigmatic of proposals: "man is a question for God himself. Of that question we are not the masters."

In Merleau-Ponty's late lecture notes we read "music, the art of perpetual betrothal" (Michaux). Only one steeped in the poetry of truth could have cited that.

8

With the twentieth century our theme becomes virtually incommensurable. Discriminations between philosophy—where it is not formal logic or the philosophy of mathematics—and literature are often meaningless. The philosopher after Bergson is simultaneously a writer. He may himself produce fiction or drama as does Sartre. He may argue his epistemological, theoretical proposals via literary examples, as does Shestov when he writes about Shakespeare, Ibsen, Dostoevsky or Chekhov. Schopenhauer is vital in Beckett whose plays in turn elicit the aesthetic philosophy of Adorno. It is impossible to dissociate philosophic considerations from poetics in what has been called "French critical theory." Literary texts and references saturate the writings of Derrida, themselves reverting to Hegel on Sophocles, of Foucault, of Lacan, of Deleuze. Often the philosopher aims to achieve a style, a voice equivalent in suggestive narrative or metaphorical force to that of the poets (Derrida on Celan, Lacan on Poe). How can one disentangle the philosophically discursive, the analytic in Stanley Cavell's playful insinuations of Wittgenstein into Shakespeare? As we have seen, moreover, novelists of the first order are also explicitly busy with metaphysics, with political philosophy and even the philosophy of science. Elements of this manifold are obvious in Proust; they are declared, indeed seminal in Broch and Musil. On which side of the classical divide does one locate Camus? Or the Platonic fables of Iris Murdoch?

How may we account for this sometimes incestuous conjunction?

The philosophic focus on language is as ancient as are Aristotelian theories of metaphor or the Johannine invocations of the *Logos*. Speculations on the origins of human speech are prolific in Leibniz and the Enlightenment. But the supposition that language is formally and substantively the core of philosophy, that the limits of our world are those of our language, that all access to the existential is in the final analysis linguistic is modern. The "language turn" in western philosophy ranges from the theological and mystical identification of word and world in, say, Franz Rosenzweig and Walter Benjamin's view of the Fall of man as generating human discourse, all the way to Quine on word and object and the notion of language-games in Wittgenstein and illocutionary acts in Austin. Conceptions of language are now crucial to epistemology, to investigations into the psyche as in Freud and Lacan, to social anthropology but also to constructs in political science and in interpretations of history. Stefan George's famous verse "Nothing can be where the word fails" has acquired axiomatic relevance throughout modern configurations of the self and of the world.

It is difficult to identify the sources and exponential dynamics of a movement, of a multiplicity of movements which come to inform modernity itself. These may embody a mutation of values and horizons as momentous as any in politics and the sciences, perhaps more so. The penetration of "linguistic" elements into intuitive and systematic thought seems to occur at diverse points in the later nineteenth century. It characterizes analytic philosophy and psychoanalysis, the experiments of Dada and Surrealism, metaphysics and the articulation of ideologies. We "are" in so far as we can emit that verb or, more exactly, in so far as we can question its grammatical status (which did not disturb Descartes). Ontology is syntax.

The very ubiquity and variousness of this language in turn alerts us to underlying forces, to tectonic shifts in consciousness and the trials of understanding. The unexamined or postulated contracts between signifier and signified (Saussure's key distinction), between verbalization and reality, between utterance and communicability which had insured classical mentalities from the Pre-Socratics to Kant, Hegel and Schopenhauer break down. They dissolve, as we have seen, into Mallarmé's intimation that nomination is absence, into the bordering on silence in the *Tractatus*, into the post-Nietzschean and post-Freudian disclosures of the essential untruths, of the illusions in all human discourse. Intelligibility signals disinformation. Intended meaning is a pretext for and of deconstruction. In turn this breakdown animates an almost febrile search for communicative, semiotic codes other than classically linguistic. Symbolic logic, meta-mathematical idioms of every kind, the quest for a political-moral cleansing of the human tongue (cf. Kraus and Orwell) tell of attempts at a "Newspeak," but this time in a positive, truth-functional register. Today the retreat from the word, from its traditional promise of meaning has become almost dramatic. Electronic encoding of information, storage and dissemination, the lexica of the Internet and the Web, the online license for individuals or particular groups to initiate and transmit their own neologisms, tribal jargon and cryptograms represent irremediable dissents from any theologically, transcendentally anchored *doxa* of universal speech and cognitive certitude. Sense is often a Magellanic Cloud of possibilities in motion. Locutions are emitted billion-fold and in fractional seconds. The avalanche of information is beyond rational intake. But less, perhaps, is *said* than ever before. A deafening volume, beyond computation, is brimful of muteness. Hearing is often radically dissociated from listening. "O Word, O Word that I lack!" (in Schoenberg's *Moses und Aron*).

The accelerando of the sciences and of technology, their mathematization have beggared both the reach and veracity of natural language. It is not only, as Galileo taught, that nature speaks mathematics: it is, to a degree he could not have anticipated, that mathematical speech would become fantastically intricate and demanding.

It is now accessible only to a mandarinate of practitioners. In consequence the commonplace relations of language to phenomena, to our daily context have become virtually infantile. They are a bric-à-brac of inert metaphors ("sunrise"), of hoary fictions and handy falsifications. Our tables and chairs have nothing to do with their atomic, subatomic, complexly mobile reality. Our vulgate inhabits prefabricated clichés. Our "time" and "space" are archaic, almost allegoric banalities out of touch with relativistic algorithms. From the perspective of the theoretical and exact sciences we speak a kind of Neanderthal babble.

But within the semantic codes of the sciences themselves the crisis is sharpening. Specialization, the construction and refinement of specific mathematical instruments such as tensorial calculus or measure theory have developed so swiftly that effective communication between branches of scientific inquiry and representation, even kindred, is becoming ever more problematic. Each section of nuclear physics, of quantum modeling, of biogenetics and molecular chemistry is generating its own nomenclatures and algebraic conventions. The pure and the applied are increasingly divided. Ramifications grow further away from any central trunk, from that universal *mathematesis* dreamt of by Leibniz and available to Newton. Fascinatingly there are today indications that certain conjectures in physics, in the physics of cosmology, notably string theory, may be beyond any adequate, let alone verifiable mathematical formulation, that they function at the edge of the inexpressible as do the most remote galaxies. What is certain is that our ordinary vocabulary, our common grammars have ceased to speak the world as the scientist or the engineer conceive and manipulate it. Topologies, transfinite numbers, nanosecond calibrations do not translate.

But it is not only the scientific and the technological revolutions which have reduced our *lingua franca* to provinciality. It is the descent of Europe and of Russia into barbarism between 1914 and 1945. The scale of massacre in the trenches, the mortalities by famine and disease altered the status of death—as Stalin put it, "a million dead are a statistic"—an alteration organically interwoven with the capacities of language to take in, to construe rationally the pressures of fact. Where thirty thousand died in a day on the Somme, where untold millions were slaughtered or starved to death for ideological reasons, neither the imagination nor the resources of inherited speech which are the generative, ordering instruments of that imagination could cope. Hence the animal cries and nonsense vocals of Dada in 1915. Even this inward collapse, however, is far outweighed by the lowering of the threshold of man, by his reversion to bestiality in the Shoah and the mass hell of the Gulag. There have been towering acts of witness, by Primo Levi, Robert Antelme, by Varlam Shalamov, chronicler of the Kolyma death-world. But overall neither documentary accounts nor fiction, neither poetry with the exception of Celan, nor social-historical analyses have been empowered to communicate the substance of the inhuman. Of that which is unspeakable in the strict sense (the Italian philosopher Agamben has stated that any verbalization of remembrance is per se a falsehood). The truths of torture, of mass extermination, of sadistic humiliation, the methodical subtraction of the human mind and body from any recognizable identity—millions of women, men and children shrunken to the "walking dead"—have defied intelligible articulation, let alone the logic of understanding. There is no "why" here, boasted the butchers. Only silence can aspire to the lost dignity of meaning. The silence of those no longer capable of speech, the so-called *Muselmänner* in the concentration camps.

The dehumanization of language, its decay into ideological hysteria, falsehoods and yawping was most obvious in Nazi Germany and has been much studied. As have the slaughterhouse rhetoric of Fascism and Stalinism. But the phenomenon is far more general. The seeming triumph of entrepreneurial liberalism, the identification of human progress and excellence with material accumulation, the virtual omnipotence of the mass media brought with it a vulgarization, a mendacity of words and syntax, an "Americanization" of discourse (though that epithet may itself be a libelous shorthand) from which numerous tongues might not recover. That Stalinism called enslavement "freedom" is a grosser but not more demeaning obscenity than the designation of American hydrogen bomb tests as "Operation Sunshine." A treasure-house of words on which a Shakespeare, a Milton or a Joyce drew thousandfold has, according to a statistical survey of telephone conversations and electronic messages recorded and dispatched on an average day in North America, been diminished to some sixty-five. No advertisement runs the risk of a dependent clause. Subjunctives, which are the wondrous vehicles of alternate life possibilities, which are the functions of hope, are rapidly disappearing even from French, once their proud abode.

Of course new terms are being created. Of course certain modes and techniques of mass entertainment such as rock and roll or rap can be verbally coruscating. But the detergent consequences of technocracy gone consumption-mad, witness China, are planetary. The daily discourse of countless men and women, of the young, the deafening babble of the media is that of a minimalist jargon. Everything I am trying to say is made lapidary in Celan's plea for "a language north of the future." Though he himself, who had forced language to the precise edge of the unsayable, felt that it might already be too late. *Sprache*, the *Logos*, had decayed into *Prosa* which, in turn, had rotted to *Gerede*, blather.

These three terms and the postulate of triadic decline were put forward by Martin Heidegger. Scarcely any component of our theme, of the relations both substantive and historical between philosophy and poetics, between performative style and philosophic argument, between poets and philosophers *in propria persona* does not have an absolutely determinant place in Heidegger's teachings. *Das "dichtende Denken," die "denkende Dichtung"*—"thought as poetry" "poetry as thought"—lie at the heart of his ontology, of his gospel of "Being." This symbiosis alone "can bring us salvation." This endowment with poetry, the *Dichtungsvermögen*, which constitutes both the primordial and the ultimate condition of man, is the source of those attempts at a synthesis of the self and the perceived world which energize the philosophic enterprise from Anaximander to Heidegger himself. Born of poetry, philosophy will at the end of time return "to the great ocean of poetry." Innumerable passages in a corpus of numbing prolixity expound this credo:

Das Denken jedoch ist Dichten und zwar nicht nur eine Art der Dichtung im Sinne der Poesie und des Gesanges. Das Denken des Seins ist die ursprüngliche Weise des Dichtens. In ihm kommt allem zuvor erst die Sprache zur Sprache, d. h. in ihr Wesen. Das Denken sagt das Diktat der Wahrheit des Seins. Das Denken ist das ursprüngliche dictare.... Das dichtende Wesen des Denkens verwahrt das Walten der Wahrheit des Seins.

It follows that the symbiosis of thought and of poetry, their existential fusion in regard to the utterance of "Being" define the authentic nature, the *Wesen*, of language itself. All legitimate epistemological inquiry is *Unterwegs zur Sprache*, "Under Way to Language," a title which could stand for the totality of Heidegger's work. Abrasively he ruled that we have not yet begun to know how to think. Which entails that we, a very few supreme poets excepted, have not yet begun to know how to speak. Or rather, that we have forgotten how to do so, how to apprehend the auroral self-disclosure and self-concealment (*aletheia*) of *Sein* in words. Here the polemic differentiation between *Wort* as *Logos* and *Wörter* as verbiage is operative.

So much is unmistakable. The relevant hermeneutic moves, the commentaries on Sophocles, George, Mörike, Rilke, Trakl are so manifold, the engagement with Hölderlin, poet of poets, is so extensive that a teeming secondary literature falls far short of any comprehensiveness. There are Heidegger's personal and philosophic encounters with, as we saw, René Char and above all else with Paul Celan. The publication of the collected works is still in progress. It looks as if the texts, notably of the lectures, have suffered omissions and falsifications (precisely as in the case of early editions of Nietzsche). Biographical data, possibly of immediate pertinence, remain opaque.

There is, moreover, a dilemma probably unique in the history of western philosophy. To many the writings of Martin Heidegger are a monstrous assemblage of impenetrable "jargon" (Adorno's scornful label), of pretentious, maddeningly repetitive obscurantism. It all amounted to an hypnotic confidence trick perpetrated by a politically tainted mountebank (cf. the parodies by Günter Grass). To others, Martin Heidegger stands beside Plato, Aristotle or Hegel at the very crest of western philosophy. The books, articles, colloquia, seminars his works have occasioned rival those addressed to Kant. The main currents of modernism and postmodernism, such as existentialism and deconstruction, are voluminous footnotes to Heidegger. No Sartre, no Merleau-Ponty, no Gadamer, no Levinas, no Derrida, no Lacan, no Deleuze without *Sein und Zeit*, without Heidegger on the nature of thought or the origins of art. Resistant though it may be to any innocent reading, Heidegger's prose represents the major revaluation of the German language after Luther. Centuries to come will ponder and debate his mesmeric *doxa*.

Until now a balanced view has seemed out of reach.

The broad outline of Heidegger's investment in Nazism have long been known despite apologetic contortions, notably by French Heideggerians. They comport his membership in the Party, maintained formally till the end of the régime, the totalitarian proto-Nazi mystique of his pronouncements as *Rektor* of Freiburg University, his nervous collapse in 1945, his lies and half-truths when seeking rehabilitation. They include a number of ugly acts or omissions in regard to Jewish colleagues and to his benefactor and sometime master Edmund Husserl. Professor Heidegger had been known to wear his swastika insignia with pride. He refused to retract his view of the inner greatness and promise of National Socialism when re-publishing earlier texts. What could not be demonstrated convincingly was any direct influence of Heidegger's politics and conduct on the genius of *Sein und Zeit*, on his immensely influential rereadings of Plato, Aristotle, Kant, Schelling and Nietzsche. The despotic raptures of his voice and rhetoric clearly predated the Nazi rise to power. Nor could they be shown to affect his ontology, his novel constructs of human existence or his scenario of being-in-the-world, *Dasein*.

This was the perplexing situation which I sought to grasp in my *Heidegger* of 1978. Which was to inform this essay arching, as it were, from Plato and the poets to Heidegger's *dichtendes Denken* and his rendezvous with Celan. But matters have changed with the recent opening of the archives and the publication, still partial, of Heidegger's lectures and seminars from 1933 to 1939. These are permeated by an almost vulgar entrancement with the *Führer* and his purification of the German nation. Heidegger's imperious idiom closely parallels the *Völkisch*, implicitly racist lingo of Nazi propaganda. The contempt for disinterested intellectuality, for the commitment of scholarship to impartial evidence is strident. The notorious remark to Karl Löwith on the beauty of Hitler's hands no longer seems a momentary aberration.

The crucial challenge still stands: does all this vileness demean, let alone refute or falsify Heidegger's principal philosophic texts? Instinctively I feel that it does not, that Heidegger on the dawn light of the Pre-Socratics, on *Sorge* ("concern") and our being-unto-death retain their stature. At the same time, however, it has made it more difficult—the inhibition is almost physical—to read, to live with, to interpret Heidegger on Sophocles, on Hölderlin and to evaluate his confrontations with Celan. What was intended to be the crowning moment in our argument no longer seems altogether accessible. Always tentative, my questions have become unanswerable. All I can do is pose a few markers knowing now how inadequate they are.

For Heidegger to read is to rewrite; to translate is to recreate. The philosophical treatise, the poem are instigations. They invite the reader's appropriation. The hermeneutic act seeks to elicit the incipient intentionalities of the author. It aims at making manifest the covert or incomplete impulses and significations in the text, bringing to light what is between and, as it were, underneath the lines. It "excavates" significations of which the author may not have been conscious. Not, however, in any psychoanalytic register. Heidegger locates the latent, the potential surge of meaning within language itself, in the central axiomatic paradox whereby we do not speak so much as we "are spoken," whereby "the word owns man" (*"Das Wort hat den Menschen"*). Thus the autonomous powers of language, notably in metaphysics and in poetry, always surpass human usage and exceed total understanding. It is the task of the true reader to apprehend how "the interior of the word becomes outwardly intelligible" while sensing that any such apprehension is fragmentary, unstable and inevitably distorting (hence Derridean "deconstruction").

Heidegger insists on the creative role of audition, of the complex arts of hearing which are obligatory in any responsible ("responding") exercise of reception and elucidation. We must learn to listen, as does the musician, to the voices of the unsaid, to the deep-lying rhythms and undertones of thought, of poetic conceptions before these stiffen into conventional and mundane speech. That atrophy defines the Fall from Adamic language and from the intimacies with Being of the Pre-Socratics. In a poet such as Hölderlin that primal audition, that overhearing of what is "wild, obscure, interwoven" at the sources of the word can still be made out. The reader's eye must listen.

The yield is a clutch of Heideggerian readings, of metamorphic auditions which exasperate philologists, historians of philosophy and literary scholars. Which strike them as crass errors or self-serving fantastications. Heidegger is fully alert to this reaction. He comes near to mocking it. It is not only that the alleged veracities and impartialities of the philological, of textual recension are replete with unexamined ideological and historically contingent presumptions; the emendations of a Lorenzo Valla are not those of an A. E. Housman. It is that philology leaves its objects as inert as it found them. The letter kills the letter. It is transformational readings, misprisions as in Hölderlin's Sophocles which make a philosophic statement, a chorus out of *Antigone* present in both the temporal and the existential sense. Which ensure their vital immediacy.

For Heidegger the history of thought is one of recurrently recaptured contemporaneity. Misreadings such as Nietzsche on Plato or, almost irreparably, Cicero's helpless rendering into Latin of cardinal Greek philosophical terms will be unavoidable. Any dolt can correct Hölderlin's Greek. But it is these mutations which keep argument and poetry electric, which guarantee the futurities of the *Ursprung*, of the seminal font and donation of possible, unfolding meanings. They make of Heraclitus—whom Heidegger translates, with a characteristic violence, into "lightning" and the "in-gathering of Being"—a thinker yet to come.

Heidegger's fixation on language stems from an illustrious lineage. It begins with Leibniz on *l'Entendement humain* of 1765 and Herder's essay on the origins of language of 1772. Heidegger's *Vom Wesen der Sprache* (1939) enlists Herder's differentiation between animal communication and human speech and Leibniz's equation of language with "audible reason." Heidegger echoes Herder's ascription of inherent creativity, of immanent poetics to language per se. He cites Herder's somewhat circular contention that "man is made solely through language, but that to invent language he must already be human" (Rousseau comes up against this symmetry). In a pre-Chomskyan perspective Humboldt postulates the innateness of language, its incision in mentality. In the very first word, asserts Humboldt, "all of speech already resounds and is posited." Heidegger refers to Jakob Grimm on the genesis of lexical and grammatical articulation. In poets such as Rilke and George, *Ursprung* becomes *Anfänglichkeit*, origins modulate into instauration. These rhapsodes create in the light of Pindar and Hölderlin. They instance Heidegger's persuasion that only poetry can lead us back to that "soliloquy of the soul" pointed to by Plato, to that luminous incommensurability of authentic discourse, of the *Logos* in logic now all but lost. Throughout this historical network we can discern the unsettling Heideggerian maxim—that philosophic thought of the first order and the mutation of such thought into poetry—has come to pass in only two languages: ancient Greek and German.

This intuition animates Martin Heidegger's language-fundamentalism and, one is tempted to say, language-mystique. It permeates his oracular hermeneutics and call for the necessity not to devise new linguistic theories but an encounter in depth with the language-center of Being itself, its *Wesensgrund*. It is verbs, particularly verbs of motion, which enunciate the otherwise inexpressible nature of Being. The verb "to be," the assertion "is" have determined the destiny of man. What Heidegger takes to be their mistranslation into Latin has generated our failure to remember the initial mystery of Being and the difference, all embracing, between Being and beings, between the essence and the existential. Of this "un-remembrance" have come the errors, the anthropomorphic illusions of western philosophy, what Heidegger entitles "onto-theology" to which even Nietzsche succumbs. Of which Sartre's humanistic existentialism and the claims of cognitive, scientific positivism are the sorry epilogue. What is "still concealed is the poetic character of thought" (*Dichtungscharakter des Denken*).

"No one has ever read like you" clarioned an entranced Hannah Arendt. Heidegger's readings of poetry, his *explications de textes*, have in turn triggered extensive commentary, laudatory or polemic, awestruck or derisive. Heidegger describes his approach as "phenomenological." In Mörike's lyric "*Auf eine Lampe*" Hegel's concept of "sensuous manifestation" is enacted. Though it need not itself be lit, the lamp is revelatory of the meaning of light. The more he deepens the reach of poetry, "the more does the poet become one who thinks." When Trakl invokes the coming of an unannounced guest in the dark blue of nightfall, he allows us to experience, however imperfectly, the footfall of *Sein* itself. Heidegger enters into dialogue, *Zwiesprache*, with the infirm poet, following him on his silent peregrination, confronting the consuming storms of *Geist*. Trakl's tragic *Untergang*, his descent into suicidal depression, is also an *Übergang*, a hallowed transit into the very homeland of language. (Alertness to Trakl is among the rare but perhaps elemental affinities between Heidegger and Wittgenstein).

Heidegger attends to the presence of Parmenides in the eighth of Rilke's *Duino Elegies*. He seeks out Rilke's thought-structure via key words. Shared by Rilke and his impassioned exegete is a sense, an experiencing of language as "other than immanent," as inhuman and even menacing in its "otherness." Heidegger locates this ambiguous transcendence in Rilke's *Windinneres*, but even this turbulent inwardness falls short of what remains unspoken.

We know now that Heidegger's immersion in Hölderlin dates back to 1929 if not before. To Heidegger, who will devote several monographs to Hölderlin's major odes and hymns, the author of "*Wie am Feiertag...*," of "*Brot und Wein*," of "*Patmos*" and the unfinished *Death of Empedocles* is more than the greatest of all poets. He stands closest to both the origins and horizon of human fate. He is the guardian of the German language and the secret ministrant of a Germany yet to come. Hölderlin's presence, as yet we read him only partially, guarantees the survival of the national genius, of its centrality in the life of the spirit after the catastrophe of 1945. He guarantees the unbroken, uniquely privileged continuities between "Germania" and ancient Greece. Owing to Hölderlin man has "a poetic dwelling upon the earth." After 1936 it is Hölderlin more than any philosopher who is the touchstone of Heidegger's designation of man as "shepherd of Being," of the conceit, substantive and metaphoric, whereby the retreat of the gods from the earth need not be irreparable. With war and *débacle*, Hölderlin comes to signify for Heidegger a symbiosis of the apocalyptic and the messianic. It is he who represents, who realizes the fusion of poetry and philosophy. A fusion whose ultimate power, "*die höchste Macht*," resides with *Dichtung*.

These exegetic celebrations (incantations?) are brought to bear on Hölderlin's idiosyncratic, technically flawed but also inspired versions of Sophocles. Notably on his *Antigone*. The triangulation is perhaps unparalleled: Heidegger reads Sophocles via Hölderlin's reading but also by means of his own lexical, philosophical, political inroads into the Greek text. These recur at diverse points in Heidegger's teachings. They are set out extensively in the 1935

Introduction to Metaphysics. Needless to say Heidegger on Sophocles and on Hölderlin's Sophocles has itself provoked a tertiary body of reverent or dissenting marginalia. I know of no more demanding example of the interleaving of the literary and the philosophical, of metaphysical and poetic impulses at their highest pitch. Heidegger opines that the choral ode *polla ta deina* in Sophocles' *Antigone* is determinant of the history and destiny (*Schicksal*) of the West. Which vatic hyperbole is calculated to shock us into utmost attention. There is, moreover, little in world literature to surpass the concentrated marvel of these stanzas, their talismanic depth.

The tragedian asks: "What is man?" The trivializing clamor in which we conduct our modern lives renders us almost deaf to the question, so Heidegger. A pedestrian translation of *ta deina* gropes toward "wondrous," none more so than man. Hölderlin proposes *Ungeheuer* signifying "monstrous," of "uncontainable dimensions." Heidegger's preference of *Unheimlich* introduces an expansive but also fiercely dense commentary. It marshals the polysemic tonalities, the aura of *heimlich* meaning "secret" and of *heim* designating "home" ("homely," but in a far more accentuated, elemental semantic field). The uncanny immensity of man, the intellectual, artistic, manufacturing skills to which the chorus points only emphasize the essential aloneness of our existence within Being, the stance of whatever is human "within the inescapability of death." The ode closes on a solemn, almost ritual admonition. He who commits lawlessness, flouting the divinities of the state, its eminence, *uphípolis*, shall end *apolis*, "a cityless outcast" unworthy of social trust or companionship. Now Heidegger's choice of *Unheimlich* comes into full play. The outlaw, the dissident collapses into "stateless confusion." Outcast from the *polis* he is ostracized from the human condition. *Apolis* is Heidegger's key term. "*Ohne Stadt und Stätte,*" cityless, unhoused. Brilliantly, *Stätte* glances at the very theme of Sophocles' drama, *Grabstätte,* the place of burial denied to Polyneices. The ideological, *Völkisch* tenor of this gloss, proclaimed in 1935, is threateningly evident. The idiom is Creon's.

To no man do the Sophoclean epithets "unhoused," "homeless," "banned from the hearth" apply more pitilessly than they do to Paul Celan. He was a stranger to life. His translations are feats of genius; they repay a lifetime's study. But in each of half a dozen languages he was a virtuoso vagrant, not an inhabitant. Celan's contributions to German poetry and prose rank with Hölderlin's. They are innovative beyond Rilke. But in that tongue his parents and millions of fellow Jews had been butchered. Its scandalous survival after the Shoah, the knowledge that he was adding to its prestige and future filled Celan with guilt, at times with loathing (he earned his precarious living by teaching German). A barely tolerated, intermittent guest of himself, Celan underwent, may have sought refuge in severe bouts of mental derangement, of *Umnachtung*, again comparable to Hölderlin's. Almost everyone whom he had trusted, whom he had granted some nuance of intimacy came to be rejected, to be bitterly condemned for failing to share wholly Celan's anguish, his despairing reading of the hunted condition of the Jew. Or for failing to embrace with sufficient public vehemence Celan's struggle against ludicrous charges of plagiarism (the "Goll affair").

Remarkable women, Ingeborg Bachmann for one, passed in and out of his torment. The late love lyrics composed on a visit to Jerusalem are a glory. But even love was in a sense contraband, a transient unearned grace smuggled across the ashen barriers of pain. It is a somewhat facile truth, but a truth nonetheless, that suicide was inscribed in Celan's early poems, in the "*Todesfuge*" whose fame nauseated him, whose reception into the German school curriculum was a final irony. From the outset Paul Celan was on leave from death.

I have within obvious limits of understanding spent many years with the writings of Martin Heidegger and Paul Celan. I have stood by their graves and visited some of the landscapes instrumental to their perceptions. These extand from the Black Forest to the island of Delos, from the Rue d'Ulm in Paris to the Almond Tree Gate in

Jerusalem. Despite the already extant and multiple secondary literature, so much of it self-serving and ill-informed, I had planned to conclude this essay with something worth saying about the Heidegger-Celan encounters and non-encounters. I had hoped to show how manifestly these crystallize and bring to their summit the history, the essence of the relations between poetry and philosophy, between thought and its poetics as these first quicken the Pre-Socratics and Plato into undying life.

I have noted that the mounting documentation of Heidegger's proto-Nazism and postwar evasions renders access unnerving. The exclusion zone around Celan is even more forbidding. Facts dissolve into gossip. Amateur suppositions as to Celan's mental state are an indecency. As Derrida says in his *Schibboleth pour Paul Celan,* "there is secrecy here, withdrawal, forever removed from exhaustive hermeneutic." To touch on the themes—I speak for myself—is to be made acutely aware of the limits of one's own intellectual resources and penetrative sensibility.

Most probably Celan first came across Heidegger's work when he met Bachmann, who had written her thesis on *Sein und Zeit.* The archives in Marbach reveal the closeness, the concentration of Celan's readings. He annotates, underlines, glosses passage after passage in Heidegger's major publications. This material is yet to be evaluated in detail. It puts beyond doubt the depth of Heidegger's linguistic, rather than philosophical impact on the poet (Lucretius imitating and recasting Epicurus). Heidegger's neologisms, his welding of words into hybrid composites, his parataxic abruptness—the omission of inert, qualifying connectives—become functional in Celan's hermetic diction. The merest hint of sympathy with the Nazi past, the most hidden trace of forgiveness or of indifference to the Holocaust maddened Celan. Heidegger's implications in Hitlerism were known to Celan. Nevertheless he familiarized himself with, he sought out "the bearer of death, that master from Germany." My conjecture is that Heidegger's pressure on the limits of language, his innovations within the crucible of violently forged syntax provided

Celan with a vital stimulus and "complementarity" (in quantum theory contrary truths may both be true). For his part Heidegger grew attentive to some of Celan's later poems and enigmatic persona. According to his son, a suspect witness, Heidegger was unaware that Celan was a Jew. This is implausible but *just* conceivable. He attended one of Celan's last public readings. The resulting photograph is mesmeric; wearing his customary black headpiece, it is Heidegger who looks like an aged rabbi. He confided to a colleague that Celan was gravely, fatally ill. The suicide certified his diagnosis. Did he ever return to Celan's poems as he did incessantly to Hölderlin's? Did he take note of the tragic affinities between the fortunes of the two? Documents, which may be relevant, are still unpublished.

All we have is the poem. And the jabber of often baseless attempts at decoding.

Although his delivery was monochrome and although he felt that his poems elicited either incomprehension or derision (many were of unprecedented difficulty), Celan gave a reading at the University of Freiburg on July 24, 1967. The next day he went to visit Heidegger in his famous hut at Todtnauberg. Had the master invited him? Had Celan requested the meeting? If so, why? What did he think might come of it? Crucial questions to which we have no answer. The poem is dated August 1st.

It tells of the well in front of the hut and of the star carved on its stone lintel. For Celan stars had gone yellow in remembrance of the horrors inflicted on those condemned to wear them. There is a guest book: "whose name did the book / register before mine?" Todtnauberg had long been the object of reverent pilgrimage. Celan added his own autograph. Michael Hamburger translates:

> the line inscribed
> in that book about
> a hope, today,
> of a thinking man's
> coming

word
in the heart ...

"Man's" is Hamburger's misleading addendum. The German is tighter and faithful to Heidegger's usage:

auf eines Denkenden
kommendes
Wort
im Herzen...

The "word" itself, metrically and typographically isolated, is "thought in advent," beyond any individual speaker. It speaks the speaker. A third party, "he who drives us," listens in. The walk—like Nietzsche, Heidegger was a prodigious walker—follows "trodden wretched / tracks through the high moors." Here translation goes limp. In Celan's *Knüppel-pfade* resound the sadistic blows of cudgels. *Moor* as in *Hochmoor* echoes the bitter, funereal chant sung by concentration camp inmates on their flogged outing to the peat bogs. The poem ends on a lifeless notation: "dampness, much."

The interpretation of "Todtnauberg" as a *memore* of abysmal disappointment, of noncommunication invaded by presences from the Shoah, is self-evident. It corresponds with the failure of the guest to obtain from his host the hoped-for word, the utterance from and to the heart. But what did Celan expect? What could, what would Heidegger have said in extenuation, in remorse for his own role and omissions in the time of the inhuman? What license did Celan have for his provocation ("calling out")?

Was *anything* said during that long walk on the sodden uplands? One school of commentary has it that both men shared that silence of which they were craftsmen. We simply do not know; we never shall. Moreover, shortly after the poem first appears, Celan informs his friend Franz Wurm in Zürich and his wife Gisèle that his day with Heidegger had proved positive and satisfying. There is no reason to suppose that this was a macabre pleasantry. But what might

Celan's mental state have been when he volunteered this report? Again, we have no way of knowing.

What remains is an image, perhaps a fathomless myth in Plato's sense. Sovereign philosophical thought, sovereign poetry side by side in an infinitely signifying but also inexplicable silence. A silence both safeguarding and trying to transcend the limits of speech which are, as in the very name of that hut, also those of death.

9

This essay has only scratched the surface. The collisions, the complicities, the interpenetrations and amalgams between philosophy and literature, between the poem and the metaphysical treatise have been constant. They extend beyond writing to music. To the fine arts (witness Egbert Verbeek's disturbing bronze bust of Socrates, 1999). The Platonic themes proliferate. I have not touched on Ficino's *De Amore* (1469), on Thomas Otway's *Alcibiades* (1675), on Wieland's influential *Gespräche des Sokrates* of 1756 or Voltaire's *Socrate* (1759), with its detestation of Aristophanes whom Voltaire held partly culpable for Socrates' fate. There is Brecht's *Der verwundete Sokrates* (1939), Alexander Goehr's musical setting of the Platonic parable of the cave in his *Shadowplay* (1970), and Jean-Claude Carrière's *Le Dernier jour de Socrate* of 1998. Shelley's 1818 translation of the *Symposion* has been staged. The fascination persists.

There are those who deny any essential difference. For Montaigne all philosophy *"n'est qu'une poésie sophistiquée,"* where *sophistiquée,* needs careful handling. There is no opposition: "Each makes difficulties for the other. Together they are difficulty itself: the difficulty of making sense" (Jean-Luc Nancy). Others have found the intimacies between the philosophical and the poetic incestuous and reciprocally damaging. Husserl, for example.

The point I have been trying to clarify is simple: literature and philosophy as we have known them are products of language. Unalterably that is the common ontological and substantive ground. Thought in poetry, the poetics of thought are deeds of grammar, of language in motion. Their means, their constraints are those of style. The unspeakable, in the direct sense of that word, circumscribes both. Poetry aims to reinvent language, to make it new. Philosophy labors to make language rigorously transparent, to purge it of ambiguity and confusion. At times it labors to transcend lexical, syntactical limitations and inherited atrophies altogether by resorting to formal logic and meta-mathematical algorithms as in Frege. But it is human discourse which remains the total matrix. This is superbly illustrated by Leopardi's *Zibaldone*. There was for him no valid poetry without philosophy; no philosophy worth acquiring without poetry. The generative access to both was an impassioned philology. Leopardi scrutinizes lexical units, grammatical ordinances and pragmatic applications with often microscopic erudition. God, which is to say the wonder of communicable meaning, lies in the linguistic detail. As it does for the Kabbalist when he derives from the single letter the very surge and magic of creation. Letters are written in primal fire. Out of which incandescence have come all philosophy, all poetry and the paradox of their autonomous unison.

I have suggested that this conception of language as the defining nucleus of being, as the donation, ultimately theological, of humaneness to man is now in recession. That neither in its ontological status nor in its existential reach the word retains its traditional centrality. In many respects this little book, the interest and focus it hopes for from its readers—statistically a tiny minority—the vocabulary and grammar in which it is set out, are already archaic. They relate to the monastic arts of attention in, say, the early Middle Ages or the Victorian library. They accord poorly with the reduction of literary texts on screens or the anti-rhetoric of the blog. The mere survival of an essay such as this depends on its availability online. The future of uncontrollably overcrowded, costly storage in public and academic libraries is increasingly questionable.

The new technologies pluck at the heart of speech. In the United States, eight- to eighteen-year-olds log about eleven hours of daily engagement with electronic media. Conversation is face-to-face. Virtual reality occurs within cyberspheres. Laptops, iPods, cell phones, email, the planetary Web and Internet modify consciousness. Mentality is "hard wired." Memory is retrievable data. Silence and privacy, the classical coordinates of encounters with the poem and the philosophic statement, are becoming ideologically, socially suspect luxuries. As the critic Crowther puts it: "The buzz inside and outside your head has murdered silence and reflection." This could prove terminal, for the quality of silence is organically bonded with that of speech. The one cannot achieve full strength without the other.

This does not mean that fine poetry and poetry of an intellectual, even explicitly philosophic concern is not being produced. Geoffrey Hill's sensibility is profoundly consonant with the values of theology and political philosophy. Anne Carson's experiments, at once forbidding and poignant, work northwards of Celan. Following on Valéry, Yves Bonnefoy is both a philosopher of art and a thinker on poetics of high distinction. Cartesian meditations inspire the *denkende Dichtung* of Durs Grünbein. The properly philosophic map is more difficult to read. Naturally enough, philosophy may be pausing for breath after Heidegger and Wittgenstein, after Bertrand Russell and Sartre. Stringent analyses prevail in symbolic logic, philosophical semantics and the investigations into the foundation of mathematics and the sciences. Prognostications as to the literary and the philosophical future are almost certain to be mistaken if not fatuous. Death knells come cheap.

Nonetheless it is permissible to suppose that the embracing systematic constructs of philosophy, the "unaging monuments" such as Comte's tomes of positivism or Jaspers on truth, which have depended on lexical and grammatical "primes," are of the past.

Together with the public, canonic authority of the poem, with its "legislation" (Shelley's proud claim). Here also the *Logos* had to be both talismanic and at the center.

It may be that hybrid genres will prove the most viable. More and more, music, dance, the figurative and abstract arts, mime and verbal utterance will interact. Already poetry is spoken against a tapestry of jazz; already philosophic pronouncements are inscribed on paintings (Anselm Kiefer). Electronic and live messages synthesize. Live performance interleaves with film. Traditional distances between performer and spectator are subverted. The provenance is twofold: ritual, mask, chorus and choreography long preceded our politically aligned literacies. They flourish still in the pre-technological world. The other source is the Wagnerian *Gesamtkunstwerk*. These modes intimate the possibility of a "post-linguistic or post-textual" philosophy, of poetry as a collective "happening." Meaning can be danced.

The radical break with the western historical past would be that of ephemerality. It would entail the deliberate acceptance of the momentary and the transient. There would be no avowed aspirations to immortality. These would be left to French Academicians. Lines of verse claiming to outlast bronze would be entombed in the archives. Citation would become an esoteric practice and arrogance. The self-destruct, the effacing sweep of death would not only be accepted but somehow enfolded within aesthetic and intellectual phenomena. Sense would be made play: *homo ludens*. Thus semantics would converge with those mutations in the status of death and personal identity to which I have referred. On the horizon lies the prospect that biochemical, neurological discoveries will demonstrate that the inventive, cognitive processes of the human psyche have their ultimately material source. That even the greatest metaphysical conjecture or poetic find are complex forms of molecular chemistry.

This is not a vision in which an obsolescent, often technophobic consciousness such as mine can take comfort. It comes after "the humanities" which so bleakly failed us in the long night of the twentieth century. Yet it may be a formidable adventure. And somewhere a rebellious singer, a philosopher inebriate with solitude will say "No." A syllable charged with the promise of creation.

APPENDIX

Select translations by the author

83: I compared the writings of the ancient pagans treating of mores to very handsome and magnificent palaces built only on sand
and mud; they exalt virtues and render them praiseworthy above all
things in the world, but do not instruct us how to know them; often
what they call by so beauteous a name is nothing but insensibility,
or pride, or despair or parricide.

84: Examining closely what I was, seeing that I could feign that I
had no body and that there was no world nor any place for me to be
in, but that, nonetheless, I could not pretend that I was not and that
in very contradiction to being able to doubt of the truth of other
things, it followed most evidently and certainly that I was.

86: He models the fallen flakes.
He rounds and circumscribes in comely curves
For which physics, swallow-swift, finds the formula.
Monsieur, reflect on what evades you if you lose your time.
For you, for you, it has snowed the night through.

100: I hate servants. I hate their odious and vile species. Servants do not belong to the human species. They flow. They are bad breath trailing in our rooms, in our corridors, which penetrates us, enters into our mouths, corrupts us. I spew you out.

113: Platitudinous, boastful, bombastic, pretentiously harsh when attacking, hysterically sensitive when attacked; swinging his sword with a vast waste of energy only to let it fall flat; constantly preaching civility, constantly offending against good manners; pathetic and vulgar in a risible tangle; concerned solely with the matter in hand but always missing the point; opposing to common sense a petit-bourgeois learned half-culture; gushing an ungoverned plethora of self-complacent triviality; plebeian form and unctuous middle-brow content; grappling with the written word so as to give it bodily substance ... raging against reaction, reacting against progress ... Herr Heinzen has the merit to be the restorer of ruffian literature and in that regard one of the German swallows heralding the approaching populist spring.

117: O Man! Take heed!
What says the deep midnight?
 "I slept, I slept,
I have woken from a profound dream:—
The World is deep
And deeper than the day bethought
 Deep is its pain—
Joyous desire deeper than heart's pain:
Grief says: vanish!
But all joyous desire wants eternity—
wants deep, deep eternity!"—

123: The waves collide, oppose one another, seek their equilibrium. A white, light and merry foam follows their changing contours. At times a receding flux leaves a little of that foam on the sand of the shore. The child playing nearby comes and picks up a handful, and is astonished a moment later to have in his palm only a few drops of water a good deal saltier, bitterer than the wave which brought them. Laughter is born like that foam.

125–26: Treading the one on the other, we perceive distinct colors, so to speak solid, juxtaposed like the diverse pearls on a necklace, necessarily we presume on a thread, no less solid, keeping these pearls together.

But it is with our whole past, comprising the best of our initial soul, that we desire, will, act. Thus our past manifests itself integrally by its thrust and in the form of a tendency, though only feeble, part thereof becomes representation.

All of animal and vegetable life in its essence seems like an effort to accumulate energy and then to release it via flexible vessels, vessels which can be reshaped, at whose extremity it will accomplish infinitely varied tasks. This is what the *élan vital*, traversing matter, seeks to obtain at one stroke.

In the instant in which the action will be accomplished, it is not rare that a revolt occurs. It is the ego from below which rises back to the surface. It is the outside crust which bursts, yielding to an irresistible thrust. Thus there was operative in the depths of that ego, and beneath reasonably juxtaposed arguments a boiling, a growing tension of feelings, doubtless not unconscious, but to which we did not wish to pay heed.

136: My solitude—which since many years is but the lack of friends met with at leisure, in depths; of intimate conversations, dialogues without preambles, without any but the rarest finesses, cost me dearly—To live without objections is not to live, without live resistance, that prey, that other person, that other adversarial person,

individual remnant of the world, obstacle and shadow of myself—
other self—rival intelligence, enemy best friend, divine, fatal hos-
tility—intimate.

142: Death is a brief anguish.
A wandering sigh from the heart
where it has dwelt long years
almost a guest and as a stranger,
and turns toward Olympus
true lodging of bliss.

145: But we must not think such thoughts uninterruptedly, we must
not think through all that we think and of which we hear, pondering; for if we do so a moment comes in which we are done to death
by this burrowing, in which we simply end dead.

158: Then the Absolute (generated by the absolute hazard of this
fact) says to all that noise: assuredly there is an act there and it is
my duty to proclaim it: this folly does exist. You are right (noise of
folly) to make it manifest: do not believe that I shall plunge you
back into nothingness.

159: Periodically, the soul is smitten by this winged mountaineer....
Of all men, Heraclitus, refusing to fragment the prodigious question, has led it to gestures, to intellect and to the habits of man without dimming its fire, without interrupting its complexity or com-
promising its mystery or stifling its youthfulness.... His solar eagle's
eye, his particular sensibility had convinced him once and for all
that the only certitude we have as to tomorrow's reality is pessimism; accomplished guise of secrecy which gives us new freshness,
alertness and slumber. Heraclitus is that proud, stable, anxious genius crossing through mobile times which he has formulated, as-
serted and at once forgotten so that he may overtake them while, in

transit, breathing within one or another of us.... His gait concludes at the somber and blazing station of our days.

189: He would have accepted the doctrine had he seen in it only a phosphorescence, a scarf tossed on the sea, unfolded, refolded by the gusts and whose truth depended precisely on its incessant and mutual involvement with the clamor of the sea.

190: Another sentiment was born: that desolate affection, tenderly funereal, brings close exhausted friends, who have torn apart so as to share only their quarrels, which quarrels have, one fine day, ceased for lack of any motive.

199: Yet thinking is poetry and not only a sort of poetry in the sense of the poem or the song. The thinking of being is the original way of poetry. In it, before all else, language becomes language, i.e. attains its essence. The poem speaks the dictate of the truth of being. Thought is the primal dictare.... The essence of thought which is the poem safeguards the dominion of the truth of being.